COMMUNITY AND ORGANIZATION
IN THE NEW LEFT, 1962–1968

COMMUNITY AND ORGANIZATION IN THE NEW LEFT, 1962–1968
THE GREAT REFUSAL

Wini Breines

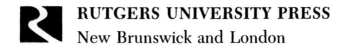

RUTGERS UNIVERSITY PRESS
New Brunswick and London

New edition in cloth and paperback by Rutgers University Press, 1989

First published in cloth by Praeger Publishers, CBS Educational and Professional Publishing, A Division of CBS, Inc., 1982

First published in paperback by J. F. Bergin Publishers, Inc., 1982

Library of Congress Cataloging-in-Publication Data

Breines, Wini.
    Community and organization in the New Left, 1962–1968 : the great
refusal / Wini Breines.
        p.   cm.
    "New edition"—T.p. verso.
    Bibliography: p.
    Includes index.
    ISBN 0-8135-1402-9   ISBN 0-8135-1403-7 (pbk.)
    1. Unites States—Social conditions—1960–1970. 2. Social
history—1960–1970. 3. Radicalism—United States. 4. Students for
a Democratic Society. I. Title.
HN59.B73 1989
320.5'3'0973—dc19   88-28300
                            CIP

For Paul, Natasha, and Raphael

Contents

Acknowledgments
Preface to the Second Edition
Preface to the First Edition

Chapter 1 • *An Introduction to the New Left: A Critique of Some Critics*   *1*

    Key Terms   8

Chapter 2 • *Emergence of the New Left*   *10*

    A Historical Sketch   10
    The Old Left and the New Left   13

Chapter 3 • *The Great Refusal*   *18*

    "The Issue Is Not the Issue"   18
    The Free Speech Movement: Students-for-Themselves   23
    "Actions"   31

Chapter 4 • *Politics as Community*   *46*

    Prefigurative Politics   46
    Means and Ends   52
    Participatory Democracy   56

Chapter 5 • *Politics as Organization*   *67*

    A Mass Movement   67
    Movement versus Organization   68
    Organizational Politics, 1964-1965   76
    Decentralization   79
    Economic Research and Action Project (ERAP)   80
    December Conference and After   83
    Internal Education   90
    Politics Is about Power   93

Chapter 6 • *Students as Agency*   *96*

 Agency as an Issue   96
 The University: New Realities, Old Notions   99
 Students as Agency   102
 New Working Class Theory and Marxism   110
 Reversals   115
 Transition Years, 1967-1968   118

Chapter 7 • *The Economic Research and Action Project*   *123*

 The Debate: Poor People or Students; Off-Campus
  vs. On-Campus Organizing   125
 The Theory of Community Unions   133
 Community Organizing: Organization as Community   135
 Democracy   139
 The Critique of Community Organizing   146

Conclusion   150

Notes   153

Bibliography   173

Index   183

Acknowledgments

Many people encouraged and aided me throughout this project. In its early stages George Ross and Maurice Stein of Brandeis University helped to improve it, as did Ralph Miliband, in part through his strenuous disagreements. A substantial number of people wrote long responses to my questions and ideas about the new left, or talked with me at length. Among these are Stanley Aronowitz, Dick Flacks, the late Alvin Gouldner, Barbara Haber, Stuart Hall, Bob Ross, Rosemary Taylor, Mike Useem, Nigel Young, and my parents, Betty and Daniel Jacoby. I especially want to express my gratitude to Kay Trimberger for extremely helpful and time-consuming comments on my ideas and on much of the manuscript, and to Todd Gitlin for his interest and suggestions and, perhaps more important, for his insights into the new left.

In the course of revising the manuscript several people wrote extensive and very helpful comments. I am profoundly grateful to them: Michael Burawoy, John Ehrenreich, Liz Ewen, and Michael Schwartz.

The hope, pain, and intelligence shared by those who participated in the SDS Reunion-Conference in August 1977 in Michigan, fifteen years after Port Huron, in the process of trying to come to terms with our new left pasts and present lives were characteristic of what was best about the new left. The experience brought back what it had meant for all of us, and I wish to thank everyone who participated.

Ros Baxandall, Linda Gordon, Allen Hunter, Ann Popkin, and Judy Stacey provided support and generous offers of help of which I generally did not take advantage. Nevertheless, the knowledge that they were there and the support that they have provided have been essential. Margaret Cerullo and Judy Stacey made my graduate years at Brandeis University a collective experience, personally and intellectually. That time provides a model for intellectual and emotional sharing that continually inspires me.

Over the years, summer conversations about the new left with Liz and Stuart Ewen have been consistently provocative and more important than they know. Margaret Cerullo has been central to the personal and intellectual unfolding of this work, and thanks are simply inadequate.

Finally, Paul Breines's confidence and encouragement have been critical. His emotional support and intellectual enthusiasm form the context for this work.

Preface to the Second Edition

It is ten years since the first draft of this book was written. By the late 1970s very little had been published about the sixties other than that written by participants during the heat of the decade and immediately afterward. It is only in the last two or three years that this is no longer true. As the new right, moral majority, neoconservatives, and the Reagan administration have shaped the political climate during the last fifteen or twenty years, the silence of those who supported the movements of the 1960s has not been insignificant. For the conservatives were not silent. Nineteen-sixties radicalism was their reference point for all that had gone wrong with America. Much of what has taken place during the last decade and a half was an implicit, if not explicit, political and cultural repudiation of the movements of the 1960s by government officials, right-wing movements, the media, and, occasionally, former activists. Reaganism has meant years of cynical reaction and ugly individualism during which visions of peacefulness, equality, and justice, even generosity, have been derided. Other than a few academic studies, sympathetic writing about the sixties was notable for its absence. That was one reason I originally wrote about and defended the new left.

In the last two or three years, however, many new books have appeared about the sixties, particularly the white new left. Significantly, all are laudatory. The new left and the student movement are being rehabilitated. One of the obvious explanations is the twentieth anniversary of the amazing year 1968, which is the subject of at least five of the new books. This anniversary provides the occasion to evaluate the 1960s from some distance, in writing as well as in the many reunions and conferences of movement groups held in the past year or two. The authors of the new books are for the most part former participants who are now middle-aged (or close to it) and thus inclined to take stock of their younger selves. A number do, in fact, consider themselves quite a bit wiser now than they were then, an evaluation I do not share about them or myself, also a former new left activist. That they are almost all white males and that they take stock in print suggests their continuing sense of their own importance. It is probably also relevant that many people now in positions of power in publishing and the media are of the same generation and were themselves influenced by sixties' movements; they are not unsympathetic to the renewed attention to their youthful experiences. (This is interesting, too, in light of earlier media efforts to portray the 1960s generation as cynical and greedy capitalists who repudiated their former radicalism. There appears to be little empirical evidence of this; in fact scattered evidence suggests just the opposite. The majority of 1960s activists are today organizers, therapists, social welfare professionals, and teachers who continue to be socially conscious if not politically active.)[1] Finally, the anticipation of the end of Reaganism is doubtless a factor in the appearance of new books on 1960s' radicalism. Hope for social movements and social change, for a more equitable and humane society, have been revived with the possibility of a more liberal administration.

In this preface I will address two critical themes raised in or by writing on the new left, including the recent work. They are themes I originally extracted and analyzed in this book, and, I believe, they still get to the heart of new left matters. The first concerns the accusation by earlier and more recent authors that the absence of effective political organization was responsible for the new left's downfall. Several of the new books (Gitlin, 1987; Miller, 1987; Isserman, 1987) share with hostile liberal, social democratic, Marxist-Leninist, and conservative academics of the past twenty-five years (Breines, this volume, 1–6) the conviction that the new left was responsible for its own demise primarily because the leadership did not build an adequately responsible, disciplined, democratic, and centralized organization that would have enabled the movement to function realistically in the world of American politics. The absence of effective organization, the mushroom growth of militancy and violence, a lack of discipline, and a utopianism irrelevant to creating serious political change in America are identified as central factors in shaping the outcome of what happened at the end of the decade when the new left and student movement seemed to let success slip away. Although they do not agree about much else and apportion their emphases differently (e.g., traditional Marxists believed the new left was infantile; conservatives, and sometimes liberals, saw them as nihilists; social democrats labeled them anarchists and wreckers, etc.), authors of every political persuasion share the conviction that the new left self-destructed in the late 1960s primarily because the leadership did not build an adequate organization.

How are we to understand what most analysts identify as the critical failure of the new left: its abandonment of the main student organization, Students for a Democratic Society (SDS), and thus the student movement, for the apparently destructive trends of the end of the decade?

Unavoidably, the interpretation of failure raises the question of what success would have looked like. The standard of success in American politics, shared by many radicals, will always condemn a movement that does not make pragmatic compromises, coalitions, and durable organizations. (Indeed, at the heart of the answer, for many recent and earlier authors, is organization.) Why was it, some of these new books ask, that the organizational political expression the authors value did not last? What was wrong with the new left?

Part of the answer, according to recent authors Gitlin and Isserman, lies in the tendency in the civil rights movement and early new left toward moralism, participatory democracy, direct action, "putting your body on the line" for what you believe in: what Gitlin, following Seymour Martin Lipset (1969:512; Breines, this volume, 1), calls expressive politics, which, Gitlin argues, found new and suicidal expression late in the decade.

Isserman suggests a link between the radical pacifists of the later 1940s and 1950s and a critical current of moral politics in the new left. This current precluded consideration of political effectiveness in customary terms, stressing instead a desire to display one's personal commitment, especially if it involved risk or injury. It is a politics associated with Albert Camus, by whom many in the civil rights movement and early new left were inspired. This is attested to clearly in Tom Hayden's recent memoir, *Reunion* (1988), and discussed in both James Miller's *Democracy Is in the Streets* (1987) and Mary King's *Freedom Song* (1987). Being effective, in this view, means making a statement of one's values through an existential act, a politics most characteristic of the Student Non-Violent Coordinating Committee (SNCC), new leftists inspired by SNCC, the resistance to the draft, and, at the end of the sixties, Weatherman. The 1960s are replete with statements by white new leftists declaring their readiness to pit themselves against the war machine, the government, or the university. Young radicals clearly found political meaning and heroism in solitary or small group acts of risk and resistance.

Such ideas stress individual morality and action as the basis of politics and assume that in concert with others such action can effect change, including the victory of a peasant nation over a superpower, an image whose power grew exponentially throughout the decade. The quiet courage and dignity of poor black people peacefully seeking justice in the face of menacing police and mobs in the American South or of Vietnamese peasants confronting the destructive force of the strongest nation on earth were seen as inspiring political models. Precisely this strand of new left thought is identified by left, liberal, and conservative critics alike as apolitical, expressive, and uninstrumental, a kind of antipolitics that led, they suggest, to the demise of organizational politics and politics itself. In Gitlin's formulation this syndrome was responsible for a "politics of extremity" and finally for a death culture in which the only politics that counted was confrontation, polarization, and disruption, and that ended, symbolically enough, in 1970 when three members of the Weatherman sect of SDS accidentally blew themselves up while making bombs.

My work on the new left identified a closely linked strand which I called prefigurative politics but which, while akin to "expressive" politics, is also different. The effort to build community, to create and prefigure in lived action and behavior the desired society, the emphasis on means and not ends, the spontaneous and utopian experiments that developed in the midst of action while working toward the ultimate goal of a free and democratic society, were among the most important contributions of the movements of the 1960s.[2] The deep desire for democratic participation was evident everywhere, particularly in the thick of political actions. Yearning for community and for a democracy in which the individual had some influence was profound among new leftists. Students rejected the instrumental rationality they discovered around them in the university, the government, and bureaucracy itself. In its place, another society was imagined and even occasionally fleetingly created.

I suggested in 1982 that the organization SDS was unsuccessful in channeling the prefigurative political inclinations of the mass of activists into a strategically effective national organization but, unlike most of the work on the new left before or since, I argued that this should not be considered a failure. I stand by this still. A centralized organization could neither have "saved" the movement, nor was it what the new left was about. Prefigurative politics was based on suspicion of hierarchy, leadership, and the concentration of power. The movement was not unconsciously unruly and undisciplined. Rather it was experimenting with antihierarchical organizational forms. Prefigurative politics was what was new about the new left.[3] The question with which we are faced is why so many authors believe the student movement and new left failed or, conversely, how they measure success.[4] This book proposes that negative evaluations of the new left were often made on the basis of instrumental criteria, which entailed overlooking the movement's radical challenge to existing society.

Critics of the new left assume that the lack of a lasting and coherent organizational representation of the movement means failure. But it was precisely this assumption about which the early civil rights movement, the new left, and the student movement raised questions. It was my view, then and now, that the demonstrations, confrontations, experiments in collectivity and participatory democracy, questioning, militance, drugs and counterculture, and the radicalization of individuals and American culture which accompanied these, were what was accomplished. The fortunes of SDS were only part of the picture.

I believe the organizational perspective expressed in some of the recent books is a narrow view shaped by some of the authors' (or their informants') male leadership positions early in the decade and their current successes, which have led them to exaggerate both the role of leadership and organization in the new left and the significance of the collapse of SDS at the end of the decade. What is overlooked in accounts that focus on the fate of SDS as an organization is the mass movement after 1968, regional and local activity not dependent upon a national organization, students organizing and grass-roots activists (including women and people of color), the counterculture, and the significance of the birth of other movements such as the women's liberation and gay movements. The enormous impact of the sixties, then and now, in other words, is diminished.

A second theme I point to in the book is the tension between the organization of SDS and the larger movement. I argue that as the "organized expression" of a spontaneous, decentralized, and growing movement, SDS faced profound political difficulties. In many areas SDS as an organization was incidental because there was a grass-roots movement with local and shifting leadership devoted to participatory democracy. Those in the leadership of SDS, particularly the early leaders, tried to channel this movement into the organization and essentially failed. As the 1960s progressed, the movement was increasingly based on an outpouring of opposition to the war in Vietnam, and although the consistent focus was the war, by the last years of the decade the discontent, expressed in prefigurative political forms, ran wider and deeper. Both factors, the experiments with direct democracy and the groundswell of anger at the war and society which sustained the movement, meant enormous difficulty for any national organization. In spite of this, many in SDS believed they could organize the movement and achieve their goals through an effective program and organization. I did not and do not believe this was possible, primarily because it overestimates the virtues of organization and underestimates the rejection of bureaucracy and hierarchy, antiauthoritarianism, characteristic of the new left. Furthermore, it underestimates the primacy of the movement that exploded during the late 1960s, and wildly after 1968.

The political tension created by SDS's effort to organize the movement is apparent in the new books, for they take, broadly speaking, either an organizational or a movement perspective. It is an interesting fact that many of the recent books on the American new left are written by (or about) former participants who were early new leftists, almost all of whom are male, and often in the leadership and/or identified with

SDS, the main white, new left student organization. They were part of the first generation of new leftists in that their activism and links to the movement began early in the decade, sometimes even in the late 1950s (Gitlin 1987; Miller 1987; Hayden 1988.) By 1968, this early generation was for the most part no longer in the leadership, sometimes marginalized, and often disaffected by the direction the student movement was taking. SDS was being taken over by a younger generation of activists who were more dubious of organization; new constituencies were developing; the movement was becoming massive; and confrontation, militancy, and violence were on the rise. Many of these early leaders turned writers or subjects date the demise of the new left from 1968. Their books celebrate the early new left until 1968 when, they suggest, SDS destroyed itself.[5] For them, the late sixties and early seventies were years of madness and confusion (in which their own political voices went unheeded).

But at least five other new books focus on 1968, which almost automatically compels their authors to examine the movement that came of age in the last years of the sixties. The new books on 1968 do just this (Caute 1988; Farber 1988; Fraser 1988; Katsiaficas 1987; Koning, 1987). No one, including those whose attention is focused on the early years, disputes the fact that the period from 1968 to 1970 (the year four white students who were protesting the invasion of Cambodia at Kent State University were killed, resulting in widespread student strikes on American campuses) was the most successful period of the movement in terms of numbers of people radicalized and active. Within the United States and internationally, the white student movement grew exponentially in 1968, 1969, and 1970.[6] As the American government continued to escalate the war in Vietnam, the main student organization, SDS, splintered and effectively disappeared while the movement as a whole exploded numerically and emotionally, affecting the lives of tens of thousands of Americans from a broad cross-section of youth, including many in the army.

The books about 1968 are written from a different perspective than those written by early new left leaders or about the early new left because national organization and national leaders receded in importance at that time. Their attention is thus on the mass movement, on contestation and spontaneous uprising, on the exhilarating experience of being in a revolt that challenged the status quo. These books focus less on leaders, less on SDS and the issue of organization, and less on the left. Thus the tension between the organization of SDS and the movement, especially the movement as it mushroomed in the last years of the decade, is reproduced in the new books on the new left through two contrasting perspectives, with a corresponding focus on the early or late 1960s. I would place my own book somewhere between the two since I concentrate on the early new left until 1968, but take a position critical of the organizationists and of a narrow focus on SDS, drawing attention to the political originality of the movement.

If we did not already know it, then, the new books inadvertently teach us that one unified movement did not exist and that one perspective cannot yield a "true" picture. People who became involved in 1966 or 1968 were radicalized in different circumstances than those who were radicalized in 1959 and 1960 (or 1964) and consequently their perspectives differ. In the short life of the new left, generations existed; *when* a student became radicalized and "joined" the student or antiwar movement shaped his or her concerns. For a complete picture of the new left and student movement, which for certain purposes must be analytically distinguished, we must listen to all the voices, even some, like those of new left women, who have not yet spoken.[7] While SDS was the central organization of the decade and its leaders articulated the political aspirations of the student movement, 1968 and the books about it demonstrate the power of the local and regional movements and of young people all over the country to express creatively their opposition to a government and society that did not represent their values.

Finally, seven years ago I argued that we ignore only at our own peril the new left's serious but ultimately unsuccessful effort to devise new forms of social and political organization that would simultaneously nurture a grass-roots social movement committed to participatory democracy and community, and effect radical structural changes in American society. I continue to believe this. All genuinely democratic movements for social change require the dual goals of changing the structure of society while creating the kind of open and free relationships the new society might embody. Although it is not certain, it may be hoped that the recent reawakening of interest in the new left and movements of the sixties points to a reawakening of the prefigurative perspective, of course in new and unpredictable forms. If the reprinting of this book contributes to that prospect, so much the better. For the moment, *The Great Refusal* takes its place alongside newer work in the more modest effort of finally giving the new left its due.

Boston, Massachusetts
July 1988

Notes

I want to thank Paul Breines and Herman Gray for encouragement and help.
1. See the "Afterword" in Fraser (1988) for a discussion of what happened to

the people who were interviewed for his book. See, too, Hayden (1988:504) and Miller (1987:321–325).

2. The oral histories in Fraser (1988) are evidence of this. Tom Hayden's descriptions of various experiences in SNCC and the white student movement also provide testimony to the liberatory aspects of insurgency (1988).

3. If after years of neglect and aspersion the new left is being rehabilitated, however, it is not based on this recognition; rather it is a selective rehabilitation which most often admires the naive belief that if only the American government could be made to see the truth, it would live up to ideals of social justice. See my review essay (1988) for a discussion of the celebration of the early new left and for more extensive exploration of some of the points raised here.

4. For an upbeat appraisal of the new left see Tom Hayden's list of accomplishments (1988:501–502). Also see Fraser, "Summing Up" (1988:353–365) and Katsiaficas (1987). Most of the other authors are at best ambivalent in their appraisals. My own approach emphasizes the less tangible contributions of the new left although I believe, along with Hayden, that the new left accomplished more than it is credited with.

5. This is particularly true of Gitlin (1987). See my essay in the *Journal of American History* (1988) for a more extensive discussion. The "self-destruction" theme is prevalent in interpretations of the new left. They suggest that the anti-authoritarian impulse and the fascination with militancy and violence at the end of the decade were responsible for the new left's demise. In other words, the new left is blamed for what is construed as failure that could have been avoided.

6. Caute (1988) and Fraser (1988) focus on the international student movement.

7. See *Eyes on the Prize* (Williams 1986) for a treatment of the civil rights movement that includes lesser known voices. The television series based on the book is also available on videotape.

References

Breines, Winifred. "Whose New Left?" *Journal of American History* 75, no. 2 (September 1988).

Caute, David. *The Year of the Barricades: A Journey Through 1968*. New York: Harper and Row, 1988.

Farber, David. *Chicago '68*. Chicago: University of Chicago Press, 1988.

Fraser, Ronald. *1968: A Student Generation in Revolt*. New York: Pantheon, 1988.

Gitlin, Todd. *The Sixties: Years of Hope, Days of Rage*. New York: Bantam Books, 1987.

Hayden, Tom. *Reunion: A Memoir*. New York: Random House, 1988.

Isserman, Maurice. *If I Had a Hammer: The Death of the Old Left and the Birth of the New Left*. New York: Basic Books, 1987.

Katsiaficas, George. *The Imagination of the New Left: A Global Analysis of 1968*. Boston: South End Press, 1987.

King, Mary. *Freedom Song: A Personal Story of the 1960s Civil Rights Movement*. New York: William Morrow and Co., 1987.

Koning, Hans. *Nineteen Sixty-eight: A Personal Report.* New York: Norton, 1987.

Lipset, Seymour Martin. "The Possible Effects of Student Activism on International Politics." In *Students in Revolt.* Edited by Seymour Martin Lipset and Philip G. Altbach. Boston: Beacon Press, 1969.

Miller, James. *Democracy Is in the Streets: From Port Huron to the Siege of Chicago.* New York: Simon and Schuster, 1987.

Williams, Juan. *Eyes on the Prize: America's Civil Rights Years, 1954–1965.* New York: Viking, 1986.

Preface to the First Edition

Among the questions posed by the social and political movements of the 1960s were those concerning the relations in intellectual life between facts and values, scholarship and politics. This book is a study of one central aspect of these movements; it follows the imperatives and goals of contemporary scholarship. However, it is at the same time a political work. I want, therefore, to outline the political ideals and values that inform my scholarship. These ideals come in large part from my own experiences in the new left movement of the 1960s. In that sense they are also part of the subject matter of the book.

Many lives in this society have been shaped by the 1960s, particularly by the new left. I know that this is true in my own case and in the case of many friends. We are, for the most part, in our thirties, with more people being on the older rather than the younger end of the spectrum; the decade of the 1960s coincided with a crucial decade of our lives, our twenties. Our experience of the new left and other radical movements of that time has marked us: our way of seeing the world, of evaluating both politics and personal life, our values and yearnings, our impulse for activism. It was not simply that we were young, or that we were part of a world-wide youth revolt that regenerated the left in Western societies, or even that we were political, which is difficult enough in America. The 1960s changed our lives because movement politics promised utopia; we believed that we could achieve an egalitarian, free, and participatory society. And, immodestly, we thought that we glimpsed its beginnings in our own political activity. We believed that we were going to make a revolution. We were convinced that we could transform America through our political activity and insights. We know now (not least from all the belittling commentators) that we were very naive.

Part of the experience of being in a radical social movement is a shared sense of efficacy. People begin to feel the power of control over their own lives, and this feeling can magnify their perceptions of just how powerful they really are. But it is not all distortion. It was wonderful to be part of a collective movement for change, to transform one's life with others for what one believed in, and to believe that it mattered. Sadly, it is a rare experience. Community and communication are experiences people do not forget in a society organized to prevent them. Those experiences helped us to believe that everyone would and could join us ("Join us, it's your fight too!" we chanted), that they would want to be part of what we were constructing. A deep enthusiasm characterized our faith in our own political and social power. This book is about just that: what the new left experienced and attempted to create politically. It examines the attempt to create participatory, non-hierarchical, and communal organizational forms.

Today the utopian hopes of the movements of the 1960s may seem bizarre, even absurd. But this is as much a commentary on our present as it is on the 1960s. Little that is egalitarian and communitarian seems possible today. Then, the future looked inviting. As most participants know, it was not all rosy and exhilarating. In fact, it is often the tedium, cruelty, and lack of caring on which numerous participants and observers have focused in retrospect. But there is another side to the story, the significant new left political experiment.

In a time of diminishing possibilities and receding potential, it is difficult to believe that the radical movements of the sixties ended only a little more than a decade ago. The post-Watergate "silent seventies" have been characterized by cynicism regarding politics. There is a widespread sense among students today that the activists of the sixties wasted themselves in hopeless idealism. They ask, "What did they accomplish?" and, as if in answer, withdraw into private pursuits. The lesson drawn is that social consciousness and activism accomplish little. This encourages self-centeredness and diminished civic consciousness. A lack of fundamental and probing questioning of society narrows the parameters of public life.

In this atmosphere a book extolling the sixties appears an anachronism. But I do not recall the new left to encourage its rebirth (although it would cheer me immensely), nor do I see simple lessons to be applied to the present. That period is over. Rather, I hope to achieve two things. First, I believe that—although there are no precise lessons to draw—nevertheless, reflection on the new left's problems and experiments, above all around the issues central to this study, namely, community and organization, is pertinent to any effort, present or future, aimed at bringing about democratic change in America. Second, the sad fact is that, at the time of writing, the prospects for movements for democratic change look slim. All the more reason for remembering and retrieving the new left's experiences, critically but with sympathy.

The new left opened everything to scrutiny. It raised questions rarely raised by a left before, about even the left itself. It broke with traditional left-wing parties and created another chance for them, although in the United States it arose in a void, with virtually no adult left wing to guide it or even to rebel against. Finally, the new left represented a notable defection from the bourgeoisie of the West. Its children turned decisively away, rejecting their parents, their values, and existing political, economic, and social structures. They looked elsewhere for meaning. This defection was in part why the new left was so controversial. In its idealism, its almost naive belief in the chances for democracy, its energetic will to collective action from below, the new left seems remote today, hopelessly at odds with present moods and expectations. All the more reason, then, for retrieving it.

It may be helpful to indicate that, although I am a sociologist, my approach is akin to and inspired by some of the recent social history, much of which has itself been generated by the movements of the 1960s.[1] Like E. P. Thompson, Christopher Hill, and others, I see as rational revolutionary behavior what other academic and establishment analysts have tended to view as irrational, antisocial, prepolitical, apolitical, and so on. With some of the new social historians, I share an interest in and sympathy for those who have resisted social control and/or tried to cope with forces apparently beyond their influence. Recently there has been a debate among social historians about the political content of cultures— customs, traditions, and movements which are not articulated in the traditional political sphere, but which are nevertheless living attempts to cope with or resist oppressive political institutions.[2] My own work accepts the notion, itself an outgrowth of the new left, that often what appears unpolitical or apolitical is in fact political. On the other hand, my work differs from these social historians in that I do not focus on the "masses" in the new left (most of whom did not come from the lower class), but on the leadership.

Integrally connected to this focus is the issue of sources. The book is based on written sources; it was usually men who were leaders and who wrote. SDS and new left leaders tended to write and verbalize more than the activists who made up the bulk of the movement. That was part of the definition of being a leader. Those in formal or informal positions of leadership were likely to be more articulate, or at least to have more of a platform for their articulateness than those who made up the grass roots of the movement. These distinctions were present even in an educated and literate student movement. The book, then, is based on understandings and articulations of a leadership that was almost exclusively male.

One of my purposes, however, was to capture the politics and experience of the mass of activists who constituted the spontaneous and participatory experiments which gave the new left its character. To gain this broader view, I have relied on underground newspapers, memoirs, and scattered leaflets and posters, which contain glimpses of experiences and moods at the movement's base.[3] In addition, I have drawn upon recol-

lections of my own role as a participant in new left activity while a student
at both the University of Wisconsin and Cornell University during the
1960s. Since I had been a movement activist, my research on the theme
of organization was particularly illuminating to me; like many other participants, I was oblivious at the time to many of the debates unfolding
within the SDS leadership circles. Our local efforts (demonstrations, mass
meetings, and interminable discussions) proceeded independently of
them, although in retrospect the parallels and links are visible. That they
did proceed independently was politically significant and informs my
interpretation of the importance of the grass roots movement. My own
experiences, because they centered around local situations, aided my
attempt to reconstruct important but elusive aspects of the movement
as a whole: the dialogues, the emergent sense of solidarity and community, the excitement of subjecting almost everything to critical scrutiny
in the process of building a new social order.

My relationship as a feminist to the new left is relevant here. It may
seem curious that as an early activist in the women's liberation movement
and a feminist whose major intellectual interest is women, I chose to
undertake a major piece of work in whose pages precious few women
appear. It is true that throughout the decade I was a new left activist in
Madison, Ithaca, West Berlin, and Boston. But, to put it very directly,
I have, in effect, reproduced the invisibility of women in the new left.
We were active and important; but as a result of sexism, women wrote
fewer documents and spoke less frequently than the men. This is evident
in almost all the original documents, which use "him," "his," and "man"
exclusively. I have added "her," "woman," or "person" where feasible.
We women were not leaders and were usually not taken seriously. As
Sara Evans has pointed out, written histories of the new left use written
sources, which confirm and exaggerate the invisibility of women.[4] This
book is guilty of that distortion.

It is important to understand some history in order to make sense of
my own project. The women's liberation movement grew out of the new
left.[5] Many of the early leaders were veterans of the new left who took
and used insights learned there into our own movement for liberation.
Very briefly, the notion of participatory democracy, small group consciousness raising, and the slogan "The personal is political," were all
central ideas and practices inherited by the women's movement from the
new left. In spite of the sexism of the new left and of all the movements
of the sixties, the political continuity between them and the women's
movement is strong. The women's movement politically inherited what
was best about the new left.[6] When women broke away from the new
left to form their own movement, influenced by the black power movement, pushed by the sexism of the white males who were the leadership

of Students for a Democratic Society (SDS), the main new left organization, and empowered by their own experiences as political activists, they brought with them the key ideas and organizational forms of the movement, many inherited in turn from the Southern civil rights movement.

What I have done, then, is to elucidate those new left ideas and actions that I consider critical for any radical and democratic movement for social change. I have gone back, using insights and political forms further developed in the women's movement in order to uncover their sources. I have sought to clarify the new left's political contribution to the women's movement and other egalitarian movements which have survived the seventies.

Finally, a word about the book's subtitle. It is in part a dedication to the late Herbert Marcuse, who spoke of "the great refusal" in his *One-Dimensional Man* (1964). Along with Marcuse's previous and subsequent writings, *One-Dimensional Man* came to exert a substantial influence on many in the new left. For Marcuse "the great refusal" summarized the protest and rebellion of those beleaguered groups who could not or would not share in the coercive consumerism and conformism of late capitalist society. Among these groups, Marcuse in 1964 included racial minorities, those living in material poverty, parts of the young generation, and maverick intellectuals. And his notion of "the great refusal" actually anticipated some of the main features of the movements that developed in the middle and later 1960s, neither based on the industrial working class, nor centered around strictly political and economic demands. In spite of the proliferation of pertinent groups today, "the great refusal" as a whole remains at least as fragmentary and marginal as when Marcuse spoke of it in the early 1960s. Yet in borrowing his term in connection with the new left, I mean also to preserve its implicitly positive side. As Marcuse saw it, the refusal was at the same time a hope, a vision, and a readiness to experiment. In all these senses, the term seems to capture both the spirit of the new left and its particular confrontation with the issue of organization in its own internal history—the main focus of this study.

Boston, Massachusetts
1982

COMMUNITY AND ORGANIZATION
IN THE NEW LEFT, 1962–1968

CHAPTER 1

An Introduction to the New Left: A Critique of Some Critics

With only a few important exceptions, commentators from the political right, left and center, from conservative social scientists to Leninists, have been almost uniformly critical of the new left. While their political standpoints diverge, most studies share the view that the new left was a utopian, anti-organizational, even anti-political movement which, for these reasons, was bound to fail. That it appeared to fail is taken as proof of the arguments. Such commentaries, moreover, presuppose or state that a coherent strategy and organization adequate to the demands of modern politics could and should have been developed by the new left.[1] "In large measure," Seymour Martin Lipset has written, "student and other youth groups tend to differ from adult political organizations by their emphasis on what Max Weber has called 'the ethic of absolute ends,' as contrasted with 'the ethic of responsibility.' " And he adds, aptly summarizing the critical thesis, ". . . Their politics is often expressive rather than instrumental. The New Left groups also have no clear concept of any road to power, of a way of effecting major social change."[2]

The bulk of social movement sociology about the new left, written primarily by an "older" generation of left and liberal academics in the university, shares this viewpoint. It is difficult, moreover, to separate the analyses from their polemical intentions. In fact, as I suggest later, important insights often get buried under the polemical weight. The venom which characterized many of their responses to the student movement and new left is intriguing in itself. Turning Lewis Feuer's own generational analysis upon its author, it seems that he, Seymour Martin Lipset, Nathan Glazer, Daniel Bell and Edward Shils, to name several, responded as if there was indeed a generational patricidal intent. In other words, Feuer's interpretation of the student movement of the 1960s as an Oedipal revolt may tell us more about the fathers than it does about the sons, or more accurately, the children. There is no way to avoid the fact that many academics responded to the Free Speech Movement at Berkeley and other student demonstrations and occupations as though they were being personally attacked—which of course they were in due time when they made their stand clear. Whether they were infuriated because their authority was being challenged by a new and youthful experimental politics or because they were being ignored, is unclear. A statement by Daniel Bell about the Columbia University 1968 rebellion indicates the characteristic tone:

> Such desperado tactics are never the mark of a coherent social movement, but the guttering last gasps of a romanticism soured by rancor and impotence. The SDS will be destroyed by its style. It lives on turbulence, but is incapable of transforming its chaotic impulses into a systematic, responsible behavior that is necessary to effect broad societal change. . . . It is impelled not to innovation, but to destruction.[3]

Edward Shils gives a further clue to their response in his characterization of student movements as intent on humiliating authority: "It is authority that the radical students wish to confront and affront—and almost any stick will do for the camel."[4] Leaving aside whether there is any truth to this assertion, there is little doubt that these professors considered themselves part of the humiliated "authorities" and reacted accordingly.

It was not only sociologists who shared this fury. Academics in the humanities, broadly associated with the left, such as Eugene Genovese, Christopher Lasch, Sidney Hook, and Irving Howe, were outspoken in their criticism of the student movement and new left. In 1968 Eugene Genovese dedicated his book *In Red and Black* to those who are restoring sanity to the ". . . remains of the miscalled and abortive 'New Left,' and to the few on the Left . . . who fought nihilist perversions." According to Genovese, those whom he singles out, as well as select other faculty members, said ". . . No to frameups, no to opportunism, no to the demagogic manipulation of the real oppression suffered by black people and no to reactionary nihilism masquerading as revolutionary action. . . . Honor to them . . . who . . . prevented momentary madness from becoming a permanent condition."[5] The words most often utilized to characterize the student movement by all these incensed professors were: nihilist, incoherent or chaotic, fanatic, irrational, moral, anti-intellectual, romantic, manipulative, extremist and irresponsible.[6]

Amidst the rancor and shrillness of these commentaries, it is possible to discern a core argument, summed up in the initial quotation from

Lipset. The kernel of sociological thinking about the new left, pronounced so widely during the 1960s, was the assumption that utopian or idealistic notions of democratic participation and an undifferentiated moral sense, both inspired by the civil rights movement, were at the heart of "expressive" politics. Expressive politics does not recognize the need for or the value of compromise. A politics with these characteristics is necessarily irrational and incoherent. It has no strategic orientation. It is irresponsible because it teeters on the brink of extremism and even totalitarianism. (Glazer suggests that the students' success in their disruption—and in convincing thousands of students and large numbers of liberals in the community of their cause—is not in itself an argument for them. "Lenin too was successful and so was Stalin, and even Hitler, for a while, and this as you all know does not settle the argument.")[7] Lipset wrote that the student movement was "almost completely uninhibited and uncontrolled, since they have no relations to the parties and organizations that have some sort of interest in adhering to the rules of the game and accept the need for compromise."[8] Shils said of the students' revolt, "The moral revolution consists in a demand for a total transformation—a transformation of undifferentiated evil to a totality of undifferentiated perfection."[9] Along these same lines, Irving Howe identified the student movement as "romantic primitivism" and as a "quasi-religious impulse which through secular nihilism and alienated idealism seeks to break into a condition of religious transcendence."[10]

The social scientists associate the issue of democracy in a social movement with the issue of refusal to compromise. There can be no democracy without compromise, in their view. In Glazer's words, the students were "unrestrained in their actions" and "indifferent to the implications of what they do."[11] The sociologists are united in their assumption that a social movement seeking democracy and freedom must accept the "rules of the game." It is not democratic if it does not. Glazer reminds his readers, "An organized society is a very fragile thing. It is amazing that it works at all. But it works on the basis of the acceptance of rules and norms of behavior which determine the kind of society it can be."[12] Those rules and norms (and roles) are anchored by the notion of compromise. These sociologists argue further that for realistic, strategic reasons a movement cannot reject compromise, since this is what politics is all about and the manner in which goals are achieved.

Compromise has for these men an ideological and specific meaning. It is clear from Lipset's analysis of the International Typographical Union, *Union Democracy,* that while he is concerned with the condition which created and sustained democracy in that union, as well as in a society, he has no difficulty whatever in equating democracy with a two-party system. The notion of democracy approved by Lipset and used to evaluate the new left is a far cry from the participatory democracy which inspired the students. In the typographers' union a two-party system was institutionalized and was the only form in which opposition could be expressed. The two-party system defined the form, process and content of differences. In Lipset's and other sociological criticisms of the new left, the model by which it was evaluated and found wanting was the two-party system which, according to Lipset, provides one of the "principal opportunities and stimulations for participation in politics by members of an organization or community."[13] Their model was the existing political reality the new left was calling into question.

The lack of comprehension and/or sympathy for the student movement's criticism of this notion of democracy and for its attempts to forge a different and more participatory version is notable. In describing the politics of the student movement of the 1960s, for example, Shils clearly and sarcastically outlines what students meant by participation and community, and rejects it out of hand. " 'Participation' is a situation in which the individual's desires and 'demands' are fully realized through complete self-determination of the individual and the institutions which such freely, self-determining individuals form."[14] Shils then comments that, while this community is similar to Rousseau's, its contemporary proponents do not think the common will is the result of rationally realized assent of its members: ". . . It is not actually a *shared* decision making; it is certainly not the outcome of consent to a compromise arrived at by bargaining and exchange."[15] While Shils's market vocabulary is noteworthy, so is his stress on what the students wanted as a "transformation of sentiment and desire into reality in a community in which all realize their wills simultaneously,"[16] instead of the bargaining and compromise which is at the heart of his notion of politics. Shils was apparently unable to recognize that the students' central project was in fact shared decision making, that democratic and satisfactory participation was often achieved in the student movement, and that it embarked on this project precisely because the old rules did not work in favor of equality or participation. Feuer says of new left politics, "One could pass directly from moral principle to direct action without the distortion of an intervening refractory political machine. One could pit one's will against the system, and it would yield. One could make history instead of being made by it."[17] This is a fairly accurate rendition of some of the central tenets and desires of the new left and yet for Feuer, too, they were dangerously out of line.

The sociologists' notion of democracy seems to me glaringly narrow. Time and again they complained that the students would not play by the rules, and agreement on the rules and mechanisms by which a society runs keeps that society together. While some argued that this was due to students' idealism and moral mood, which led to their desire for a "totality of undifferentiated perfection" (Shils), others suggested it was because they were manipulative and did not really care about their demands. They wanted instead to disrupt, as an end in itself. Lipset, Bell and Glazer, among others, accused the students of having no real interest in any specific demands, of being indifferent to legality and of ignoring the conventional channels by which, the academics claimed, the students could have attained these demands. The rules by which they are accused of refusing to play were (1) compromise, (2) representation (a two-party system preferably), and (3) a commitment to the rules. The rules, in the sociologists' view, were more important than democracy, which is as clear an example of formal rationality as any. This, then, was the issue between the students and those who defended the status quo. The sociologists' democracy, moreover, contained a delimited, electoral path to social change. By 1964, white students were rejecting it by sitting in, demonstrating or organizing, because the traditional path did not appear to permit significant social change.

The criticisms we have been examining, as well as most social movement sociology, are based on organizational, or paraphrasing Lipset, instrumental political biases. That is, they assume not only the efficacy but the necessity of certain kinds of instrumental politics or certain kinds of organization. I believe that in connection with studies of the new left such approaches lead to two serious problems. First, they tend to prohibit the analyst from looking at the new left through new left eyes, which did not accept certain conceptions of politics. While one needs to do more than this, one ought to do at least this. A major goal of this book, then, is to approach the new left with the assumption that when its politics was what some would term expressive rather than instrumental, it was nevertheless operating politically. Specifically, I believe that the utopian and "anti-organizational" characteristics of the new left were among its most vital aspects.

The second problem intrinsic to organizationally or instrumentally biased approaches to the new left is related to the first. Such approaches generally fail to recognize the degree to which the new left sought to discover organizational forms and instrumental mechanisms that could be both effective within the given political arena and consistent with the so-called anti-political motifs of the movement. It may be that any such attempt, which in Max Weber's terms would amount to a synthesis of an ethic of responsibility with an ethic of absolute ends, is doomed to failure. But the fact is that a substantial part of the story of the new left was its attempt to accomplish this. A second major goal of the present work is to analyze the new left's effort to grapple with and resolve the problem of organization and instrumentality, and to a lesser extent, of agency, and in so doing to fill a substantial gap left by the bulk of the studies of this movement.

The unresolved tension between the spontaneous grass roots social movement committed to participatory democracy, defined in the 1962 guiding document of SDS, the Port Huron Statement, as the equal participation of each individual in all the social decisions that affect the quality and direction of his or her life, and the intention, necessitating organization, of achieving power or radical structural change in the United States, was a structuring theme of the new left. This tension and the ambivalence about organization is the axis on which the book turns. An underlying theme is the issue of agency: What groups are able to effect major social change in America? The contradictory demands of a national political organization, SDS, and the impulse towards local, utopian and spontaneous politics were projects pulling in conflicting directions. Furthermore, the depth, breadth, and complexities of what was a genuine grass roots social movement form part of the subject of this work since it was precisely these characteristics which presented obstacles to organizers and leaders. The disordered, anti-authoritarian movement of students regularly resisted attempts by leaders to centrally "organize" it. This discloses what I consider the kernel of insight beneath the layers of ideology in commentaries such as Lipset's. For what he and others tendentiously term the "expressive" and apolitical features of the new left, are, I believe, among its central features. Where those commentators see pathology, however, I see the healthy and vital heart of the new left, its prefigurative politics.

The term *prefigurative politics* is used to designate an essentially anti-organizational politics characteristic of the movement, as well as parts of new left leadership, and may be recognized in counter institutions, demonstrations and the attempt to embody personal and anti-hierarchical values in politics. Participatory democracy was central to prefigurative politics. "Anti-organizational" should not be construed as disorganized. Movements are organized in numerous obvious and often hidden ways.[18] My use of the term anti-organizational should be understood to mean principally a wariness of hierarchy and centralized organization. The crux of prefigurative politics imposed substantial tasks, the central one being to create and sustain within the live practice of the movement, relationships and political forms that "prefigured" and embodied the desired society.

The notion of community is integrally connected with prefigurative politics. The new left sought community as it sought to unite the public and private spheres of life. By community I mean a network of relationships more direct, more total and more personal than the formal, abstract and instrumental relationships characterizing state and society. "Community is founded on [man] conceived in his wholeness rather than in one or another of the roles, taken separately, that he may hold in a social order."[19] In saying that the new left sought community I refer not only to the desire to create a sense of wholeness and communication in social relationships, but to the effort to create non-capitalist and communitarian institutions that embodied such relationships, for example counter-institutions. In this sense, prefigurative politics, by attempting to develop the seeds of liberation and the new society prior to and in the process of revolution through notions of participatory democracy, often grounded in counter-institutions, meant building community.

There is a case to be made that community refers to a set of relationships, experiences and institutions that have been and continue to be destroyed by the development of capitalism and which consequently became relevant in the late nineteenth century and remain so in the present.[20] The search for and/or struggle to defend community, both the "sense" of community and actual community institutions, becomes political in the context of the changes that capitalism has brought in the everyday life of the individual—changes characterized by lack of control at work, school and play; impersonality and competition in all areas of life.[21] The desire for connectedness, meaningful personal relationships and direct participation and control over economic, political and social institutions on the basis of the needs of the individual and community, takes on radical meaning in a period such as ours.

Certain organizational forms were precluded or controversial, since they undercut the anti-hierarchical and direct nature of prefigurative politics. To cite by way of anticipation an example: to the extent that the new left embraced the concept of community, it faced great difficulty when events compelled it to develop formal organization in order to function in the customary political arena. This forced the new left into the dilemma of being unable or unwilling to create hierarchical organization which undermined, from the participants' point of view, its values and organizational forms. This does not mean that the new left was not political.[22] Once again, the central impulse toward community and democracy was precisely its political content.

Within and alongside the new left's prefigurative impulse was what I have called *strategic politics*, which was committed to building organization in order to achieve major structural changes in the political, economic and social orders. Organization-building and strategic thinking were central to strategic politics. In these terms, then, the book reconstructs the conflict between strategic and prefigurative politics.

Throughout the years in question the decentralization and grass roots nature of the movement informed the ideology of participants. Around the country activists functioned politically with little regard for what the SDS National Office or specific leaders suggested ought to be done. The genuine ambivalence about leadership, about representatives speaking on behalf of the group, derived in part from activists' sense of their *own* autonomy and self-direction. The fact that self-directed political activity sprang up all over, that mass insurgency often spread in spite of the lack of organizers and leaders, that a "thousand flowers bloomed" during the sixties, reinforced anti-organizational ideology. There seemed little need for centralized organization when local organization and political activity mobilized itself.

If the new left as a whole had merely rejected organization, strategy or instrumentality, as many commentators have insisted, then the story would not be of particular interest to many. But the new left's intense and finally unsuccessful effort to devise forms of social and political organization capable of effecting major, radical structural changes in American society, that would at the same time nurture a grass roots social movement committed to participatory democracy and community—this has bearing on both past and future social movements in the West. Much of the story I have reconstructed here is of course specific to both one decade and the social groups which constituted the social movements in that decade. I believe, however, that especially with regard to problems of organization and democracy, the experience of the student movements of the 1960s can be ignored or scorned only at risk by others interested in revitalizing democracy and communitarian life in modern society.

KEY TERMS

I shall be employing the term 'new left' in a specific sense, namely, the largely student and racially white social movement that emerged in the United States in the late 1950s and early 1960s and which called itself the new left. The perhaps final elusiveness of the term itself, however, is in many respects central to its meaning. That is, unlike the terms Communist, Social Democrat, anarchist, Trotskyist, and so forth, new left is: a) "new" and not linked to historical forms of affiliation and labelling within the left; b) lacking clear institutional loci and membership and/or identification with the outlook or program of a political party; and c) an especially complex term in the American context where a substantially visible "old left" presence has been lacking from the political picture.

More specifically, I have utilized a distinction suggested in 1971 by Richard Flacks:

> . . . It is neither historically accurate nor analytically helpful to regard the New Left as simply another name for campus revolt, anti-war pro-

test, or other youth-based insurgency. Rather, the New Left may be defined as a *particular segment* of young activists who were self-consciously radical ideologically, but disaffected from all "established radicalisms," and who self-consciously sought to provide political direction, theoretical coherence and organizational continuity to the student movement.

The notion that there was a "layer of people who specialized in organizing, theorizing, rationalizing and planning, and who therefore were relatively distinctive in their degree of politicization,"[23] differentiated from the general student movement, helps to define the different layers of people with whom I am concerned. The theorizing, debates and organizational preoccupation were undertaken by a self-conscious sector of the student movement, its largely male leadership, in this case found mainly in SDS. For the purposes of this work, the term *new left* refers to those most self-conscious and articulate groups and persons concerned with both political analysis and strategizing the transformation of capitalist society. This includes SDS as well as other political organizations of the 1960s. It also incorporates the most self-conscious activists on campuses, in draft-resistance activity, journalism or communities. In contrast, the term *student movement* is used to designate the upsurge of protest and opposition by students and ex-students usually (but not exclusively) to the war in Vietnam and university complicity with the war.

In the context of what has been formulated regarding the central tension in the new left, the student movement was the constituency that presented difficulties to new leftists; the movement was a challenge not only to society but to the movement's own leaders and organizers. The continual attempts to channel movement activities into centralized organization usually failed. One serious warning is in order about accepting these definitions literally; they were not clear cut. A grass roots social movement is by definition in flux and during political activity, usually direct action, this division between new leftists and movement participants blurred. Often participants became new leftists at such times. In the heat of activity consciousness changed: the participant was forced to take sides and risks, commit himself or herself, change a world view. Action might force a passive observer to become a historical actor, in the process becoming radicalized.

CHAPTER 2

Emergence of the New Left

A HISTORICAL SKETCH

During the 1950s two movements appeared which were crucial for the emergence of the white new left. The first, not really a movement, was composed of beatniks, artists, and dropouts from suburban and middle-class America. As early exponents of the rejection of dominant American values through a non-materialist lifestyle, they were forerunners of a mass counterculture. In retrospect they are more important than they seemed at the time. They signaled the birth of something new and critical in white American culture and society of the 1950s, the underside of the great American celebration. Little more than a decade later, the beatniks became the heroes of the 1960s counterculture.

Second and more important was the civil rights movement, which can be dated from the 1955 bus boycott in Montgomery, Alabama and early attempts at equal schooling in the South. The next step came in 1960 with the first sit-ins and then the freedom rides, which caught the media's, and thus the nation's, attention. With them the civil rights movement was in full stride, shaping the 1960s ahead. In particular, it galvanized the early new left. The Student Non-Violent Coordinating Committee (SNCC) was the most radical and important youth civil rights organization. The beat sub-culture and the civil rights movements shared a moral critique of American society, a critique the new left would inherit.

As soon as the civil rights movement erupted, northern campus support was organized. In 1960 picketing of Woolworth's and other national chain stores in support of black people's rights was the first political activity for many northern students and young people. In the ensuing years large numbers of white students went south as freedom riders (to desegregate public facilities) and to work in all aspects of the civil rights movement, primarily with SNCC. The movement was formative for the politics and outlook of the new left; styles of work, ideas and organizational forms were learned directly from SNCC.

SDS (Students for a Democratic Society) was formed in 1960 as the youth group of the League for Industrial Democracy (LID), an old left social democratic, anti-Communist organization.[1] From June 11 to June 15, 1962, a group of approximately fifty students met in Port Huron, Michigan, and adopted a guiding document which was to become known as the Port Huron Statement of SDS. They elected officers and planned to organize on the campuses in support of the civil rights movement and other student-oriented political issues. Many activists of those early SDS years went south and worked with SNCC as did many who participated in the 1964 Free Speech Movement in Berkeley. The experience was critical in the conception of the northern community organizing projects (Economic Research and Action Project—ERAP) sponsored by SDS beginning in 1963.

Between 1962 and 1965, the year of the first national anti-war demonstration called by SDS, intellectual and political ferment intensified among students. SDS, while numerically small, was central to what was happening. Its initial impact was intellectual rather than organizational. The first SDS'ers, drawing on the works of Camus, Paul Goodman, and above all, C. Wright Mills, formulated and began to disseminate the ideas that would constitute much of new left thinking in the 1960s. The first years of the decade saw the formation of an analysis of the structure of power, powerlessness, inequality and foreign policy in America. The intellectual work was in turn pushed progressively leftward by its immediate context, the violent and illegal response of white Southerners to civil rights activities and what seemed to be the less than principled response of the federal government to the peaceful and legal demands by black people for their constitutional rights. The impact on the developing new left of the Democratic Party convention in Atlantic City, in 1964, cannot be overestimated. The voter registration drive in the south culminated in the Mississippi Freedom Democratic Party's challenge to the all-white, racist Democratic Party delegation from that state. Had the national party recognized the Freedom Democratic Party in Mississippi, participants and supporters of the civil rights struggles would surely have been impressed with the Democrats' commitment to serious reform and with the general efficacy of pursuing politics within the established channels. What actually happened was no less impressive. By taking its stand with the racist side in Mississippi, the Democratic Party convinced whites and blacks in the civil rights movement of the party's hypocrisy, and of the obstacles built into the established channels. Instead of being forestalled, the momentum toward disillusionment with the existing system and more radical protest against it was intensified. For many black activists, black nationalist ideas quickly acquired meaning. Whites, particularly students, in and around the civil rights movement began to look for other paths.

One such path had already appeared. Just one month after the Democratic Convention in the autumn of 1964 the first decisive development occurred outside the framework of the southern civil rights movement: the Free Speech Movement (FSM) on the campus of the University of California at Berkeley. FSM was critical because, as the first major white student rebellion, it laid down the terms for many others during the rest of the sixties. The ideas, demands, and experiences at Berkeley were enunciated time and again, and may serve as a characteristic scenario by which to understand the politics of the early student movement. FSM forced the white student movement's attention and focus back to the northern campuses.

April 1965, with the prior bombing of North Vietnam and the first demonstration against the war in Vietnam, marked the beginning of the anti-war movement on a national scale and the expansion of the student movement into a mass movement. The anti-war movement continued to grow throughout the sixties and although SDS often did not assume organizational responsibility, it was symbolically and politically at the center, particularly as the strength of the anti-war movement lay on the campuses. A moral position formed its core. From 1965 onward a proper history of the new left must focus on the growing opposition to the Vietnam war, increasing support for the black revolutionary movement and growing disillusionment with the university, due particularly to its connection and cooperation with the government in the form of military research, and military and corporate recruitment. The new left's sophistication developed as the analysis of capitalism became more refined and the connections between the corporations, the universities and the government more apparent. The moral critique was politicized as the new left became conscious of itself and the organization of American society. The war and the black movement together seemed to provide proof of the analysis of colonialism abroad and at home. The exploitative relationship of rich white capitalist America to the rest of the world's peoples became one of the most pervasive themes of the new left, particularly at the end of the sixties.

By 1968 the intensity of the political situation domestically and internationally moved many in SDS towards a militant revolutionary program and rhetoric, with the sectarian Progressive Labor Party making a concerted effort to take over the organization. The 1968 SDS National Convention marked the beginning of the end of the organization; 1969 saw it split completely into competing factions, one of which identified with Third World guerrilla revolutions and the other with the American working class, though neither faction was in touch with the mass student movement. While the student anti-war movement continued to expand, the most significant organization, SDS, imploded, leaving the student movement leaderless on a national level, and enabling the anti-war movement to remain the single-issue movement it need not have been. Although the student movement alone could not have produced fundamental social change in the United States, its disintegration and especially the disappearance of the new left, deprived American society of a source of radical analysis and of a significant force for egalitarianism and liberation.

THE OLD LEFT AND THE NEW LEFT

The problematic relationship between the old left and the new (and implicitly new left's relation to Marxism as a theory) haunts any work on the new left. Tension dominated the relationship. In specific instances, one can find old leftists who became new leftists and vice versa. On the whole, however, the old and new lefts stand as conflicting political traditions/orientations/sensibilities. My own work echoes that conflict; specifically it echoes some of the criticisms the new left made of the old left. In any case, my concern in the present chapter is not to assess the old left but to examine briefly the new left's attitude toward it.

The American Communist Party (CP) was the most important institutional expression of the old left.[2] For new leftists, the CP was the main symbol and most visible reality of old leftism. But it was not the only expression. As was noted, SDS was the youth group of the League for Industrial Democracy (LID). The LID was a small old left organization of socialists who were, however, hostile to both the Soviet Union and the CP. LID played a role in the early fortunes of SDS, but beyond that its influence was largely negative. That is, although SDS never developed sympathies for either the Soviet Union or the American CP, it quickly grew impatient with the LID's vociferous anti-Communism and its commitment to moderate reforms. In this context, some SDS'ers described their position in the early 1960s as "anti-anti-Communism." The Socialist Workers' Party (SWP) and its youth group, the Young Socialist Alliance (YSA) represented still another old left current: Trotskyism. The SWP and YSA along with smaller Trotskyist groupings were active throughout the 1960s, particularly in large-scale coalitions against the Vietnam War.

Beyond these old left organizations, there was, as the 1960s opened, a range of individuals and small groups gathered around pacifist and anarchist ideas. They were old left only in the chronological sense, having been on the left during the 1930s, 1940s and 1950s (as well as since). But such radical pacifists as A. J. Muste and David Dellinger, the Catholic

Worker movement or anarchists such as Paul Goodman or Murray Book-chin were politically not old leftists. Their ethically oriented criticism of capitalism, emphasis on the activism of moral witness and distrust of hierarchical organizations distinguished them from the old left parties and organizations proper. Their impact on the new left may not have been extensive; nevertheless, the pacifists and anarchists are among the new left's real forerunners.[3]

As far as the tensions between the old left and the new were concerned, the CP occupied the main position. Between the end of World War Two and the end of the 1950s, the CP was battered and weakened by official and popular anti-Communism on the one hand, and American capitalism's post-war economic boom on the other. Yet it endured and during the period of the new left's emergence, it was the CP that embodied the old left. In response to the new left, in fact, the CP formed the W.E.B. Dubois Clubs, which sometimes took part in and sought to recruit members from new left activities in the mid-1960s.

The DuBois Clubs, however, represented only the surface of a more complicated tie and tension between the two lefts. There were in the new left, for example, many children of old leftists, Communist Party members or their sympathizers, referred to as "red diaper babies." For a variety of reasons, the most salient being the repression of the McCarthy period, which forced parents to hide or change their politics, young people who had grown up in old left families and became part of the new left cannot be assumed to have transmitted old left politics lock, stock and barrel. The family connection, particularly when parents were afraid of and/or repudiated their own left politics, meant that old left politics were not cleanly handed down, if politics ever are. The children were shaped by a great deal more than their families, as any elementary sociological analysis of American culture and institutions makes obvious. Even so, Jonah Raskin was not wrong to write in 1974:

> . . . The children were frightened by McCarthyism and the FBI and conformed, but in the thaw of the sixties they surfaced and rebelled. They joined the movement, the crowd in the streets, looked like freaks and hippies, lived in communes, dropped out. They connected the old left with the new left, they linked the thirties with the sixties.

> In the sixties the children of thirties radicals pushed their middle-aged parents into politics again. Maybe the parents were at first unwilling to march or protest again after so many years. But by demanding that their parents demonstrate, the children were applying their parents' own original values. In a true, historical sense they were thanking the old leftists who kept alive the sparks of the thirties in the cold, cold fifties.[4]

The existence of these children in the new left demonstrates the power of an old left culture and of its values, a continuity of generations in spite of adverse odds. There is, in fact, some evidence that family life was particularly close and intense among the old left; it was, as Raskin noted, the values and not the politics that in many cases were passed on.[5] But the new left as a movement *did* have to reckon with old left politics (and vice versa). In part, the new left defined itself in and through this reckoning, giving shape to its own politics in the process of contrast and confrontation.

What were the salient characteristics of old left politics? Briefly, the old left was oriented towards the Soviet Union, the first country to experience socialist revolution. The CP viewed the Soviet Union in almost religious terms as a socialist paradise; the LID and other Social Democrats saw it as the great evil; and the Trotskyists took up a position somewhere in between. But for all of them, the Soviet Union was the central point of reference. Second, the old left as a whole shared the idea of the industrial working class as the agency of the transformation of capitalism to socialism.[6] Specific differences aside, the old left viewed industrial workers generally and labor unions in particular as the locus of its potential constituency. While often preoccupied with such questions as racism, the old left nevertheless did not consider sectors of the population outside the working class to be pivotal to socialist transformation.

Third, the old left by and large espoused an economic interpretation of history, capitalism and left politics. With some exceptions, the old left was thus prone to see such questions as alienation, bureaucracy and culture as secondary at best; as products of flawed economic arrangements which would be rectified naturally by appropriate changes in the economy. Fourth, the old left believed in "progressive" reforms of capitalism from above. They worked easily and with dedication in electoral politics, sometimes for their own candidate, often within the Democratic Party. Finally and perhaps most significantly from the point of view of this work, the old left groups were oriented toward strategic politics. There were of course important differences in this area, but on the whole the old left viewed the political party (be it Leninist or not) as the chief organizational form of its activity.

Some of the flavor of the differences between the old and new leftists can be grasped when the main experience of each is outlined. The old left was shaped by the Depression, by fascism in Europe and by the Second World War; the Russian Revolution was critical in its vision of alternatives. The Cold War and McCarthyism were powerful determinants of its world view. The new left was shaped by the post-war boom, the consumer goods and suburban explosions, mass culture, especially television (it was the first television generation), and a general sense of prosperity, power and expanding horizons.

Participatory democracy, central to the new left, pointed naturally toward a critique of the Soviet model of socialism and the traditional American model of electoral representative politics. It was not at first consciously a critique of the Soviet Union, but developed into one. Moreover, the question of the Soviet Union was not a pressing one for the new left, which was profoundly American-centered—only later becoming internationalist, and then with a primarily Third World focus. The vision of the new left, developed in affluence rather than depression and fascism, was of a cornucopia of possibilities. A social system which provided for everyone, and in which everyone participated equally, seemed desirable and possible; class was not critical to its vision. Predictably, given its secure economic situation and mass media developments in America, the new left became interested in culture and hegemony: concepts central for understanding the hold which advanced capitalism had on people's consciousness. The old left was preoccupied with "objective conditions" of revolution, while the new left highlighted the importance of "subjective conditions."

The old left was more socialist than the new. On balance, the early new left and the student movement were not traditionally socialist. They did not believe in a working-class revolution, or in a Marxist analysis of social change and of political organization; they were largely ignorant of the history of the left in this country and globally. Existentialism and not Marxism was relevant to them and captured their mood. Symptomatically, for the new left corporate capitalism and liberalism were the enemies, whereas for the old left the enemy was the right wing.

I have already noted that while it was not the sole representative, the Communist Party tended to dominate the old left picture. In certain instances, then, it makes sense to speak of relations between the old left and the new primarily in terms of the role and legacy of the Communist Party. This has been the focus here. Other instances would require that attention be given specifically to pacifists, or Trotskyists and so on.

In fact, there is still another aspect of new left-old left relations which pertains to my theme. For although the new left generally rejected the models and styles embodied in the older communist and socialist parties, it found in the process another old left with which it felt closer ties. This old left, and not its immediate generational predecessor, as Richard Gombin has shown, was a leftism which included a critique of bureaucracy, the centrality of everyday life and which incorporated the thought of Lukács, Korsch, Gramsci, Luxemburg, the Frankfurt School and the council communists.[7] According to Gombin, all currents to the left of the Communist Parties, and previously unknown to all but a few, were revived. *This* left tradition, both theoretically within Marxism and politically in history, had a more positive influence on new left intellectuals than did the official Communism of Moscow and its member parties.

The new left experiment, prefigurative politics, was near the heart of struggles among European Marxists early in this century. In the context of a working-class movement, Rosa Luxemburg and Antonio Gramsci and the lesser known Anton Pannokoek combined hostility towards centralization and the bureaucratic conception of the workers' party, with a faith in the spontaneity of the masses and support for the councils which were both an organ of struggle and future unit of government by and for the producers. They mistrusted the party apparatus, believing like Robert Michels, author of *Political Parties,* that it turned into an instrument of domination over the workers. Mass actions and revolutionary consciousness were underscored in this radical leftist tradition, as were councils, natural groupings of the masses, revolutionary forms of organization. These political activists and theorists wanted to bring together prefigurative politics and the conquest of power, issues with which the new left struggled, further removed from power than even the council communists, but nonetheless with seriousness. In times of insurgency and upheaval social movement theorists or historians often discover other and hidden traditions which seem suddenly profoundly relevant and inspiring. As always happens, new social movements tend to introduce new ways of looking at the past and new pasts to look at. In this case the immediate old left and, indeed, *its* relationship to the leftist tradition, served not as inspiration but as warning signal to students passionately interested in forging not only a new but a different left.

CHAPTER 3

The Great Refusal

"THE ISSUE IS NOT THE ISSUE"

Writing in 1970 Todd Gitlin said of the Free Speech Movement (FSM): "That mass movement is not simply 'about' free speech, nor even simply 'about' the right to organize for political action, but finally it is 'about' the necessity of revolt from the gargantuan, depersonalized, mass-production multiversity." And in a related article he stressed the point that a social movement is never simply "about" its object, but "is always 'about' the deepest identities of the participants . . . who . . . stoke it and shape it."[1] Throughout the sixties specific grievances against the university and opposition to the government's domestic and foreign politics sparked student revolts. The trajectory of these grievances and revolts travelled from domestic issues, civil rights and civil liberties, to foreign policy concerns, particularly the war in Vietnam. Often opposition to the Vietnam War was directed at university complicity with the government's war effort, specifically against class ranking for the draft, campus military research, and campus recruitment for the military and war-involved corporations, such as the Dow Chemical Corporation, makers of napalm. Although the bureaucracy, rigidity and often the violence of the university's response to student demands always provided additional issues, and although the horror of the continued escalation of the war provided the single most powerful impulse for the student movement, these were not all the student movement was "about." A Berkeley slogan put it this way, "The Issue Is Not the Issue."

In the following pages the pervasiveness and strength of prefigurative politics is explored, as is the actual experience and meaning for activists of direct political activity. This was the movement from 1964 to 1968, the grass roots insurgency on the campuses, the never quiet, always eventful environment in which the political debates and analyses took place. It becomes clear that while specific issues gave the movement its impetus, the American student movement of the 1960s was about the "necessity of revolt"; students' deepest identities wished to create a "world turned upside down."[2] It is interesting to note that every one of the liberal and sociologist critics of the student movement, including Lipset, Glazer and Shils, accused it of not seriously caring about the issues around which it rallied and demonstrated. They charged that the students "used" these demands to destroy the university and the fabric of society, to express hostility against the government, to sow chaos. They are not entirely wrong. But while they see in this phenomenon malevolence and conspiracy, I am suggesting that often the revolt was about more than the issues articulated by the students.

In the first section of the chapter I suggest that underneath the liberal rhetoric and the demands for university reform lay a more profound and explosive conception of political possibilities. Following that, I examine the Free Speech Movement for themes and experiences critical to prefigurative politics which were continually reproduced in subsequent movement activity. The final section presents material from events, short-lived, extraordinary or characteristic political actions, from across the country, which illustrate their power to release hopes, energies and ideas which anticipated a new and radical society. The character of these hopes and meanings, widespread in the movement, is the heart of prefigurative politics.

Social science accounts tend to reduce student rebellions to quantifiable or at least highly specific factors. Most analyses of the student revolt dissected it, evaluated each component—such as the demands, the administration's response, the role of the faculty, the external pressures, the actual conflict, and the outcome, at face value (often based on questionnaire responses)—and finally put it back together again, having lost or ignored the radical hopes, experiments and vision of the students. This means, in effect, that the cultural, personal and social implications, the deeper subjective political meaning has often gone unnoticed or unrecorded, and has been excluded from an analysis of the political significance of the movement. Consideration of the words and meanings of the participants makes accessible an alternative notion of politics, a politics of community in action.

Michael Miles, a commentator concerned primarily with educational industrialization as the generator of the student movement, nevertheless points out, "University conflicts release transforming passions because all parties understand . . . that the rebellions are not exclusively 'student' rebellions and that the stakes are not only university 'politics' and 'structures.' "[3] He refers to the symbolic dimensions of student rebellion, which account for the release of powerful passions and resentments triggered by apparently unimportant events. And Alain Touraine helps to explain this by suggesting that the student movement was not "primarily an effort to reform the university but a basic indictment of society and its culture."[4] The ideas and forms of revolt were expressions of a radical and utopian upsurge on the part of students and young people. Although I have made a distinction between the new left and the student movement, it is critical to remember that the line between them, particularly in the midst of action, was often difficult to distinguish. Participants were transformed during political activity, lines blurred between new leftists and the masses of movement activists. As Eric Hobsbawm has written in his book *Primitive Rebels*, "In the intoxicating and ecstatic moments of revolutions the great surge of human hope may sweep even reformists into the camp of revolutionaries. . . ."[5]

Most discussions and analyses of the new left have ignored the political content of the cultural and personal revolt and the cultural and personal content of the political revolt. Commentators have interpreted the political and cultural components of the revolt as two very separate spheres.[6] Specifically, there has been little recognition of the cultural dimensions of the student revolt.[7] A letter to the *Berkeley Barb* in 1967 articulated the close ties between Haight-Ashbury, the counter-culture and hippie center in San Francisco, and the anti-war movement:

> There would probably by no Haight-Ashbury without the war and perhaps the anti-war movement would not have reached the cold brutal turning point from disobedience and submission to rebellion and violence had there been no "hippies"; the pre-hippies, hippies and past hippies who marched, got arrested, sang, screamed and cried . . .

> Hippies are more than just people who walk down Haight Street with beads, bells, long hair, stoned on drugs. They are a concept, an act of rejection, a militant vanguard, a hope for the future.[8]

Notions of personal and cultural transformation, sometimes but not always involving drugs, were inherent in prefigurative politics. In the period until 1968 there was great continuity between the hippie and political wings of the movement. Student demonstrations, occupations, and other rebellions against the university and federal government, as well as the life style changes embodied in the counter-culture, were groping attempts to create a more meaningful, free and moral existence. The student movement was anti-war and anti-authoritarian as well, an "expression of rejection and revolt,"[9] a search for a democratic community. The full meaning of the student movement can be grasped only by inclusion of these dimensions.

One of the most characteristic features of the social movement of the 1960s, at the time and in retrospect, is the developmental leaps it took and the speed with which it took them. Each stage of development generated its successor, often literally overnight. Perhaps the most vivid example is the French student movement of 1968, which began as a small protest against a ban on coeducational swimming at Nanterre University and culminated within about a month in a massive student rebellion and finally in a general strike. The movement in America did not develop with quite the speed and scope of its French counterpart, but it was nonetheless carried forward by a familiar dynamic. Most of the left-of-center campus groups in the early 1960s, for example, had such mild names as the Liberal Discussion Group or the FDR Club. Their activities often centered around protesting dormitory curfews and visitation rules. But it is not accurate to characterize such a focus as petty, liberal, or reformist. In retrospect it seems clear that the small matter of parietals, for example, entailed such larger matters as a sense of powerlessness among students and the beginning of a refusal to accept established authority as given.[10] Many left analyses of the new left fail to see this underlying dynamic, preferring instead to highlight the early new left's lack of economic and class-structural perspective.[11] It makes more sense now, and made more sense at the time, to see the moral, subjective and middle class aspects of the early campus rebellion, its liberal packaging, as a groping toward a new radical politics. Traditional left intellectuals tend not to err in the same way when considering working class movements, which are habitually given theoretical room to develop erratically. In this regard, a number of early SDSers at the time and later referred to participatory democracy as another term for socialism.[12] Such claims are reminders that the young movement's impulses pointed beyond the language and the specific demands through which they were first expressed.[13]

Early black and white student activists petitioned the government for protection, and guarantees of civil rights and equality under the law. There were those, the majority, who assumed that the people in power in the federal government and universities shared their ideals and would naturally act on them, but this was not necessarily because they believed the state would or could comply. When the federal government seemed at best to drag its feet or when, at its 1964 convention, the Democratic Party seemed to side with racism, or when university administrators told student protesters to return obediently to their studies and partying, what Todd Gitlin has called "radical disappointment" was generated among white and black students who had internalized ideals of democracy, equality, and constitutionality.[14]

In his study of the English working class, E. P. Thompson pointed to a "dialectical paradox" in the years 1770 to 1790 in which ". . . the rhetoric of constitutionalism contributed to its own destruction or transcendence," which sheds some light on a similar process for the new left.[15] There was both hope and ambivalence. The southern civil rights movement in the early 1960s provides a good example of this process. Initially activists used the Constitution as the document protecting the rights of blacks; they continued to do so, but since they had no power with which to enforce the law, they were progressively radicalized by the federal government's consistent refusal to protect those rights. They expected and hoped for support and protection, were confused at first, and horrified and infuriated later when the federal government rarely intervened on their behalf. Historians of radical social movements often point to the fact that these movements look backwards to older traditions and documents, or upwards to unsympathetic authority for justification and support for their ideas and actions. While it may appear conservative, or in the case of the student movement, "liberal," such appeals to the past cannot be dispensed with too facilely.

Appeals to past documents or traditions were used as weapons for creating resistance and developing new left politics. Familiar vocabulary and conditions were indicated while the revolts were often "about" other only vaguely communicated and sometimes unarticulated experiences. Once spontaneous and collective political actions unfolded, new modes of communicating, decision-making and analysis developed, as did solidarity and a new kind of caring, which in turn became the basis of future protests and changing notions of politics. Rebellion often initially took familiar complaints and issues, those at hand, and infused them with radical content. As the decade wore on, the understanding and articulation of a critique of American society became more accurate, sophisticated and realistic.

A good example of the lack of sophistication and the existence of liberal illusions is Carl Oglesby's November 1965 speech at one of the earliest national demonstrations against the war in Vietnam called by SDS. He outlined his shocked realization that *liberals* were responsible for the war and for supporting right-wing tyrannies around the world. He named the system, "corporate liberalism," and remarked, ". . . Others will make of it that I sound mighty anti-American. To these, I say: Don't blame *me* for *that*! Blame those who mouthed liberal values and broke my American heart."[16]

It took at least some time and learning for vocabulary and analysis to catch up with the dissatisfaction and moral revulsion, linking these to a more sophisticated understanding of American society. The political milestones in this process may be pinpointed by looking at the speeches and demonstrations from the Port Huron Statement onward. The vital point, however, is that stated demands and grievances were not the whole story. A close examination (which university administrations and/or faculty occasionally did, and often did not do) of students' demands does not yield all that the student revolt was "about." Writing in 1968 about the upheaval in Berkeley, a reporter stated, "The politics of this struggle can never be reduced to a set of demands. Political demands are not the same as political goals."[17]

THE FREE SPEECH MOVEMENT: STUDENTS-FOR-THEM-SELVES

At the December 2, 1964, Free Speech Movement rally before the Sproul Hall sit-in at the University of California at Berkeley, Mario Savio announced:

> There's a time when the operation of the machine becomes so odious, makes you so sick at heart, that you can't take part, you can't even tacitly take part. And you've got to put your bodies upon the gears and upon the wheels, upon the levers, upon all the apparatus, and you've got to make it stop. And you've got to indicate to the people who run it, to the people who own it, that unless you're free, the machine will be prevented from working at all.[18]

The Free Speech Movement was politically the first and most important major white student demonstration of the 1960s. It is often inaccurately viewed as initiating the "student movement"; it did however articulate most of the issues and enact many of the experiences of later student revolts. Savio's short speech prior to the Sproul Hall sit-in, widely quoted and reprinted, perfectly expressed many of these issues: the university and the society as a machine (bureaucracy); the conviction that an individual must refuse to cooperate, refuse to be a cog in that machinery, or in the case of the draft, a body for war; a belief in freedom and the individual's right to resist an unfree society until freedom is attained; and the notion that a political movement is created by thousands of individuals who say "no" to the structures and politics of the dominant society, who refuse to take part and in so doing create a crisis of legitimacy that stops the machine. In this version of revolt strategic and economic considerations lose their primacy, and individual resistance turns into mass insurgency.

Resistance in new left terms required total commitment and risk, often physical: "putting your body on the line" (a sixties slogan). This derived from and resulted in a politics of activism.[19] Becoming radicalized and joining the movement often meant changing one's life, breaking with the past and with values of prevailing institutions, being part of the solution instead of part of the problem. Part of the explanation for students' ability to engage in this sort of politics lay in their sociological position as students: specifically their lack of everyday responsibilities, their convergence in large numbers in one institution, and the concern with humanistic values fostered in the university.[20]

The Free Speech Movement is the most discussed student movement of the 1960s.[21] FSM provided the first example of students acting politically for themselves, raising issues and questions central to their own lives and acting spontaneously on them. As has often been noted, FSM was informed by the tactics of the civil rights movement and was the first example of participants in that movement using what they had learned on their own behalf. Lewis Feuer quotes Jack Weinberg, a major actor in FSM, as saying, "I became an activist before the FSM. I worked with CORE [Congress of Racial Equality] in the South in 1963 . . ." Weinberg was not enrolled at Berkeley at the time of FSM and Feuer refers to him as the "leading nonstudent of the Berkeley Free Speech Movement." Feuer seems particularly discontented with "nonstudents," stating they lived compulsively in generational revolt. "To every virtue which his father upheld he counterposes an antivirtue . . ." and, ". . . the nonstudent is a luxurious excrescence of the affluent society."[22]

Savio's statement, cited above, begins with the notion of the society as a machine and people as cogs, fuel, or raw material for the social system, who are turned into finished products. In the Berkeley rebellion and repeatedly thereafter students expressed opposition to a faceless and inhumane bureaucracy organized for industry and profit, and the necessity of non-cooperation in order to force it to stop. At Berkeley the machine was the bureaucracy of the multiversity which identified and treated students as IBM cards. A Berkeley student, Larry Spence, suggested that the multiversity was a factory turning out personnel for an advanced industrial economy, and that it had, as well, to produce a steady stream of teachers and professors to meet the rapidly increasing requirements of the "knowledge industry." "The 'multiversity,'" Spence charged, "is the anteroom of the power structure and of monopoly capitalism, where managerial cadre are recruited and young men on the make are made."[23]

Later, particularly in the draft-resistance movement, the machine was the manpower channeling apparatus of the Selective Service System and the structure of the state in general. The imagery, as in Mario Savio's speech, derived from an analysis of the United States as a society of giant bureaucracies over which people had no control, devoted to asocial, profit-making and destructive ends. At bottom, according to Saul Landau and Paul Jacobs, this perception was a "challenge to the quality of life, to the essence of modern American values, and the social system itself."[24] The revolt against liberal bureaucracy was a revolt on behalf of participation, a revolt for democracy. As many participants and analysts pointed out, surges of FSM activity were always a response to being administered and manipulated. Discussing life at Berkeley, Savio said in 1965, "There is a sense that there is a class of managers and a class of managed."[25] He pointed out that the managed were an overwhelming majority who were prevented from participating in the direction of their own lives and who were impersonally dictated to by managers who served the bureaucracy.

Clark Kerr, president of the University of California during FSM, was one of the chief architects and spokespeople for the multiversity as a bureaucracy servicing government, industry, finance, labor and national defense.[26] In Kerr's view the university was to be run like an efficient business by skilled managers and administrators. Only a small place was given to critical or humanist knowledge in such an enterprise, now a major growth sector of the national economy. Scientific and technological knowledge were replacing older disciplines in importance. And by necessity students were excluded from major decisions. For many students, experience in the university simulated in microcosm the experience of most citizens in the major institutions of American society, where freedom and control over one's life were severely constrained in the interests of profit, property and efficiency. From the beginning, students linked their struggle with the southern civil rights struggle. And it was linked directly at Berkeley by those who participated in the movement in the south and then returned to Berkeley in the fall of 1964. Commenting on FSM, Savio suggested that the irrationality of a society which denied a dignified life to Negroes was the same irrationality that denied autonomy and freedom to students and had caused the uprising.[27]

Freedom versus the machine was the main image. "Unless you're free, the machine will be prevented from working at all," Savio stated. Inspired by blacks, students took a stand on behalf of freedom. Holding the police car that had arrested one of its members (the "nonstudent" Jack Weinberg), rallying and sitting in, were meant to indicate to "the people who run it, to the people who own it" that freedom was more important than the efficient functioning of the machine. A central theme came directly from Max Weber via C. Wright Mills. Spence, a participant, had written, "Bureaucracies become ends instead of means. Nearing the end of industrial slavery, men become, instead, slaves of their own industrial creations."[28] The "iron cage" of bureaucracy figured powerfully in new left ideology. The fear that bureaucracy and centralized organization took on lives of their own and subverted original goals was responsible for the movement's wariness of even its *own* political organizations and for many of its political dilemmas, as well as for its opposition to large-scale bureaucratic institutions in the society at large. Larry Spence's analysis of the University of California pointed to a "great discrepancy between the size and power of today's giant organizations and their effectiveness." He argued that this ineffectiveness was evidence relevant to the American government's inability to "conquer an oversized rice paddy called Vietnam" (a comment exposing the prejudice and ignorance of even those opposed to the war in 1962). And most tellingly: "The bureaucracy of the largest university in the world cannot admit simple mistakes—or negotiate with dissident students without calling in the state police.["29] The trajectory of student revolt was always affected by bureaucratic responses of a university administration which never failed to underscore the students' original critique. Spence remarked that the rallies increased in size after each administrative intransigence and that students' consciousness was radicalized by the spectacle of organizational machinery grinding their lives into "atomic fragments."[30]

As evidence of the intimate connections between the university and the government's war effort in Vietnam became available, students perceived themselves and soldiers as instruments for the corporate liberals who ran the country. Early on they began to articulate an analysis that permitted them to see those responsible for waging the war as part of a "system" of corporate liberalism, as Oglesby stated in his speech in 1965. These were not evil men, he noted. They had, rather, been divided from their compassion by a "system that inherits us all. Generations in and out, we are put to use. People become instruments. Generals do not hear the screams of the bombed; sugar executives do not see the misery of the cane cutters—for to do so is to be that much *less* the general, that much *less* the executive."[31]

Perceptions of the lack of connectedness and meaning in their lives— the feeling of being IBM cards—lay at the heart of students' critique of large scale organization, and lent urgency to their experiments in democracy, which were in large part precisely quests for connectedness and meaning. Explaining the outbreak of FSM, Savio said:

> The people are all cut off from one another and what they need is a spark, just one spark to show them that all these people around them, likewise, are quite as lonely as they are, quite as cut off as they, quite as hungry for some kind of community as they are . . .

> Free speech was in some ways a pretext . . . . Around that issue the people could gain the community they formerly lacked.[32]

The desire for community may have, in fact, *sensitized* students to the issue of bureaucracy; their experience of alienation may have facilitated their formulation of a condemnation of their society. It is helpful to see students' critique of American society and their own political experiments flowing from their desire for community. Without alternative notions of democracy, participation or communication they could neither have zeroed in on their unavailability in most American institutions nor struck such a profound chord among students.

Following from this, the sense of community and temporary community institutions that *were* created by students in the midst of movement political activity were critical and formative for new left politics. The process was one of energetically, even joyfully, creating and experiencing connectedness and meaning, which often dissipated quickly, only to be recreated and dreamed of long after, shaping an alternative vision of society. These feelings and experiments were among the driving inspirations and goals of the movement and new left, attained briefly in just such actions as FSM. In Jack Weinberg's words, "The FSM . . . has been the most complete experience of my life, the most all-encompassing . . . . It gave me a sense of comradeship we had not known existed."[33] Experience demonstrated that collective political activity released feelings of connectedness and participation whose absence had called the opposition to life in the first place. This had been learned first in the civil rights movement, and later on the campuses. A basic if rarely articulated purpose of the movement was to create communities of equality, direct democracy and solidarity. In bold contrast to the values of competition, individualism and efficiency, the movement yearned for and occasionally achieved the community it sought.

In FSM direct communication and democracy were often achieved in the midst of demonstrations, strikes and occupations, through dialogue and talk. Discussing FSM, Sol Stern wrote in 1965:

> Most of the education that took place in the next few days came outside the classrooms, in the innumerable knots and crowds of students and faculty that sprang up everywhere on campus. They argued and discussed the nature of democracy, the rule of law, and civil disobedience. The FSM organized classes off the campus at their "Free University of California." It was truly an amazing scene. Nothing less than a revolution, though a gentle one, seemed to be taking place.[34]

Public dialogue on political issues, the feeling of being engaged with others in real education, the power of talk to transcend individual and private woes and launch students into political engagement, were novel, exhilarating and often contagious experiences. They became hallmarks of student politics. Participants almost always compared this orgy of talk favorably to the official education they received in the university. Unlike many classes, it was inspiring. Michael Rossman has described events which triggered FSM following the university's action forbidding the solicitation on campus for off-campus political activity; the immediate reaction to the ban and the arrest of a student was to surround a police car that held prisoner one of those who had been soliciting on campus:

> So it's Thursday night, and there are still well over a thousand of us. And by this time we realize simply that we have to hold that car. That car is the only thing we've gotten in six years. It's our car; it isn't the

cops' car anymore. And so we start bringing our sleeping bags. And the dialogue on top of the car continues. People are getting up there and talking, and people are listening. And people are voting on this, and people are voting on that.[35]

The democracy and spontaneity, the sheer amount spoken by people who usually said little, the give and take, and the disappearance of the isolation and loneliness experienced by many students, all became rudiments of the new left's emerging sense of itself. New left dialogue encouraged and enabled many to participate.

Participants in the student revolt were quickly struck by the fact that in the university, as in the society at large, talk leading to political action was discouraged or trivialized. Savio had remarked that the free speech fight indicated that "Students are permitted to talk all they want as long as their speech has no consequence . . ."[36] As soon as they had *acted* on their own loss of democracy or liberty, the university stepped in. Words in the classroom, meaningless with respect to their desire for relevancy and freedom, were unsatisfactory. When the connection was made between words and actions, students understood by the university's response that they were becoming relevant.

Paradoxically, in light of popular stereotypes of the new left's anti-intellectualism, the eruption of dialogue and discussion went together with a positive evaluation of the potential of the university. We will see below the early new left's idealistic belief in the university as a center of learning and as a community of scholars devoted to the pursuit of truth. The FSM allied itself with this image of the university *against* the administration, separating the administration from what they believed was the real and ideal purpose of the university, learning. In a pamphlet revealingly entitled, "We Want a University," FSMers said: "We are beginning to *build* a great university. So long as students stand united in firmness and dignity and the faculty stand behind us, the University cannot be destroyed."[37] It was the administration and not the students who were destroying the "real" university.

The charge of anti-intellectualism against the new left, discussed below and again in Chapter Six, was often inaccurate, particularly in the early years. In fact, new left analysis and criticism grew directly from ideals pertaining to the university. The early new left idealized the pursuit of truth and freedom; it was in part the university's divergence from this ideal that precipitated students' actions. They were amazed and thrilled by the dialogue and learning, by the discussion of ideas as well as tactics and the sense of community created in the process; from their point of view these should have characterized the university but did not. The "free universities" arose out of these experiences. The interest in learning and ideas that school often crushed rose to the surface during FSM and was interpreted by activists as support for a true university community. Their pamphlet stated, "The university cannot be destroyed unless its core is destroyed, and our movement is not weakening that core but strengthening it."[38]

Commentators remarked that because FSM included so many, it was characterized by inefficiency and duplication. Yet it was surprisingly effective. Observers repeatedly stressed the open nature of FSM, which enabled it to enlarge its base of support. Leaders and spokespeople were committed to publicizing what was happening and to arriving at decisions as democratically as possible. At large rallies, ". . . extensive discussion about options open to the FSM took place right at the rally and a voice vote decided the issue."[39] The price for this participation was a good deal of inefficiency which took the form of groups duplicating each others' activities. An observer remarked that, while this was not particularly efficient, it indicated the "popular nature of the participation in the strike."[40]

No central political organization was responsible for popular mobilization. People participated because the issues struck a chord, because many students believed in FSM's principles (civil libertarian at first), and because they were generally both dissatisfied and hopeful. This was also true of the movement at large. While it meant duplication, it also meant that participants did what was necessary in order that the revolt, strike, sit-in or demonstration should survive. Division of labor was not hierarchically organized from above, but arose out of obvious need. It did not escape students' notice that this contrasted sharply with the centralized and hierarchic institution against which they struggled. Michael Rossman asked, "Who were 'members' of FSM? No one ever knew, or defined what membership meant." It did not matter, because when work was needed individuals always did it. "If a need for a function was clear enough, people puddled like rain to fill it . . . ."[41] The duplication this process produced was also obvious but it was consonant with the spirit of the movement. A nonhierarchical community was created in which groups and individuals were dependent on each other but on no central person or committee. This permitted grass roots initiative and required interdependency for support, strategy and analysis.

It may be that such political experiences and forms are possible only in the context of insurgency, the highly charged early phases of social movements. Much historical evidence and certainly the traditional wisdom on social movements point to such a conclusion. The implication is that to survive in the political world, a social movement must and inevitably will transform its initial libertarian interest in democracy and community into viable organization, with structure, hierarchy, division of labor, and so on. Experimentation with democracy and community, therefore, can be at best transitory. The new left, however, questioned and grappled with this view of the fate of social movements, although it never finally found structure appropriate to the values of community and full, active participation. Yet it would be a mistake to continue, in the name of some idea of fate or higher realism, to overlook the effort. This seems especially true in light of the socialization in political passivity so characteristic of American life. I suspect that the level of participation and commitment people are able to maintain is much higher than appears or feels possible in the present situation.

Several commentators have pointed to what I think is a more useful approach. According to Irving Louis Horowitz, ". . . Victory was not defined as taking over the operations of the machine, not the classic capture of organized political power . . ."[42] Stephen Spender remarked on a similar phenomenon in France, saying of Daniel Cohn-Bendit, one of the leaders of the French student movement, that he "believes much more in revolutionaries than he cares about revolution." In an important statement Cohn-Bendit said that the aim of revolutionaries was to launch "an experiment that completely breaks with that society, an experiment that will not last, but which allows a glimpse of a possibility; something which is revealed for a moment and then vanishes. But that is enough to prove that something could exist."[43] What the students often achieved was a rupture with the status quo and the momentary creation of a liberatory community not possible through centralized organization or by simply replacing the machine operators. The conviction that centralization or a change of personnel would not result in a society different from the one in existence was a strong current in prefigurative politics. A fear that victory might mean *running* the machines, becoming bureaucrats and leaders of the system, and thereby its instruments, infused new left debates on organization. This, coupled with the idea of a total break with the status quo, an interest in the experiment and the "means" to the end, which might allow a "glimpse of another possibility," was central to new left libertarianism.

All these elements signified, then, a break with traditional politics. Civil rights and new left leaders were often dropped or forced out by movement suspicion of leadership and entrenched power. Students wanted neither to "take power" nor to create alternative institutions informed by centralized and hierarchical models. Those who espoused prefigurative politics were convinced that the process and the changes in people which transpired in the movement could not be separated from the goal of structural political change, while those more firmly in the strategic camp emphasized the latter goal alone. And finally, an FSM participant wrote that the events at Berkeley should be ". . . an impetus to American radicals to finally 'kick the labor metaphysic' and drop the vulgar Marxist belief (shared by administrative liberals) that men must be hungry or unemployed or discriminated against to participate in radical political action."[44] The writer suggested that what was required to bring about radical political change was radical consciousness, not hunger or expropriation of one's labor. Radical consciousness could be created by "successful acts of dislocation." The Free Speech Movement inspired a general interest in a new working class consisting of students and sectors of the middle class and acceptance of students as a potential oppositional agency (see chapter 6). It was still a year or two before the idea that the student movement might be considered part of a new working class received widespread circulation. This idea would be strengthened by knowledge of how the draft worked, suggesting that students and youth were raw material for future bureaucratic jobs or fodder for war. FSM put on the agenda the possibility, and perhaps necessity, of politically taking students' experience seriously, seeing the university and its functions as vital to an advanced industrial society. It legitimated students-for-themselves. Writing about FSM, Michael Rossman put it this way: "For the first time, we acted collectively on a condition of our immediate life, acted on behalf of ourselves as a class whose responsibility is the future, rather than on behalf of oppressed minorities, or of humanity in the abstract."[45]

"ACTIONS"

> The Cornell contingent, numbering in the thousands, was led by its "We Won't Go" organization and draft card burners under a large banner, "WE WON'T GO" emblazoned in the school colors. Locked arm in arm they were literally dancing down the street, joyful, defiant, irresistible. "Hell, No, We Won't Go," their words vibrated between the sterile buildings on Madison Avenue and echoed up and down the canyon-like side streets.[46]

The April 15, 1967, peace marches in New York City and San Francisco attracted a half million people; the New York demonstration saw the first massive public draft card burning, a significant event in the history of the Resistance, the organization of draft resisters, at which between 150 and 200 young men burned their draft cards. The tide was beginning to turn in favor of the anti-war movement. Hundreds of thousands of people were willing to demonstrate for an end to the war in Vietnam. The Cornell group had spearheaded the draft card burning on Sheeps Meadow in Central Park and its success helped to create a spirit of exuberance, joy and defiance. Others in that and many demonstrations during these years experienced similar feelings. Dotson Rader's account[47] of April 15, 1967, in New York City underscored its transformative effects; the act of demonstrating, the numbers, the chanting and posturing, all released a sense of individual energy and power. He wrote: "It is a kind of theatre, with banners and songs and ritualistic language, a moment unto itself creating the illusion of power, absolutist, making the unreal, the wished-for, seem within reach. It is a place where one can say things and mean them which one could never speak anywhere else." Thinking about his friend Philip, a moderate, upper-class liberal, who had come along on the march and had been clubbed by the police, Rader noted his friend's "remarkable anger and his ability in the shortest time *to become other than what he was.*"(Emphasis mine.)

That the "unreal, the wished-for" seemed within reach, that one became other than who and what one was ordinarily, created joy. The power of collective action, the solidarity "creating a feeling of omnipotence that comes when your side invades the center of the city and holds captive the physical symbols of power" (to continue with Rader's account), is critical in understanding the attractiveness of the movement for thousands of people. Collective insurgency enabled participants to attain a sense of cohesiveness and collectivity, a sense of themselves as more important, powerful or connected to history than they ordinarily were. This was heady experience in a society in which the young are virtually disenfranchised and expected to become wedded to the routine of daily life in order to survive, with little opportunity for meaningful political participation. A future with more meaning and fulfillment beckoned to them.

The accounts of occupations of university buildings communicate a sense of ecstasy generated by working together for a shared ideal, making use of a building of inhuman scale or purpose or previously off-limits, by cooperation and caring. Participants described the evolution of a community at the Free University founded at Berkeley during the strike. "Graduate students taught in the stairwells; . . . We set up a kitchen and a first aid station. Blankets were distributed. We governed ourselves. Peace and order prevailed."[48] The occupation of the Mathematics Buildings at Columbia University in 1968 had similar meaning for Rader. Outlining the risks and problems they faced, he concluded, "But it did not matter. None of it. Not the bust to come, nor the degrees and careers in jeopardy, nor the liberal faculty insulted and lost. All that counted was the two hundred of us in solidarity for the first time together, together in our place in our time against the cops outside and the jocks outside." Rader said the occupation "was the first event in most of our lives where we felt effective, where what we were doing belonged to us. *Never before had I felt as effective* as during the Liberation."[49] (Emphasis mine.)

There is a remarkable kinship between these feelings and those expressed by Rossman four years before, referring to the police car incident during FSM. ("And by this time we realize simply that we have to hold that car. That car is the only thing we've gotten in six years; it isn't the cops' car anymore.") Both of these statements are about doing or taking something the students considered theirs by virtue of the justness of their struggle. The implication is that he, and others, felt *ineffectual*, a not uncommon sense for most Americans. Feeling effective enabled participants to give their own meaning to a symbol of the establishment; they transformed what they considered authoritarian symbols into their opposite. The occupations in particular released communal visions and creative attempts to reconvert premises to more humane and collective spaces. "Our building—*our* home for Christ's sake!—where we slept and talked and bathed and worked together. . . . Our tolerance of each other was immense. In the week, I heard not one word said in anger against anyone in the commune."[50]

On October 21, 1967 a national demonstration against the war took place at the Pentagon in Washington, D.C. Across the country in Oakland the week of October 16–20 was called Stop-the-Draft Week, with massive demonstrations at the induction center and the city streets. Both of these were important milestones in the history of the anti-war movement and the movement in general. Many of the accounts of the march and occupation of the Pentagon steps lingered on the feelings of community and cooperation of those who camped outside. Norman Mailer described the march earlier in the day when the crowd of marchers "surged back and forth like a wash of waves caught by the change of tides in a channel," and the promise of chaos was omnipresent. But instead the mob was good-humored as it inched its way along the bridge towards the Pentagon, waiting, sitting, singing and marching again; Mailer proposes that "any other group so large . . . would have erupted" but that the "underlying composition of those gentle troops," the pacifism and good will of the crowd, prevented it.[51]

What finally happened in both demonstrations was a "massive improvisation from below, unplanned by leaders."[52] The accounts, mainly in underground newspapers, stress this point. A report in the *Fifth Estate* from Detroit stated, "The actual storming of the Pentagon was something few had really expected. So there was no pre-established structure to deal with the situation; people had to use their heads and work together."[53] Because it was unplanned, "The confrontation itself created a dynamic spirit of community."[54] And then with three thousand people holding the Pentagon steps and determined to stay there, "organization grew, communication systems were set up, water and food brigades brought in supplies. Political discussions and news broadcasts from other fronts were conducted through bull horns."[55] Later on: "Soon diggers started bringing in food, and joints were in evidence. A real festival atmosphere was in the air. People laughed and hugged. And they began to talk to the soldiers."[56] Reports were that three soldiers defected to the protesters' side. Throughout the long hours a friendly interaction took place between the troops and the anti-war demonstrators; and until they were ordered to arrest those left on the steps early in the morning, "an amazing magic was created. Everyone chanted "Join us! Join us!" And they really meant it. That was why it was important. It wasn't just empty rhetoric . . . *we knew we had something to offer,* something good.[57] (Emphasis mine.) George Dennison said, "Our sense of ourselves as a community—the community that could be, the one we felt we *had* to be . . . was acute. And there before us . . . was the vast engine that is in fact destroying the modern world."[58]

The accounts of the Pentagon demonstration included many of the central themes of the movement and new left: the juxtaposition, in this case graphically, even physically, of a free community against the destructive "engine," the machine; the talk, sharing and festival atmosphere versus the authoritarianism and violence of the bayonets; the theatrical improvisation from below; the movement versus the leaders; the development of elementary organization for survival; activists' sense they had created something desirable and attractive, that they had something powerful to offer. Within the confines of this event, a national anti-war demonstration, the participants acted spontaneously (although there had obviously been much planning for the event) and in the process had created among themselves an "amazing magic."

In a more concrete political way, Marvin Garson, writing for the *L.A. Free Press* about the Oakland Stop-the-Draft Week, said that same week that what had happened in the demonstrations on Friday was going to be happening everywhere soon, but he cautioned it would happen in "its own pace and its own way." He suggested that the key to this kind of demonstration was not correct leadership but "confidence in your brothers and sisters." In Berkeley, that confidence was developed through five mass meetings in three days ". . . with never less than 2,000 people in attendance, freely discussing the tactical issues and sometimes voting against what the leadership planned." He stressed the community of protest that had developed in Berkeley over the years as the key to the successes, since people came together not because of a call by leaders but as a community responding to a crisis, ". . . and once together we didn't need a leader."[59] In the journal of the Free University of Berkeley, a participant described the Friday Oakland demonstrations in which people instinctively spread out in the streets and blocked traffic, saying, "They acted, I think, in a spirit of anger and revenge without leaders and certainly without a plan." He described what they had learned: to stay on their feet and keep moving, how to build barricades, and most importantly, they discarded the notion that their strength lay in their leaders and their plans, understanding it resided in each other.[60]

There are three ideas contained in these statements about Oakland on Friday. The first is the development, over a long period of time, of the Berkeley community, which had generated trust, cooperation, and a sense of political tradition. It may be that this happened in only a few places in the country. Participants suggested that the traditions and community Berkeley had developed were in part responsible for political initiative and trust, reinforcing the sense of community. The long Berkeley political history enabled activists to disregard their leaders and to act with others on their own instincts. It is also true that this sort of initiative and solidarity was achieved in other sorts of situations, such as the Pentagon demonstration, where people had come together momentarily from all over. Yet throughout the sixties Berkeley activists continually pointed to their community history as part of the source of the strength and appeal of their movement, responsible for the immediate responses to political emergencies and for its creativity and mass nature. They considered it a critical resource.

The complexity of the relationship between community and organization is raised here; the Berkeley insights suggest that political activism and organization are often based on and generated by, *must* be based on, networks and community ties if they are to be viable and sustaining. In other words, significant political organization must be built on community of some sort. The new left understood this, if not always consciously, and sought to construct community institutions based on democratic participation as the foundation of organization. Successful organization must be built on shared values (or be characterized by social control mechanisms); the new left built those values and connections, sure of their necessity in the movement, less sure about the organization that might be built upon them.

The second theme is the resistance of the *movement*, the thousands of people who sat down at the Pentagon or fought the police in the streets of Oakland, to the *leadership*, the organizers, the organization. The tension between the spontaneous and undisciplined movement and its organizers, the underlying conflict between the grass roots insurgency and the goals of organizational leadership, is a structuring theme of these years. Whether in a demonstration or over a longer period of time, politics and activities were very much an outgrowth of a struggle between those who identified with national organizations such as SDS (or national antiwar coalitions) and those who were locally-based, anti-organizational and suspicious of centralized organizations or national political "lines." In late

1967 the underground newspaper *The Seed* printed the following poem entitled "Leaders," a striking expression of the wariness of "systems," leadership and bureaucracy:

> Beware of leaders, heroes, organizers.
> Watch that stuff. Beware of structure freaks.
> They do not understand.
> We know the system doesn't work because we're living in its ruins. We know that leaders don't work out because they have all led us only to the present, the good leaders equally with the bad . . . What the system calls organization—linear organization—is a systematic cage, arbitrarily limiting the possible. It's never worked before. It always produced the present . . .[61]

These sentiments were widespread.

The third crucial ingredient of the Oakland demonstration and characteristic of the movement demonstrations throughout the sixties were the enormous mass meetings, in Marvin Garson's words, "freely discussing the tactical issues and sometimes voting against what the militant leadership had planned." David Harris described the Tuesday night meeting of the California Stop-the-Draft Week in which the following day's activities were being debated. When he arrived the rally had been going on for an hour and a half at the open mike from which people were debating whether to march on the chancellor's office or on city hall in protest of police brutality. He spoke, saying he thought everyone ought to return to the induction center and sit in and "after debate, the group [3000 people] decided to go back . . ."[62]

That three thousand people engaged in a discussion and debate appears not to have distressed or inconvenienced them. It seemed, in fact, the natural and necessary way to decide how to proceed or to share analyses, and created enormous exhilaration. Time and again during the decade, huge meetings formed in the midst of political action to debate and discuss politics. This was a central characteristic of the student movement, and one which is often overlooked as a simple by-product of political activity. The meetings were usually democratic, often with open mikes, and infused with interest and passion. Referring to a strike at Berkeley in 1967, a reporter for *The Paper*, published in East Lansing, Michigan, wrote that even though it was clear that the strike would have to end and although the meeting began in a depressing atmosphere, "the spirit in here is amazing." This was due to the fact that the microphone was opened to the floor and the "widest assortment of people began to speak."[63]

For people who were rarely given an opportunity to express their political views and effect an outcome—and students were afforded it more than most people—such collective democratic forms were thrilling and confirming. Irving Louis Horowitz and William Friedland described a sit-in at Stanford to protest the suspension of students who had demonstrated against CIA recruitment on campus.[64] Describing an early meeting, they pointed to the "political socialization" of many who had joined the demonstration, in which the emphasis was on spontaneity and the inevitable confrontation with university officials and involved the entire group of demonstrators. They were surprised that student speeches were short and sentences clear and simple in contrast to the usual "convoluted" expressions that the faculty find characteristic of students. And most astonishing, many students who hardly ever spoke in the classroom spoke to large numbers of demonstrators often urging them to a particular tactic or strategy. Nathan Glazer said of FSM, "Certainly many professors have been given quite a start to discover what stores of energy are locked in our students and untouched by the normal educational routine."[65]

In a reconstruction of the Dow Chemical Corporation (makers of napalm used widely in Vietnam) demonstration at the University of Wisconsin at Madison in October 1967 in which students protested Dow's recruiting for employees among the students on campus, the underground newspaper *Connections* described the possibility of an on-the-spot agreement between the administration and the protesters which entailed the protesters leaving the scene of Dow recruitment, and the administration ensuring that Dow would leave the campus, thus preventing violence or arrests. The demonstrators were euphoric that an agreement had been reached, but a student speaking through a bull horn said that no "deal" had been made and it had-been decided that ". . . if the agreement was to be reached, the administration would have to come down to the demonstration with a written document to be voted on by the obstructors."[66] Again the mass was to decide.

These accounts indicate the importance of group discussion and decision making and, in the case of the Madison Dow demonstration, the unwillingness to have representatives negotiate for the group: the whole group would have to decide; responsibility could not be delegated. If the whole group must decide, then the whole group must discuss. Democratic mass meetings occurred spontaneously, providing models of participation and collectivity that enabled students to envision a democratic and participatory process and to constitute it as a goal of their movement. This process also generated novel emotions, feelings of collectivity and engagement, since it was so different from everyday political experience. Engagement, listening and being listened to, determining political decisions collectively, although seemingly unrealistic, particularly in the climate of the present, *inspired* activists. Being political meant actively participating with others as equals; it did not seem beyond the pale that this might be possible in America. Dwight MacDonald, writing about the

1968 Columbia revolt said, "I've never been in or even near a revolution before; I guess I like them. There was an atmosphere of exhilaration, excitement—pleasant, friendly, almost joyous excitement. . . . Everybody was talking to everybody those days, one sign of a revolution; Hyde Parks suddenly materialized and as abruptly dispersed, all over the place; even the jocks were arguing."[67]

The account presented here may be accused of being overly romantic. I have selected experiences and reports that stress participation and engagement and have not discussed the tedium of interminable mass meetings, the frustration, the elitism that often developed, and the desire of some to be led. I have suggested that sometimes those who did not speak in class spoke eloquently in meetings, and have stressed the excitement rather than boredom or frustration. It is particularly interesting to consider the case of women in this light. As many have charged, sexism was a powerful ingredient of the new left, and to a large extent, one of the generators of the women's liberation movement. New left women were often afraid to speak up and when they did they were often ignored. They were, as Sara Evans has written, critical but invisible.[68] They were treated as secondary citizens by new left men and yet it is curious that they did not always *feel* invisible. How was that possible? Part of the reason is that sexual discrimination in the movement replicated sexual discrimination in the society at large, and women had no intellectual preparation for recognizing it at first. It was the movement *itself* that raised the contradictions for many women.

Evans suggests that the strength and skills women derived from their political activity in the movement simultaneously made them stronger and permitted them to perceive the sexism of the men. Naomi Weisstein describes the 1966 University of Chicago anti-draft sit-in in which she had been ecstatic, believing the activists would remake the world according to their vision of justice and democracy, and points to a terrible and striking paradox, "that schizophrenia of not being able to talk, of being terrified to talk . . . and yet feeling the ecstasy."[69] Weisstein was afraid to speak up, but despite the feelings of fear she felt ecstatic, powerful and joyful. Bernice Reagon, an important black activist in the civil rights movement said of her experiences, "There was a sense of power, in a place where you didn't feel you had any power. There was a sense of confronting things that terrified you, like jail, police, walking in the street . . . you were saying in some basic way, 'I will never again stay inside these boundaries.' "[70]

Without going into the specifics of women's situation in the new left, it is fair to say that the learning and strength acquired in political action, the step into another way of being, the risks, all of which meant becoming other than who one ordinarily was, empowered women. It began the long process of changing consciousness that led to feminism. We have, then, several contradictory elements side-by-side, each representing a facet of the truth. Women were discriminated against and yet were empowered by the movement. Participants were manipulated or afraid or frustrated in mass meetings, and yet mass meetings were high points of the movement, the stuff of the movement in which the uniqueness of the new left was expressed. While there are an abundance of examples and memories of elitism and deformation of prefigurative politics, on balance the power of the collectivity, community and communication was *more* important. The significance of the new left's contribution lies in its break with the past, in new forms and standards for decision making and personal relationships that attempted to anticipate the future liberated society.

Stephen Spender's description of the student movement in America and East and West Europe in 1968, *The Year of the Young Rebels*, stresses characteristic huge meetings, discussions and talk. He explains, for example, how in a huge mass meeting at the Odeon in Paris a young man got up in the gallery and described how he had taken into his care some adolescent delinquents whom he was having trouble helping, and asked for suggestions. Speaker after speaker stood in this huge meeting to discuss the problem seriously and sensibly, continuing the discussion for over an hour. On another occasion Spender tells of an overfilled lecture hall, with people hanging from the rafters, lots of noise and disruptions, waiting for Sartre to appear. When he finally arrived, ". . . in some extraordinary way the audience did succeed in turning itself into a spiritual entity like an attentive small group." The mammoth audience transformed itself, able to listen and appreciate others. In Spender's words:

> That May, at the Sorbonne, for a few weeks, the students lived the communal life of sharing conditions, of arriving at decisions by the method of "direct democracy"—that is to say by consulting the action committees of the movement (*les bases*) and not imposing decisions from the top—of having meetings which were as far as possible spontaneous, with different chairmen for each meeting, resisting the "cult of personality."[71]

Practically every prolonged demonstration or struggle in the United States was characterized by mass meetings, intense debate and discussion, tremendous cooperation and receptivity to ideas. It was this rudimentary council form or town meeting characterized by spontaneous direct democracy that emerged at the heart of the student movement. And the rudiments of self-organization developed. *The Rag,* published in Austin, Texas, described a common process in the student movement:

> Following the hearing a rally was held on the South Mall with about
> five hundred people attending. . . . Committees were formed to handle
> grievances, faculty contact, organizational contact, speakers, demon-
> strations, defense and finance, and distribution and press. A five-man
> steering committee was elected to coordinate activities and to act as a
> non-negotiating representative of the group.[72]

Horowitz and Friedland suggest that the key element in these meetings
was the political socialization of the many individuals who had joined the
demonstration. This was clearly an important function of such mass meetings: a political learning experience and further initiation into the movement. As such it was a significant formative process which impressed
upon participants a notion of participatory democratic politics. Mass meetings, like demonstrations, both characterized by direct democracy, transformed self-images and political ideas. They changed consciousness about
what it means to "do" politics, or to "be" political. Discussion was at its
center. Spender describes Paris in 1968 in these terms: "The spring fever
of talk which overtook not only the students but almost everyone in Paris
seemed so like the euphoria of camaraderie and open-heartedness which
overtakes people after revolution, that many people mistook it for this."[73]
Ferber and Lynd stress the importance of genuine communication, for
bringing people into the Resistance:

> To talk and listen in an involved and authentic way is a liberating act,
> and in a society where talk is reduced to hollow bombast or merely
> functional symbols it can be the beginning of a political movement. If
> the movement is to be true to its initial insights it will maintain its direct
> and personal approach in speaking and living together.[74]

The release of suppressed expression was liberating. Most had never
experienced anything like it. It went against all the formal and controlled
notions of liberal politics, releasing genuinely political, democratic instincts while underscoring the manipulated and anti-political nature of
the American political system.

There has been, in recent years, a large body of social scientific work
about language. Basil Bernstein, Jürgen Habermas, Claus Mueller and
Alvin Gouldner have devoted their attention to varying aspects of communication, language, and talk.[75] I want here only to spotlight the student
movement with some of their insights. Mueller attempts to explain the
nature and existence of middle-class protest and dissent in the ability to
communicate in an undistorted manner, which for him means full discussion of ideas and problems with public relevance. Distorted communication, fostered by the status quo, prevents the formulation of
meaningful alternatives and therefore restricts political life. In other

words, the articulation of needs and ideas on the part of classes and groups in the society depends on their access to and use of undistorted language. For Mueller the ability to abstract and universalize is essential for critical thinking, for transcending and transforming one's private situation into political demands. The university is one of the few places where categories with which to analyze society are provided, and, thus, contradictions of the system may be discovered. The individual using elaborated language may consciously oppose a political system and articulate interests other than those that have been defined by the state. From this vantage point the ability to formulate counter-institutions and utopian alternatives derives from students' ability to utilize undistorted speech. The problems with this theory, particularly its elitism vis-à-vis poor and working class people who know very well how discriminatory the society is towards them, will not be explored here. The insight it sheds on the flowering of talk is suggestive.

Gouldner, focusing on intellectuals more than students in particular, underscores their interest in writing and ideas as instruments of social change. He has stated, somewhat expansively, "In the end, there is probably no more powerful mechanism of social change than people's talk."[76] It should be clear from the foregoing that talk and discussion were not "mere" words but a process of people changing, discovering new individual and group selves, and new capacities and possibilities. The "release" of words was part of a new kind of political socialization in which words were given new meaning and ideas were renewed and created. Discussion of democracy outside the classroom, for example, on top of the police car at Berkeley or in draft resistance groups, meant something very different for participants than it did in a traditional classroom. The words and effort to give them new significance were also a *goal*, not uniquely a means. Dialogue was important as an instrument of communication, a medium through which to create connections between people, understanding, and a community. The activity of talking politicized both speakers and listeners.

The work on language by Gouldner, Habermas and Mueller must be seen within the context of the new left movements of the 1960s because it was in significant measure provoked by them. The work theorized the spontaneous practice of the movement; it was inspired and informed by the historical developments of the decade. The importance of ideas, language and talk in affecting consciousness and its role in political passivity or activity in our society begins to uncover part of the explanation of the explosiveness of the new left for the participants and society at large. It required a more active level of participation. The new left was able to reflect on the quality of life in relative ease, in a university setting, raising non-material moral and cultural issues outside conventional political arenas. It could explore, both in words and in practice, those kinds of issues defined as illegitimate or apolitical by the hegemonic society. The non-instrumental and non-hierarchical political forms it was able to create had democratic communication at their heart.

Reflecting on the Free Speech Movement, two meanings of "free speech" present themselves. "Free" in the civil liberties sense, so that citizens and students were able to express their political ideas and platforms without fear of punishment; and "free" in the sense of liberated, unrestricted communication that may foster political visions and political forms that transcend the existing framework, enabling utopian ideas to inspire individuals toward becoming political actors on the basis of their unmet collective and individual needs.

One other component of the discussions was respect for thought and the university. We have seen that FSM took a position defending the "true" university. In a 1966 sit-in at the University of Wisconsin protesting the administration's provision of class rank to the Selective Service System, one saw students grappling actively with the issues, and, in contrast, the university showing disinterest and disengagement. The student newspaper reported a sit-in in the Administration building and a large mass meeting in which the issues of student Selective Service deferment and university complicity were debated for hours:

> One of those who spoke . . . alluded to the writings of Plato and Hegel in asserting the important social functions of philosophy and the social sciences in finding the truth in any social organization and that for the University to compromise with the Selective Service system is to "pervert these social functions."[77]

After the faculty voted to continue to provide students' class rank to the Selective Service System, students were disconsolate in their feelings of betrayal and defeat. A speaker at a rally, reminiscent of FSM's sentiments of wanting a university and seeing themselves as the representatives of the "true" university, said:

> What you saw today was proof that no university exists here. In every historical, every rational way, the men who voted against our resolutions today are not faculty. They are not men of ideas . . . [and] it was the students' duty to distinguish between "the real faculty" — those interested in ideas — and those who see the university community merely as "an ongoing business concern."[78]

In response to the faculty decision, the student newspaper editorialized that while the faculty had met for only two hours and discussed for one-half hour, the student body had discussed the problem of the university and the draft for the last seven days. It was the students who were worried about the weakening of the academic community through the draft exam and Selective Service use of student ranking:

> WSA [Wisconsin Student Association], the Committee on the University and the Draft, I-F [Interfraternity Council], the campus religious leaders, the teaching assistants and some of the faculty have deeply questioned over the last week the relation of the University to the Selective Service System. In meetings that lasted until dawn, ideas have developed, dialogues raised proposals.

> Students who had never exposed their personal thoughts outright were in the middle of discussions portraying a most significant educational experience not found in the classroom. Yet the faculty decided in two hours.[79]

Almost millenarian expectations generated by demonstrations and revolts, personal and collective transformations, feelings of well-being, strength, solidarity and caring, "massive improvisation from below," decentralization and spontaneity, undirected and chaotic mass meetings in which everything was discussed, participation and community, were all part of nontraditional and unstrategic politics, a politics of process and means, personal and moral, a seed sprouting straight out of the heart of the alienated politics and of youth America. It instilled thousands with an experience of active and democratic political participation, with a taste of community.

The Resistance provides a good example of a less flamboyant political style based on individual and moral conscience combined with a dramatic tactic of opposition which may be characterized as prefigurative. The New Haven group stated that they had decided that the kind of public organizing that issued calls and printed newspaper ads encouraging people to act was not consonant with their notion of organizing or with their goals. They continued, saying that ". . . only after the basic groundwork is laid over the next few months (i.e., building strong committed local groups by the field staff) will we pull out the stops on publicity." And commenting on the size of the country they posited that ". . . if there is regional strength and unity this will help in the struggle that is to come."[80] The politics of the Resistance insisted on grass roots local support; it tried to encourage the movement, to downplay central organization and facilitate the formation of small groups as the basis of its political network. This was perhaps dictated by the risk and security involved in draft resistance, but ideologically the Resistance was committed to a decentralized and personal politics. A Resistance organizer stated that he "would be suspicious of the validity of actions that have to be planned over and over by the same people. It's better that things fan out and that people take on different styles and forms, involving always larger and more diverse elements." The kind of organizing the Resistance engaged in was similar to what later became known in the women's movement as consciousness raising. The same organizer gave an account of a regional meeting:

> There was tremendous respect for the opinion of each person who spoke and there was virtually no interruption of someone speaking. Everyone who wanted to could express his or her opinion thoroughly. I had the definite sense that the issues were being considered in a deep clear manner and that we moved into a consensus quite naturally.[81]

Describing another conference on noncooperation in October 1966, a participant said, "It began with each of them telling us why he chose this path. Speaking to others out of one's own personal life, rather than in political abstractions."[82] And a participant in the Resistance commune in Palo Alto said, "Part of the process was creating a sense of intimacy between us which, whether we articulated it or not, we felt was the basis of our organization."[83] The sense, again, as in Berkeley, was that community and trust were the foundation of organization.

Because what the Resistance was doing was illegal, it was important to create trust and confidence in both the person and the group. One of the ways this could be achieved was through a very personal and locally-based politics. The authors of a book on the Resistance, Michael Ferber and Staughton Lynd, explain, "What both the SDS and Resistance leaders tried to do was to understand personal liberation and political effectiveness not as opposites, things to be chosen between, but as aspects of a single process." And a Resistance leader stated, "Our lives and our politics are really inseparable." [84] "The personal is political" became an influential notion, particularly in the late sixties with the development of the women's movement. It meant that all aspects of one's life, including personal problems, behavior and needs, had a political dimension and explanation.[85] The idea that personal and community transformation was part of the process of building a radical organization and movement was seen earliest in ERAP and continued as a deep movement current. Greg Calvert, president of SDS at the time, stated that the slogan "Not with My Life You Don't," the slogan of the Resistance, was basic to new left politics. "People are capable of doing extraordinary things when they are in resistance. They can walk out of their studies and take on new lives, if necessary. They do not walk to gas chambers." Calvert continued that in the process of resistance, in the struggle against the powerlessness imposed on people by capitalism, ". . . there is a rediscovery of self in the midst of a dehumanized society."[86] For new leftists the assertion and discovery of self were linked to meaningful political action. Personal liberation, the escape from loneliness, meaninglessness and manipulation were attained through collective political action. Community was created in the midst of fragmentation and inhumanity, and the self liberated.

One of the peculiarities of prefigurative politics was its out-of-the-ordinary nature. "The movement formed and transformed itself out of its immediate action. . ."; "immediate struggle" did in fact "nourish the general revolt," in Alain Touraine's words.[87] We have looked exclusively at demonstrations in order to indicate the widespread occurrence of spontaneous, democratic and communal politics. This does not mean that long-range projects precluded some of these same experiences or goals; although less dramatic, they were, as we shall see, similarly informed by prefigurative efforts. Yet confrontational or direct action politics *were* extraordinarily seductive and powerful, like an epiphany; they reveal vividly the heart of prefigurative politics. The appeal was in the ability to release buried democratic impulses, to transform politics and individuals into forms more human and meaningful than any of the participants dreamed possible.

There was and still is a community out of which such political action grew and by which it was sustained and supported. The ongoing political efforts that structured the movement community were critical to the emergence and success of spontaneous and utopian expressions of opposition. Although their profile was lower, their importance was great; I state this here so that the everyday and less dramatic work the movement and new left engaged in is not lost sight of, particularly as it outlasted the "actions" and must be the basis of any serious movement for social change.

We have seen, in the words of participants, the communitarian nature of much movement political activity. As Cohn-Bendit suggested, these were experiments that broke with existing society but which could not last, experiments which allowed a "glimpse of a possibility" which was "enough to prove that something could exist." They created models and images of an alternative that remain alive even today in the recesses of the minds of those who were there. Although students were not "properly" revolutionaries, perhaps it is not an accident that Eric Hobsbawm's description of *Primitive Rebels* accurately described their experiences in the 1960s: "Liberty, equality, above all fraternity may become real for the moment in those stages of the great social revolution which revolutionaries who live through them describe in the terms reserved for romantic love."[88]

CHAPTER 4

Politics as Community

*Abandoning corporate–liberal authoritarian America
in favor of a centrist organization
is like converting from Jesuitism to Stalinism.*[1]

PREFIGURATIVE POLITICS

Groups characterized by direct democracy and dialogue seemed to form
naturally in action situations during the sixties. Spontaneous assemblies
arose and were incorporated into the emergent new left culture and
experience. Referring to the occurrence of councils or spontaneous democratic groups during revolutionary upheavals in history, Hannah Arendt
notes "the regular emergence, during the course of revolution, of a new
form of government that resembled in an amazing fashion Jefferson's ward
system and seemed to repeat, under no matter what circumstances, the
revolutionary societies and municipal councils which spread all over
France after 1789." And somewhat elliptically, she adds that ". . . no
tradition, either revolutionary or pre-revolutionary, can be called to account for the regular emergence or reemergence of the council system
ever since the French Revolution."[2]

Although the links between the new left and earlier radical and reform
movements in the United States are substantial, the spontaneous emergence of councils ties it to rebellions and yearnings for democracy which
cut across cultures and ages. A deep desire for democratic participation
surfaced in new left political practice, mandating its inclusion in the
history of radical and democratic insurgency. Michael Rossman described
the birth of the Free Speech Movement at Berkeley, stressing just those
elements that created the vision of a communal and equitable alternative
to American society and higher education. Writing at the time, he said:

And the dialogue on top of the car continues. People are getting up there and talking, and people are listening. And people are voting on this and people are voting on that.

It's almost enough to make you believe that if it were given a chance, the democratic process might work. It just might work. People quoted books as if books were relevant. They talked about the Greeks, and they talked about theories of politics, as if it all *meant* something. And listening to them, I almost believed for the first time in years that it did mean something.[3]

Hannah Arendt spoke of the experience of people in the French Revolution in almost identical terms:

An enormous appetite for debate, for instruction, for mutual enlightenment and exchange of opinion, even if all those were to remain without immediate consequence on those in power, developed in the sections and societies; and when, by fiat from above, the people in the sections were made only to listen to party speeches and to obey, they simply ceased to show up.[4]

A sense of the predominant political climate in the new left in the mid-sixties is captured in an article in *New Left Notes* in the fall of 1966. At the August 1966 Clear Lake, Iowa SDS National Convention a decentralized, anti-bureaucratic and anti-organizational politics had been affirmed. As the decade progressed, theoretical sophistication about left ideology and particularly about the uniqueness of the new left in relation to the old left and to Marxism developed and spread. Specifically, the problem of bureaucratic manipulation and control in left movements and socialist countries began to be explored. The article stressed the bureaucratic and hierarchic nature of institutionalized communist parties and pointed to the tradition of worker's councils and democracy at the grass roots. The author favorably contrasted tactics leading to a society of participatory democracy with a vision of centralization and control of economic power by a bureaucratic state in which the citizenry is at best appeased.[5]

Connections with earlier liberatory socialist movements began to be made, as the intellectuals in the new left attempted to place themselves within a historical tradition. Throughout 1966 and 1967, as anti-draft and anti-war activities multiplied and intensified, so did reflection on their organization and significance. One of the most impressive spokespeople at this time was Greg Calvert, elected National Secretary of SDS at the Clear Lake Convention. He was an articulate leader of prefigurative politics.[6] In an important dialogue that revealed the heart of prefigurative politics, Calvert explored the meaning and ramifications of the attempt to create *community*, so central to new left politics.

He responded to an essay written by Pat Hansen and Ken Mc-Eldowney, itself evidence of similar concerns. They had said, significantly, that they did not think it was SDS's position on Vietnam or its leadership in calling demonstrations that was causing its growth and the growth of the movement, but it was instead "a sense of community and opportunity to affect at least a portion of our lives." They went on to say that they were working not only for changes in the structure of society and its institutions, but ". . . also bringing about real changes in the individuals that we involve as well as in ourselves." SDS's priority, they thought, should be to increase the number of people who will not be content with small reforms or improvements but want radical change, especially in the ". . . way that people relate to each other."[7]

The notion that the movement represented a community which it had continually to regenerate and communicate to others can be traced from the civil rights movement, through ERAP into the student movement proper. The community organizing projects in ERAP had attempted to build a community out of their organizations. Recognition that the movement should represent something more genuine and human, a way of life that called for equal and caring relationships, meant that it could not strive only for small restructuring or reforms. Such reforms could not guarantee profound changes in individuals, changes required by a truly radical movement. By the same token, the way people treated one another was interpreted politically, something to "work" on; the problems people had in relating were perceived politically, created by growing up in America, and presumably remediable. Often individual failings or difficulties were understood to be caused by forces larger than oneself; "the personal is political." Hansen and McEldowney downplayed organization in their concern for individual change and exemplary community.

Calvert responded in a piece called "Beyond the Beloved Community," clearly revealing the impulses and the difficulties in forging a prefigurative politics. He agreed that the desire to love and know others, the need for community, were central to the struggle for freedom. "Cynicism easily dismisses such sentiments as naive. And yet, no sentiments seem to be more revolutionary in the society in which we live—because there is no clearer denial of human freedom on the most immediate level than the destruction of the kind of *community* which makes human relatedness and love possible." This was what our movement was about: "While struggling to liberate the world, we would create the liberated world in our midst. While fighting to destroy the power which had created the loveless anti-community, we would ourselves create the community of love—*The Beloved Community*."[8]

But, according to Calvert, there was a division in the movement between those who denied the legitimacy of striving to create "the beloved community" and those desperately attempting to enact it. He disparagingly called those in the first group "politicos" or the "old guard," a reference to the older leadership group in SDS and their lack of receptivity to newer political ideas, ideas less organizational than their own, and more influenced by the counter-culture. However, and poignantly, Calvert did not hide the fact that the attempt to implement the beloved community in the movement was less than successful; it simply had not worked. This was the tragedy, pure and simple, and there seemed no alternative but to conclude that the movement could not afford to seek community, relatedness and personal change *before all else.* This did not mean, however, that the impulses and the attempts were invalid. On the contrary, Calvert saved his anger for the "politicos" and the strategists:

> *Above all, I would never abandon the freedom struggle for what the politicos call "politics."* The alternative which is offered by those who disparage the "anarchist" freedom movement is "political realism". . . . Talking about "politics" rather than talking about "freedom" is being "realistic." Being "realistic" is not being "sentimental" or "romantic." Talking politics is talking "realistically" about "realities." The interesting thing about anti-freedom "politics" is that it defines reality in terms of an existing system which lacks everything that I consider important.[9]

Extensive quotations are included here because they clearly articulate the concerns informing prefigurative politics. The impulse and its fragility and contradictions are exposed. Politics as the transformation of relationships, the promise and construction of "the beloved community," as freedom and even love was attractive, inspiring, difficult, utopian. Much hope was directed towards these notions and was to a certain extent responsible for feelings of disappointment and despair when they did not materialize. (This may be seen in much of the writing and reminiscences of new left activists after the sixties.) But often they did materialize, if only briefly.

When Calvert spoke of the "disaster" associated with the attempt to implement the beloved community, he referred to the complex pressure on SDS, to behave and function as a national organization. Those pressures were experienced as contradictory: it was no easy task to build new relationships and a community when mailings had to be gotten out, the newspaper written and printed, new membership processed, leadership provided, decisions of all sorts made. In spite of this, Calvert and others were not ready to concede to the "politicos." They were "realistic" in their disparagement of "the beloved community" and thereby willing to lose what was most precious about the new left experiment. Significantly, in Calvert's formulation "realistic politics" was equated with "anti-freedom" politics, and with not being "sentimental" or "romantic." Being realistic was associated with traditional politics, with instrumentality and organizational strategy. He resisted the negative connotations associated with "romantic" and "sentimental." These were criteria used by the on-going political system, judgments which trivialized the new left experiment.

Sheldon Wolin makes an interesting distinction relevant to Calvert's categories. He suggests that the modern dialectical tension between community and organization is present in an older dualism between church and sect. Modern communitarians, following the sect-tradition, stress the "spontaneous life of the group" in contrast to institutionalized organization, while organizationists who belong to the church-tradition, revere a "structure of authority" and distrust spontaneous expression.[10] The following statement by Calvert in early 1967, when he was president of SDS, is illuminated by this distinction:

> SDS just simply was not interested in talking about organizational problems or about political analysis; it revealed its deepest concern in talking about what people can do with their lives . . . and with their bodies . . . At its present stage of development, SDS cannot be understood in terms of traditional political organization. Neither ideological clarity . . . nor organizational stability are fundamentally important to SDSers. What counts is that which creates a movement. What counts is that SDS be where the action is. What counts is that SDS be involved in the creation of a cutting-edge in the freedom struggle.[11]

Here is the anti-organizational impulse, stressing the movement before the organization, and an almost existential notion of politics. SDS was identified less as an organization than as a state of action, of risk-taking, of challenge and contestation. In all his statements Calvert argued intensely for politics as an act of resistance, as the creation of community, in which one was morally transformed in collective effort with others. This represented a rejection of politics as students had been socialized and schooled to understand them. The attempt to create "the beloved community" was, in Henri Lefebvre's words "unthinkable in terms of the mental categories of specialized politics."[12]

This developing prefigurative politics represented, in political sociological terms, a questioning of instrumental rationality. Beginning with Max Weber, the instrumental rationality of bureaucracy at the expense of individual freedom and autonomy has been a well-documented phenomenon of modern life and a major sociological theme. Generally ignorant of the theory, student activists were familiar in their own lives with the manifestations of instrumental rationality. The sense that the "system," the "machine" (the university, the government, the corporation, and other large institutions) functioned hierarchically, in spite and in ignorance of members' consent or participation, that such systems had a logic of their own, informed and to some extent inspired the student revolt. Students spontaneously attempted to create forms that did not duplicate the instrumentality characteristic of institutions in the larger society. When activists asked what was the point of organization, they meant that the movement as well as SDS could not be based on policy or politics which simply replaced hierarchical structures with others equally undemocratic. In addition, the movement was viewed as an avenue of freedom, a way to express oneself and decide with others on political strategy. Paradoxically, given the stereotypical image of social movements and collective behavior, the movement was considered a way to express one's individuality.

While Max Weber is pertinent, it is impossible to study the new left and ignore the work of Robert Michels. His *Political Parties* (1911), the classic statement of the degeneration of a democratic organization into an oligarchic structure, seems almost to have been internalized by the anti-organizational currents in the student movement, though few had read the work. Students often rejected representative democracy in favor of direct democracy, refusing to have representatives in negotiations with authorities because they were suspicious of formal organizational delegation. They rejected centralized and permanent structure as well. Michels analyzed the attempt of the German working class to "secure a sufficiently vast and solid organization in order to triumph over the organization of the state" which resulted in "acquiring a vigorous centralization of its own, based upon the same cardinal principles of authority and discipline which characterize the organization of the state."[13]

In the student movement of the 1960s the distance between leaders and participants, between national officers and membership, was vigorously solved by eliminating leaders, office functions, the division of labor, centralized decision making, formal democracy. SDS and the student movement criticized all the oligarchic tendencies towards elitism, bureaucracy, rigidity and conservatism of which Michels warned when he suggested that ". . . the mechanism of the organization, while conferring a solidity of structure, induces serious changes in the organized mass, completely inverting the respective position of the leaders and the led.[14] Most of the requirements of organization were perceived as undermining the values of the movement and rejected.

Michels warned that ". . . from a means, organization becomes an end";[15] the student movement was wary of bureaucracy, leadership and representation because each appeared to preclude participation and autonomous democratic decision making. Each of the factors about which activists were suspicious found an historical precursor in Michels. The concern about the growing power of leadership at the expense of membership participation, for example, although not arrived at through experience in a large socialist party (or even knowledge of that experience) nevertheless was extracted and created by experience in the mammoth bureaucracies of advanced capitalist society and were similar to Michels' conclusions. Yet Michels stated unequivocally that "Democracy is inconceivable without organization," that organization is the weapon of the weak against the strong, and is absolutely essential for political struggle of the masses.[16] In essence this was rejected by new left anti-organizationists.

MEANS AND ENDS

In August 1967 David Harris, a West Coast leader of the draft resistance movement and of the organization "The Resistance" stated:

> To choose resistance means that there are no longer simply issues, there are no longer simply problems to argue solutions to: beyond innuendo and beyond observation and conclusion, there is an act with the totality of our lives against the machines of the state. The act begins with a refusal to cooperate with conscription; as long as America continues to mean oppression, the act has no end.

Michael Ferber and Staughton Lynd suggest that the Resistance was part of the movement in the second half of the sixties in which "the spirit of SNCC and SDS in the early 1960s was still, for better or worse, most evident." They refer to David Harris' words, quoted earlier, as evidence of this affinity.[17] The resemblance to Mario Savio's FSM statement three years before is striking: "The operation of the machine . . . makes you so sick at heart . . . you can't take part. . . . You've got to put your bodies upon the gears and upon the wheels, upon the levers. . . . You've got to make it stop . . . unless you're free, the machine will be prevented from working at all."[18]

Counter-institutions (institutions outside the established order organized along radical egalitarian principles as a means of building the new society within the shell of the old) were one of the most important new left efforts. In the white student movement they developed initially in ERAP. An emphasis on the political "means" in contrast to the political "end" was at their heart. The counter-institutional moment in prefigurative politics stressed, in Carl Boggs's words, the "embodiment, within the ongoing political practice of the movement, of those forms of social relations, decision making, culture and human experience that are the ultimate goal."[19] In the case of ERAP some of the community organizations began to serve functions, provide services, and exercise some minor power in a manner that "embodied" the future society. Later free universities, alternate and underground newspapers, affinity groups and communes developed out of the notion that the left had to create institutions and social relations that embodied its values. Critics asserted that the goal of achieving power was lost in these experiments which stressed means, values and process.

For those who embraced prefigurative politics, if the new society were to be characterized by participatory democracy, anti-authoritarianism and liberation, the political means of achieving these goals had to be consonant. The category "utopia" introduced by Mannheim is applicable and helpful here, and has been utilized in an analysis of the European student movement by Gianni Statera in *Death of a Utopia*.[20] According to Statera, the thrust of the student movement was the negation of the existing order and the transformation of contemporary society. The spontaneity, notion of individual liberation, emphasis on means before ends, the conviction that the revolution was a value *in itself* and not only for what it might bring—all these elements qualify the student movement as utopian (or "chiliastic," according to Statera). Mannheim's description of utopian movements, which Statera utilizes, includes the belief in the realization of transcendent ideas in the immediate present. There is a stress on means as opposed to ends and the lack of a conception of the development of progress, which propelled new leftists in this case, to stress the movement over and above the organization. The reality-transcending nature of utopian thought, with action the instrument through which reality is disclosed, is a good characterization of the student movement. Although the word "utopian" is generally used negatively in our political culture— not least because, as Mannheim indicates, it is the dominant group in full accord with the existing order that determines what is considered utopian—it is used positively here. The utopian vision, a negation of what exists, served as a guide for social change. And while material conditions were not in accord with the vision, as they so often are not, the isolation of the students (their most important liability as well, perhaps) the source of that vision, utopianism with all its naive, humane and liberatory connotations, tells us a good deal about the student movement.

In 1963 SDSer Don McKelvey stated as one of the central tenets of the new left:

> . . . One cannot divorce means from ends for no other reason than because men's consciousness and values are shaped at least in part by their actions and their (and others') perceptions of those actions. . . .
> We must strive to create—here and now in our everyday functions—a certain mode of relating to other people which will serve as a counterweight (for both ourselves and others) to the manipulative, dehumanized, coercive relations which we so rightly criticize in the society all around us.[21]

Here were the basic political conceptions that lay at the heart of prefigurative politics. Massimo Teodori, another commentator on the new left, makes sense of these conceptions and new left practice by suggesting they were attempts to realize in the present those social relationships and values which will be the basis of the future society. He remarks that "counter-communities, parallel institutions and alternative structures to capitalism and bureaucracy" were the new left's attempt to effect a synthesis of utopia and existing reality.[22]

In a 1965 review of Howard Zinn's book, *SNCC: The New Abolitionists* (1965), Tom Hayden outlined the significance of SNCC. He underscored that black people in the south and in Newark, where Hayden was an organizer, were not being organized simply on the basis of material gain, but on the basis of their alienation and outrage. The needs expressed by poor blacks, focusing on participation and control of their lives, could not be absorbed by the reform tradition of organizing people around material benefits. At the same time, however, SNCC was experiencing tensions and contradictions in its functions. On the one hand it sought to make itself an efficient organization, which meant growing, making decisions quickly, carrying out its stated purposes effectively; on the other hand it sought to make as many people as possible competent to decide on policy, to de-emphasize elite control, to overcome specialization which led to hierarchy, and to extend power to everyone affected by the organization, in sum: to demonstrate by example another way of life. Hayden, echoed by Calvert one year later, stated that an entirely new society could not be constructed by utilizing existing methods and organizational forms. "But it is just as impossible to revolutionize this society by employing its prevailing styles of bureaucratic organization, because these styles are meant to work only for groups that want integration into the existing pluralist structure of rewards, privileges, roles and opportunities."[23]

This, then, was the dilemma inherited from SNCC and perceived and experienced throughout the sixties by those interested in radical political change free of bureaucratic and hierarchical social relations. Means and ends could not be divorced, since traditional organizational forms undermined goals of freedom and democracy; simultaneously there were organizational demands that were not easily met in this manner. One of the major theses of Nigel Young's *An Infantile Disorder? The Crisis and Decline of the New Left* (1977) is that the newness of the new left inhered in the "belief that new structures, institutions and relationships could themselves represent a revolutionary process"; this was the new left's "crystallization of its own experience. . . ." Young states that the classic revolutionary seizure of power model was rejected by the new left in favor of a utopian model that labored to close the gap between means and ends throughout the movement itself, the movement that "should foreshadow the type of society which would emerge during and from the revolution."[24]

The dualism which developed is easy to discern. The first and oldest leftist tradition, in Hayden's words, accepted the "prevailing styles of bureaucratic organization" (historically embodied most clearly in Leninism) and the second, which prevailed in the new left, believed the movement should foreshadow the future society. However it is neither just nor accurate to accuse as "bureaucrats" those who believed in the importance of organization. In the heat of struggle positions were polarized and the dualism exaggerated.

Nor, on the other hand, is it legitimate to characterize the prefigurative effort as an obvious flight from power and fundamental structural change, a consistent criticism of prefigurative politics. Nigel Young, for example, suggests that the new left retreated from participatory democracy and counter-institutions in the late sixties, and he sees this as the most important factor in the movement's loss of identity. He interprets counter and parallel institutions as the way the new left closed the gap between the political means and ends, an attempt to create the good society and live happily ever after in the womb of the old. But Young and others miss the complexity and ambiguity of such efforts; for most activists the emphasis on the "means" did *not* automatically signify a rejection of achieving power. Prefigurative politics were never flatly at odds with all and any idea of organization and power. The new left worked to forge new organizational forms that would accomplish *both* goals. This was its novelty.

Activists in ERAP, for example, did not believe that they "could empower the poor" in Young's phrase, nor did those creating free universities believe they could supplant the existing multiversities.[25] In fact, counter-institutional experiments often developed directly out of a sense of powerlessness, with little illusion they could replace the power that be. They represented instead an effort which simultaneously enabled participants to live according to new values while attempting to build bases of power. Movement activists involved in such projects labored in an ambiguous situation. They agreed consciously or instinctively that the new world could not be built using, in Richard Gombin's words, the "reified instruments of the opposition movement inherited from the past,"[26] and yet new institutions were needed as seeds of the future society.

The attempt to close the gap between political means and political ends did not entail the rejection of the goal of organizing for and achieving power, but rejection of a certain *kind* of organization and power. Many in the new left recognized that the two sides had to be combined, and sought to do so. If new leftists finally "gave up" counter-institutional experiments, as Young argues, it was not, as he suggests, because they embraced, in their stead, a more hierarchical and violent politics. Here the political context is important. From 1965 onwards, the escalation of the war, the development of a mass student movement, the black rebellion, media focus, and repression, played a major part in the trajectory of the movement. The new left's "relinquishment" of prefigurative politics around 1968 was neither as voluntary nor as complete as Young indicates. The difficulty of sustaining parallel and alternative institutions in a hostile environment while simultaneously fighting on other fronts was very real. The isolation of the student movement, with few allies in other sectors of the population, was a further hurdle facing new left experiments.

Young, a pacifist, links participatory democracy and counter-institutional experiments with non-violence as the novel characteristics of new left politics. For him it was the embrace of violence in 1968 that signaled the demise of the new left. In a famed formulation, Max Weber wrote that "He who seeks the salvation of the soul, of his own and others, should not seek it along the avenue of politics, for the quite different tasks of politics can only be solved by violence."[27] This warning might have been the secret drummer to which the early new left marched. Young is correct to attribute the novelty of new left politics to counter-institutions, democracy and non-violence, because as Weber suggested, politics and violence are traditionally joined. Violence may be of the literal physical sort or of a more diffuse political kind in which a small number of powerful individuals determine the welfare of the majority through forced decisions and secret deals. I do not agree with Young's voluntarist interpretation of the turn towards violence and militarism around 1968. I do, however, concur that the non-violence of the early new left was a powerful ingredient in its politics, one that was initially learned directly and indirectly from SNCC, the Student Non-Violent Coordinating Committee.

It is my conviction that the attempt to seek the "salvation of the soul" *in* politics, to forge a new definition of politics in which violence, authority and hierarchy did not reign supreme is the most unique and powerful legacy of the new left. Throughout the sixties the new left, ironically in light of the widespread association of the movement with violence, sought to dissociate politics from violence, to find salvation through a nonviolent and nonhierarchical politics. Resistance politics, "an act that had no end" in David Harris's words, had the same goal. To refuse to cooperate with the machine, literally to refuse to fight, and to build instead a community which might serve as an alternative moral and personal standard, was to separate politics from violence and power hierarchies. It is not accidental that the new left was an anti-war movement, that saying "no" to the war in Vietnam was the central issue of the movement, conscientious objectors, conspicuous actors; it was a dramatic demonstration of the dissociation of politics from violence.

PARTICIPATORY DEMOCRACY

> . . . Participatory democracy is often like a chronic and contagious disease. Once caught, it permeates one's whole life and the lives of those

around. Its effect is disruptive in a total sense. And within a manipulative, bureaucratic system, its articulation and expression amounts to sabotage.

Carl Davidson, a national officer of SDS from 1966 through 1968, added that he hoped those who were exposed to participatory democracy while they were building a movement would "never quite be the same," particularly after they had left the university.[28] Davidson was not overstating the case; participatory democracy was at the heart of the movement called the new left.[29] It was discussed and enacted throughout the community, anti-war, counter-institutional and campus projects during the sixties. It *was* infectious, compelling, and persuasive as an ideal and organizational model for those in leadership as well as for those at the grass roots. It developed directly out of the separation of ordinary people from the decisions that affected their lives; it entailed an emphasis on the process of radical transformation. In 1962 Tom Hayden stated the basic notion underlying participatory democracy, rejecting the idea that only a privileged few could be autonomous. Rather, Hayden asserted, ". . . Independence can be a fact about ordinary people. And democracy, real participating democracy, rests on the independence of ordinary people."[30] Ten years later, in 1972, Richard Rothstein noted that the 1962 Port Huron Statement contained the central ideas behind participatory democracy. It had expressed the goal of a society in which "the individual shares in those decisions determining the quality and direction of his life; and that society [is] organized to encourage independence in men and provide the media for their common participation."[31] Interestingly, in 1972 Rothstein would say that SDS's founding articulation of participatory democracy ". . . was largely a generalization adding up to socialism without the word. . . ."[32]

Participatory democracy was a means of transforming powerlessness into shared competence and responsibility and rested on operationalizing the participation of everyone in the group. New left participatory democrats assumed that everyone was equal in their potential understanding and contribution, and sought to create both a community within the movement and structural transformation in the larger society. Large-scale change, whether it was called economic democracy, independence for ordinary people, or socialism, was unsatisfactory if achieved from the top down. Participation was critical.

Participatory democracy contained the notion of transforming people's relations to institutions and each other in the process of large-scale change; more accurately, they were unified processes, inseparable. A dual process was always taking place: the creation of alternative communities, incorporating new modes of relating and deciding, and organizing for power. Since participatory democracy was both a goal and a means leading to that goal, new leftists were often on the horns of a political dilemma. Political differences derived from differences of emphasis. While virtually all new leftists agreed that participatory democracy required a concern with means, process and cooperation, many did not believe that this process should be the primary goal of movement politics. Others, as we have seen, believed that the attempt to build a participatory community was the very heart of the movement.

An important implication of participatory democracy was stated in 1966 by Don McKelvey: ". . . What the New Left has been calling participatory democracy is really direct democracy. . ." He suggested that this implied decentralization, since economic and political units had to be sufficiently small that individuals could participate directly in decisions. McKelvey defended direct, in contrast to representative, democracy because it retained the integrity of the community, stating that the usual form of decision making was voting and majority opinion, but that "the alternative form of consensus—widely used by the New Left—more perfectly recognizes and enhances the community's integrity and unity."[33] He suggested that the voting/majority method led to factionalism and lack of community while participatory democracy, particularly consensual decision making, did not. In insisting on the notion of decentralization inherent in direct democracy, McKelvey highlighted an important feature of new left politics, one that came into its own in the late sixties and during the seventies. Community control advocates, counter-institutional experiments, and the women's and ecology movements, all embraced notions of decentralized control and community participation. Organizational forms based on participatory democracy led in the direction of decentralized and manageable units with small-group decision making. In his 1969 *Essay on Liberation*, Herbert Marcuse pointed to the democratic and delegitimizing aspects of direct democracy: ". . . Direct action and uncivil disobedience become for the rebels integral parts of the transformation of the indirect democracy of corporate capitalism into a direct democracy in which elections and representatives no longer serve as institutions of domination."[34]

Staughton Lynd, concerned throughout the sixties with participatory democracy, suggested that its implicit strategy of social change was one of parallel structures. These ranged from the Mississippi Freedom Democratic Party to community unions. Their possibilities included transforming existing institutions to building anti-establishment networks that would form the basis of the new society. What the movement sought, according to Lynd, was community. "The spirit of *community, as opposed to organization*, is not, We are together to accomplish this or that end, but We are together whatever life brings."[35] (Emphasis mine.) This tension, community versus organization, is the decisive one from our point of view, and was rarely so consciously articulated. Community was sought by the movement and attained through the practice of participatory democracy. Parallel structures or counter-institutions were both communities *and* strategies for social change. Above all, the movement came together not only for instrumental reasons, not primarily to accomplish a specific end (as the "politicos" might advocate), but to be together in a more basic experiment than "organization" implied.

According to Lynd, the political direction indicated by participatory democracy seemed to be toward building a "brotherly way of life even in the jaws of the Leviathan." He characterized the nature of participatory democracy as conscientious objection not only to war but to a dehumanized society. Lynd also acknowledged some of its difficulties. It could not specify how to clothe and feed people. It was neither a clear strategy nor could it answer hard, tangible questions about strategy and outcome. And while Lynd maintained that the creation of community and parallel institutions was the new left's main task, he also asked: "Like the conscientious objector, however, the participatory democrat has unfinished business with the question: Is what's intended a moral gesture only, or a determined attempt to transform the American power structure?"[36]

Many charged that those most committed to participatory democracy, those identified here as advocating prefigurative politics, intended a "moral gesture" and little else. Or that their embrace of participatory democracy crippled other more significant political efforts. I have suggested that the attempt to close the gap between means and ends, the project of prefiguring future radical transformation, was not a rejection of politics or a failure to be realistic. Rather new leftists attempted to hold on to both sides of the tension, understanding that both were necessary. There is no question that they were more vulnerable than those supporting a more strategic politics since they were in fact making a moral as well as an organizational statement, and were much less clear about how their efforts would transform the American power structure and economy. The demand of critics and radicals to be pragmatic and realistic, to come up with a blueprint, makes those who are concerned with other things appear guilty of idealism.

Kenneth Keniston interprets the appeal of participatory democracy by suggesting that the "fear of the abuse of power or irrational authority, and of dominating leadership is . . . a legitimate reaction to a world in which power, authority, and leadership are used cruelly rather than benignly." Participatory democracy in this light was an attempt to develop new forms of organization and action based on humanistic values and criteria.[37] While this provides us with psychological insight into the appeal of participatory democracy, the latter's practice began to generate its own critique. These were criticisms derived through experience, which we will explore more extensively in Chapter Five. For now, they may be grouped around two issues: one, the development of elitism and the actual undermining of democracy and two, the failure to function adequately in large groups. Two articles written in the early 1970s by new left participants looked back on baffling problems facing activists. Both Richard Rothstein and Norman Fruchter were active in the community organizing projects of SDS, ERAP, and utilize their experiences there to outline the weaknesses of participatory democracy.[38] Rothstein's "Representative Democracy in SDS" is one of the most extensive and damning accounts of participatory democracy in SDS. Rothstein argues that participatory democracy was responsible for some of the worst anti-democratic developments, particularly the development of an elite not answerable to the membership, but with enormous prestige and power in the organization. This elite made decisions that *should* have been made in a more democratic manner, using the representative forms which had been dismantled precisely because they had been judged hierarchical and anti-democratic. "As each representative institution in the organization was destroyed, the organization became, in fact, less democratic." Rothstein places the rhetoric and confusion about participatory democracy, which issued in the mistrust of leaders, skills, administrative concerns and structure itself, at the core of SDS's failure.

As an example, he points out that regular rotation of high offices was unquestioned since it seemed to combat bureaucracy and the accumulation of power. However, the result was not to eliminate leadership, but to make it inaccessible to the membership. Behind the scenes the power of certain leaders grew, as did the power of the national staff. Because there was no recognition of the importance of developing skills and no mechanisms for instructing leaders, there was little organizational continuity. In this vacuum the staff became crucial to the maintenance of the organization. The staff, needless to say, was not formally responsible to the membership. According to Rothstein, the rhetoric of participatory democracy was used to abolish positions, offices and membership participation under the misconception that this would create democracy. All the mechanisms for participation were abolished until political differences issued in factions in the national offices. "Fighting out political battles within a national office is far less democratic than having those battles fought in a general election campaign for control of the office."

Rothstein refers to the extension of what he calls the "ultra-democratic" mystique, suggesting that it resulted from a refusal to define and enforce SDS National Council membership (made up of delegates from all chapters) so that by 1967 random members who showed up at meetings outvoted chapter delegates, making it possible for non-chapter members to relate to SDS only at the top (National Council meetings) and undermining the chapter as the basic unit of the organization. This happened because it was seen as "oppressive and in violation of 'participatory democracy' to prevent from speaking anyone in the room who might have something to say. In due time this was carried further and it was felt to be embarrassingly 'bourgeois' to ask for voting credentials." Rothstein also believed that lack of structure in ERAP projects gave the student-organizers inordinate power, although the objective was precisely the opposite. Rothstein ends his analysis by suggesting that "fully participatory democratic organizations were probably impossible in the politically naive days of the early New Left, but formally democratic organizations would have been a good place to start."[39]

In his 1972 article, Norman Fruchter also focuses on the organizational difficulties SDS had faced. Fruchter suggests that SDS as an organization was a "premature political form," which articulated only the *values* of the developing social movement. It was an organization formed by leaders who were responsive to these values but not sufficiently self-conscious and consequently still tied to traditional notions of role, structure, politics and ambition.[40] Fruchter argues that SDS's failures could be traced, among other reasons, to its inadequate traditional organizational structure and forms. He points out that SDS's initial structure was actually traditional: national officers and a National Council were elected by the membership annually at a national convention; the Council, officers and a hired staff were responsible for the functioning of the organization; National Council meetings were held several times a year to discuss policy and formulate program. However, although the *form* of the organization was traditional, the emphasis on openness, communication and consensus created ambiguity. The elite created a new national organization at a time when "new forms of opposition" were just beginning to develop. "What resulted was a hybrid, an organization proclaiming a set of new values as its goals, yet attempting to achieve those new values through a traditional set of structures and forms."[41]

The national elite, according to Fruchter, did not in fact accept the responsibility required of them by the national structure. The rhetoric of democracy and humility used to criticize SDS's organizational structure was indicative of a deeper ambivalence about leadership, role and ambition that characterized the SDS leadership. These leaders did not have an adequate historical self-consciousness with which to recognize that their own developing forms of association and relations might offer some clues toward building a more workable structure. "They were unable to be responsible to the national structure they had initiated because it did not correspond to the actual forms of their own work and relationship." Fruchter suggests that, had there been more time, the experiences and experiments in small group activity, projects and relationships "might have generated the political forms and structure necessary for a national political organization attempting to embody new values."[42]

In summary, Fruchter shrewdly sees SDS as the elite of a developing social force, created by the contradictions of advanced capitalism, and embodying new oppositional values. This elite assumed it could directly translate its new values into political practice, but used traditional forms which could not incorporate them. Fruchter proposes that as a result of a variety of factors—time, inexperience, personality traits, and personal goals peculiar to the "elite" of SDS—an organizational form appropriate to the new culture and politics was not developed. Instead, traditional representative forms were formally utilized but practically ignored because these forms were inappropriate vis-à-vis the new values and politics. Implicit in this argument is the assumption that there *existed* an organizational form which coherently articulated or represented the values of the new left.

In contrast, Rothstein argues that serious determination to make representative structures work would have created a more democratic organization. Fruchter, however, maintains, and, I think, more to the point, that the difficult question is why SDS leadership had to "*make* these structures work." For Fruchter, the answer lies in the fact that these traditional structures did not correspond to their real relationships and politics. Clearly, as Rothstein argues, representative structure did not function well in SDS and the rhetoric and ideal of participatory democracy contributed to that. At the same time, Fruchter says little about potential alternative organizational forms. He does not take the further step of formulating what organizational form would have corresponded to SDSers' real values and politics. It remains an abstract possibility, as perhaps it did for other participants as well, who understood the dilemma and yet could not solve it. There is no question that the "ultra-democratic mystique," which in large part derived from SNCC and lodged in ERAP most profoundly, did not translate well into large-scale organization. But the rhetoric to which Rothstein critically points was *not* simply willful and manipulative. New leftists, committed to the values embodied in participatory democracy, were unable satisfactorily to operationalize participation, particularly decision-making, in a mass political organization. In some cases they attempted to utilize participatory democracy inappropriately, unintentionally producing elitism and making it almost impossible to make decisions.

Two examples illustrate difficulties in decision-making. A letter in the *ERAP Newsletter* about the 1965 SDS National Convention complained that lack of structure consistently impeded decisions. "Everyone talked about everything but did not come to any decisions." This, it was said, was because people did not really expect decisions to be made.[43] Here was evidence, alluded to by Rothstein, of the difficulties created by the breakdown of representative structure. It was evident to most participants in mass assemblies that representative structure provided guidelines for the procedure and process of delegated decision-making, while participatory democracy did not. And a report from the Newark ERAP project stated straightforwardly that the problems of operating democratically with a staff of forty-five were overwhelming. "Although many of us regard voting as undemocratic, there is a real question about whether we can afford to take eight hours to attain consensus on every issue." They wondered how it might be possible for everyone to understand and communicate with one another so that a "real consensus [could] be attained."[44]

Consideration of Rothstein and Fruchter's 1972 retrospective analyses should not obscure the fact that these sorts of concerns developed during the sixties out of the ongoing practice of the movement. It dawned slowly but profoundly on partisans of participatory democracy that it worked well in small groups, but they had not yet devised appropriate forms for large-scale organization. By the second half of the sixties, even those most committed wondered uneasily how participatory democracy could be operational in a mass organization. A 1967 article by Greg Calvert, spokesperson for prefigurative politics, entitled "Participatory Democracy, Collective Leadership and Political Responsibility," stated that the basic problem with participatory democracy was not with its analysis or vision, "but in its basic inadequacy as a style of work for a serious radical organization." Evaluating what he saw as a critical organizational problem, Calvert suggested that SDS recruited people on the basis of that analysis and vision and then attempted to do political work "as if the rhetoric were sufficient to create, here and now, the non-repressive society of equals."[45] This was, needless to say, a sober self-criticism and political appraisal on Calvert's part less than one year after his "From Protest to Resistance" statement.

Another movement veteran and staunch defender of participatory democracy, Staughton Lynd, wrote an article called "Prospects for the New Left" in which he explored its problems. He, too, was chastened, and suggested that new left organizational concepts were better suited for small and homogeneous groups. In an analysis similar to Fruchter's, he pointed out that there had been an initial "fit" between SDS staff existence and new left rhetoric and ideas of democracy. Large organizations, heterogeneous, more prosaic, less romantic and run by "others," "probably have less capacity to anticipate the lineaments of a future society than the small staff groups in which intellectual and physical labor can be combined, authority and rewards can be made equal." Understanding this on some level, the new left consequently shied away and "failed to give organizational birth at all . . ." Lynd stated very clearly:

> If we are talking about a mass movement then we are talking about
> representative government and voting. This doesn't mean . . . that small
> groups taking direct action after consensual discussion must disappear.
> On the contrary. But there has got to be a way for hundreds and thou-
> sands of people to set policy together regarding fundamental issues, and
> consensus is not it.[46]

The foregoing analyses indicate a practical dilemma faced by the movement and recognized by participants: the necessity of incorporating participatory democracy into a large-scale organization. We have seen how
many SDSers understood that the movement and SDS recruited on the
basis of their vision and promise of community and of meaning in one's
life through collective participation. Calvert reiterated in both the earlier
celebratory statement and in the more sober appraisal that the values and
promise of SDS were the basis of its appeal.

Yet the challenge was to translate the community and democracy espoused by SDS into organizational mechanisms. These statements (other
than Rothstein's) were *not* repudiations of participatory democracy. They
were, rather, signs of political development and maturity. A second kind
of historical explanation for these appraisals was the escalation of the war
in Vietnam and the riots in the ghettoes of American cities, both of which
reinforced a strong sense that a white student movement was unimportant
in the wars of liberation waged by people of color against the white ruling
elite in America, and which created a sense of horror and desperation.
Many were led to re-evaluate their optimism.[47] Early libertarian hopes
ran into the enormity of the tasks, and the fragilities and failings of SDS.
In the midst of the frenetic and violent events of the sixties, participatory
democracy presented difficulties in a large organization that was feeling
pressured to *lead,* to fix priorities, to focus on specific programs and
politicies, to incorporate masses of people, in other words, to utilize their
energies in an effective and focused manner. In this context, participatory
democracy appeared too fragile and uninstrumental,

Such reassessments signified becoming more "prosaic" and less "romantic," in Lynd's words, as well as the worry that this might mean
relinquishing the "anticipation of the lineaments of a future society."
These concerns, along with the criticism of participatory democracy's
propensity to create elitism, might well be interpreted as the failure of
participatory democracy in the new left. But this is not an accurate appraisal. It is true that the conventional forms of politics, of bureaucratic,
hierarchical and/or representative organizations, began at this time to
appear more adequate to exerting power on the federal government than
did the movement's own experiments and examples. Participatory democracy seemed unable to halt the government's war in Southeast Asia,
in the ghettoes, often even in the university itself, and for many in the

new left, organization seemed part of the solution to the new left's dilemmas. This led some into Marxist-Leninist organizations and others to become disciplined quasi-military cadre in new groups working for socialist revolution. Second thoughts, then, evolved from the realization of the immensity of the political tasks and out of the sense of isolation and despair that the movement began to experience.

These thoughts were not simply reversals of early optimism in the direction of a more traditional politics, or an end to the "world turned upside down" in which everything seemed possible, and politics had taken on a new meaning. They must not be overinterpreted. For neither participatory democracy nor prefigurative politics was abandoned. They were the single most powerful attraction and inspiration of the movement for thousands of people, and were responsible for the appeal and growth of the new left. Participatory visions and experiments were the fuel that fired the movement's grass roots, even while the debates within the leadership and in the organization unfolded. It is useful to make the distinction again between the new left and the student movement, and the organization and the movement. These had to two levels of evaluation. The first, which we have been considering, was national and organizational. It was here, among those most concerned with the health and effectiveness of the organization, that most of the discussion took place. These analyses reflected the material situation of those on the national level; they were concerned with the whole, with masses of people whose participation had to be guaranteed. The second was the grass roots, local level, where prefigurative politics was powerful and less problematic. Calvert and others like him were attempting to make prefigurative politics viable on the national level.

And to add a complicating factor, there is serious question whether the converse might have been true, whether on the national level strong representative and disciplined organization would have made the new left and the movement more "successful." Most commentators, and many leaders, were probably wrong to argue that strong organization was the key to success. For what did success mean? The movement was successful. It created significant social and cultural changes in the direction of equality and participation, especially among youth and the disadvantaged of America; it had a large part in ending the war in Vietnam; it created a climate of questioning and cynicism about those in power; it was responsible for local political gains that have continued into the present; and it changed much about the universities. The apparently self-evident truth that organization is what succeeds is only apparently true in the case of the new left.

It is inaccurate to interpret worried and critical thoughts as a rejection of participatory democracy. Rather, as I have suggested, many new leftists held on to both sides of the dualism expressed in prefigurative and strategic politics, struggling to develop organization which accomplished the goals of both. Their efforts were a challenge to Michels and all the preceding social movements that had resulted in organization at the expense of democratic and direct participation.

Yet Lynd was not wrong in his suggestion that there had to be a way for hundreds and thousands of people to participate in an organized manner; it was the task facing the movement. Those who attempted to operationalize participatory democracy in the mass movement, who searched for appropriate organizational forms, were part of the challenge to Michels. The reassessment on the national and organizational level was a new stage for a new left that went from an ecstatic optimism to a more sober effort to create participatory organizational forms on a mass scale.

And, finally, while the re-evaluations were not reversals or political turnabouts, there is no escaping the shattered utopian hopes hidden within them. Max Weber warned that the salvation of the soul, the beloved community, could not be sought along the avenue of politics. Time and again the word used by administrators and government officials faced with disruption and protest was "unrealistic." They might have said "utopian" as well. The direct democracy and community "buried in the disasters of the twentieth-century revolutions," according to Hannah Arendt, have been persistently looked upon "as though they were a romantic dream, some sort of fantastic utopia come true for a fleeting moment to show, as it were, the hopelessly romantic yearnings of the people, who apparently did not yet know the true facts of life." New leftists were learning the "true facts of life"; they had initially articulated an anti-authoritarian and anti-hierarchical politics, understanding the undemocratic potential of bureaucracy and centralized structure, and in the midst of their success were overwhelmed by the task of listening to and drawing everyone into an effective political formation. In Arendt's words, the impetus behind revolutionary politics was a "hope for a transformation of the state, for a new form of government that would permit every member . . . to become 'participator' in public affairs. . ."[48] To many this "hidden treasure" seemed a "romantic dream," hopelessly unrealistic. For most it was all that mattered. It represented a rupture with the present and most of history, which held out a hope that politics could directly embody the democratic instinct liberated when people are able to organize themselves, that the salvation of the soul might be attained in politics. It seems rarely to last.

CHAPTER 5

Politics as Organization

A MASS MOVEMENT

Everything changed in 1965. The escalation of the war in Vietnam and the development of the anti-war movement, created a mass movement in the space of several months. Organizational issues and strains of the middle period of the decade were partially the result of the enormous growth and proliferation of the student and anti-war movement around the country. Todd Gitlin has suggested that the media's role in controlling and constraining the movement at the same time that it "spotlighted" it, transformed SDS at this time into a mass movement with which it was unprepared to deal. By simplifying and making immediate the new left's issues and consequently speeding up the movement's timetable, Gitlin proposes that the escalation of the war, and the role of the media, dissolved the movement's organic rhythm and progression. From then on, the movement developed in relation to the media rather than its own constituencies.[1]

In June 1966, Paul Booth, National Secretary of SDS at the time, stated that the December Conference closing the year 1965 was "the occasion of our recognition of SDS's new character as a national student organization." SDS had become a new feature of American life, and, according to Booth, the conference was an "exercise in collective self-definition," which struggled with the organizational and internal problems caused by SDS's rapid growth.[2]

However one accounts for the difficulties of the movement, there is no question that 1965 was the turning point, the shift from the "new left" to the "student movement": from a face-to-face network of acquaintances and primary groups, a family, to a mass movement and a mass organization. But the change was not only quantitative; it involved the very character and quality of the movement. Several commentators have proposed a useful way of depicting this by noting a generation shift within the new left around 1965. Gitlin suggests that movements divide into generations. Regarding the new left, he proposes a model of a primary generation which was recruited personally and a secondary generation which was recruited through the media. The second assumed the movement *was* its media stars, while the first resented both this assumption and the stars themselves, which created a strain and discontinuity making it difficult to pass on one generation's experience to the next.[3]

The differences between these generations were important. Milton Mankoff studied the changes in generations in the movement at the University of Wisconsin and observed that when the radicals were small in number they were atypical of the college community at large; they were likely to be from politically liberal and active homes and much more exposed to political ideas in comparison to the general student population. Mankoff found that the growth of the student movement brought into the vanguard students who were unlikely to have come from liberal families and were less politically sophisticated than the veterans.[4] More specifically, Gitlin, following Kirkpatrick Sale's analysis in *SDS*, identified two groups of new membership, in contrast with the original "old guard": the first flooded in in the wake of the SDS-sponsored anti-war march in April of 1965; the second, called the "prairie dogs" (because they were not from the east coast, not obviously intellectuals nor from left-wing backgrounds) who inherited the organization in August 1966 at Clear Lake, Iowa. These two groups, who blend into one another, the new less politicized recruits and the prairie dogs, mostly from the midwest, more alienated and anarchistic than the original leadership, made up the bulk of the student movement from then on; and on balance they stood for anti-organizational and prefigurative politics.[5]

Sale and others suggest that SDS's organizational structure broke down under the waves of new membership in 1965. Fragile and limited structure accounts for complaints of national office hegemony, absence of communication between staff and local chapters, lack of internal education and difficult and unproductive national meetings. It was some of these difficulties that the advocates of participatory democracy addressed in their concern for its ability to function well. SDS as an organization simply was unable to handle all the demands made upon it by the new membership and by the urgency of the national political situation; this was particularly true since so many did not consider organization a high priority. It is to those who did that we turn in this chapter.

MOVEMENT VERSUS ORGANIZATION

Analyzing SDS and the movement in the mid-sixties, Michael Rossman wondered how much SDS was responsible for what was happening. Despite the fact that SDS initiated many fronts of conflict and rebellion, the number of those who counted themselves official members was not enormous. Instead:

> . . . SDS is less an organization than a broad penumbra of feeling present in every heart. Indeed, at most demonstrations . . . less than a quarter of the protestors belong to any organized political group. Young activists, like the rest of their peers, are reluctant to create formal groups. The organization of resistance and revolution is informal and interior.[6]

One of the more perplexing and complicated issues facing SDS was its relationship as a national student organization to the student movement, a broad, mass insurgency that SDS either directly or symbolically represented. The fact that the movement was signified by a "feeling present in every heart" and the "interior and informal" organization of resistance made it difficult indeed for leadership to gauge and analyze their own organizational responsibilities and effects. The student movement was a grass roots, often spontaneous, political expression of discontent, opposition and desire for change and SDS was the organization that most obviously represented it. As Kirkpatrick Sale put it, SDS "stood as the catalyst, vanguard, and personification of that decade of defiance." While SDS was only part of the movement and the movement only a part of the larger cultural upheaval of the time, it was "the organized expression of that Movement, its intellectual mentor and the source of much of its energy, the largest, best known and most influential element within it for a decade."[7]

As an "organized expression" of a movement which was often internal and informal on an individual level and decentralized and spontaneous on the local level, SDS faced profound political challenges and difficulties. The organization wrestled with the tension between an apparently thriving and growing grass roots movement and the conviction held by many in SDS of the necessity of creating centralized institutions and of channeling the political activity. From 1963 onwards, and especially after 1965, when SDS, instigator and beneficiary of grass roots political dissatisfaction, began to grow significantly, it was faced with the problem of distinguishing itself from that generalized movement and providing organizational leadership. Representation of the movement by a central student organization, through elected officers and an elected National Council, raised classic political issues for the new left, issues that bourgeois as well as Marxist theorists alike have analyzed: the relationship of political parties to participation and to the masses of activists, specifically, the nature of democracy in a representative system.[8] The rapid growth and the exigencies of the movement forced SDS leaders to confront political problems they had barely thought about.

Many in the leadership of SDS believed strongly in the importance of forging a strong left student organization as a means to political change. The movement, on the other hand, was a locally-based, spontaneous outpouring of opposition to the war in Vietnam around the country. Its existence did not depend on strategy or formal organization. New left organizations were based on the movement; they did not create it. As a SNCC member remarked on the civil rights movement, "No one really needed an 'organization' because we then had a movement."[9] The "organization vs. movement" tension was not based on differing material interests between leadership and "membership." Many in the movement sought organization of one or another type; however, their only obvious difference was that those who became part of the leadership generally became more committed to organization. But even this was not true across the board since there were always leaders who were ambivalent about centralized organization. The line-up was not simple.

In winter, 1965, Robb Burlage, an early SDSer, asked, "How can SDS be responsible to its diverse constituency and build solid local bases while being responsive to national crises not so clearly linked to our campus and community bases?"[10] The organization was not directly responsible for the growth at the base, and yet, in Sale's words, stood as its "catalyst, vanguard and personification." The challenge was to represent the movement in concrete political organization.

From 1962 onwards reports from SDS chapters remarked on the energy and enthusiasm at the local level. Often this political activity developed with little input from SDS leadership. As early as 1962 and 1963 Burlage noted a Boston chapter's vitality and activism on the one hand, and the problems stemming from the chapter's lack of connection to leadership in the national office, on the other. He specifically pinpointed their lack of intellectual analysis, suggesting that the leadership might have provided it.[11] As SDS grew so did the difficulties of simply keeping track of membership and political activity on campuses. In April 1965 Paul Potter, president of SDS, announced: "As all of you know, SDS is growing at an incredible rate. Chapters seem to come in the mail, almost mystically on occasion, coming as often as not from campuses where there has been virtually no direct contact with SDS."

Here was an indication of the power of the movement at the local level and the growing numbers of people who identified with SDS. There were no rigorous requirements for a group of people to constitute itself a chapter; in fact, they had only to call themselves an SDS chapter. Potter acknowledged that most of the people who were working for SDS seemed to reach them with no contact with an SDS chapter, much less an SDS card. Organizational difficulties were created, according to Potter, by this phenomenon of people working outside any formal structure.[12]

In early 1966, the following year, in an article in *New Left Notes*, Paul Booth, SDS National Secretary, reported that it required little from the national leadership to keep people active and enthusistic.[13] And later that same year, Dick Flacks worried that SDS National Council meetings and programs ". . . don't represent the reality of the organization." The decisions and activities of SDS occurred at the local level, "in the chapters, projects, regions—and at that level organizational life is rich, developing, relevant." There was no question, according to Flacks, that at the local level SDS had never been better off. New leadership was emerging and varieties of action taking place in conjunction with a growing group of people, on campus and off, who identified with SDS.[14]

Flacks was describing the discontinuity between the base and the national program, structure and leadership, what Sale calls the "distance problem." Flacks discussed the deep organizational malaise consisting of the inability of the national organization to capture the reality of the movement, symbolized by bad national meetings filled with speech-making, abstract debate, ideological posturing and rhetoric. He, along with many other SDS leaders, suggested that the sources of this malaise at the national level reflected the fact that SDS had no national program to provide a focus for the movement. In part this was the result of the greatly increased size and internal complexity of SDS. Flacks pointed out that only two years before SDS members had been connected to one another by ties of personal friendship. All this had changed since the March on Washington against the war in Vietnam in April 1965 and SDS's leap into national prominence. The organization had literally been swamped with thousands of new recruits of every sort of viewpoint, aspiration and sophistication.[15] Repeatedly SDS leaders pointed to the divergence between strength at the local level and the organizational and programmatic chaos at the national level.

But is is not accurate to attribute the growth of the movement uniquely to opposition to the war in Vietnam. The burgeoning grass roots movement signaled the start of a multi-layered, multi-causal critique of American society, a rejection and withdrawal from its dominant goals, a period of experimentation, a rupture—all of which added to the pressures on SDS and the organizational question. Jeff Shero, vice-president of SDS in 1965–66, reporting on his work as a campus organizer, captured the upheaval taking place among young people on the campuses around the country. According to Shero, students were increasingly rejecting mainstream life patterns, resistance was everywhere; the central expression of this resistance was the "fantastic growth in the use of drugs." Another principal form of resistance was the movement to avoid the draft. "Draft dodging is the most unorganized and universal sign of disaffection," but there were scores of other signs as well. Shero's point, however, was that SDS had had "a failure of imagination in developing [a] program that is relevant to much of the dissent that is taking place."[16]

It is not self-evident that a national program *could* have captured and channeled the dissent he noted, or even been more effective, although Shero and other leaders consistently assumed it would have. In fact, the summer 1966 Clear Lake SDS convention had signaled a triumph of a decentralized, regionally-oriented organization, prefigurative politics, with less emphasis on national program and structure and a rejection of leaders, parliamentary procedure, structure and top-down organizing. This was considered by many leaders and ordinary members the way to give organizational expression to the movement. Despite this the assumption throughout the discussion in national SDS seemed to be that it was possible for the national organization to represent the movement: to guide, control and focus its energies, and perhaps determine its outcome. This is, of course, always the assumption of people involved in building or maintaining organizations.

The national organizationists are supported by sociological work on social movements. Much of the sociological literature assumes that for success, leadership, structure, division of labor, specific goals, and hierarchy in some combination are required.[17] Joseph Gusfield, however, points out, basing himself on Max Weber's "routinization of charisma" and Michels' "iron law of oligarchy," that while a semipermanent organizational structure is often essential to the achievement of movement goals, this organizational structure often sets in motion forces that *defeat* the very ideals that gave birth to the social movement.[18] And literature within the Marxist, specifically, Leninist tradition, routinely considers the party the self-evident representative of the working class.

In arguments of this sort there is a tendency to confuse organizational form with organizational effectiveness. How people are incorporated into an organization and how pressure and influence are exerted to attain goals are not the same thing. A "disorganized," or rather, non-hierarchical, insurgent movement may be as effective as a more organized one and according to some analysts, for example Francis Fox Piven and Richard Cloward, is often more so. The equation of national program and structure with influence in oppositional movements is one traditionally made by social scientists and by leftists. But according to Piven and Cloward, ". . . it was not formal organizations but mass defiance that won what was won in the 1930s and 1960s."[19] In the paperback introduction to *Poor People's Movements*, they criticize the left for stubbornly holding to the idea that formal mass-membership organizations are the way the working class can successfully wrest power. And they state unequivocally, the thesis of their book, that bureaucratic organizations blunted the militancy that was the critical source of various movements' influence. Piven and Cloward, considering poor people's movements, argue that mass insurgency and disruption are often the only recourse open to poor people—further, that it is often politically strategic for them to disrupt institutional life since historically they have achieved more this way than through building their own, ultimately bureaucratic, organizations. They argue strategically: the poor have no other leverage and sometimes it works. It can be maintained that the student movement was as successful as it was due to *its* disruption of "business as usual." But more than that, the Piven-Cloward argument is pertinent for interpreting the debates between organizationists, *usually* early new left leaders, and those who rejected organizational concerns as a priority. The latter group stood for prefigurative politics, more an ideological and political choice and less a pragmatic or strategic one, based on the understanding that traditional institutional politics excluded the radical goals they pursued. Those who embraced prefigurative politics, worried, too, about the co-optive and deradicalizing potential of electoral politics. This choice was based on their fear that organizations take on a life of their own, creating hierarchy and conformity. However, I do not want to imply that those who supported strengthening SDS organizationally were bureaucrats. On any scale one could devise, new leftists, no matter where they stood, would rate very low in inclination towards bureaucracy. Rather, those who embraced strategic politics articulated a more traditional, and traditionally left, political position.

SDS leaders were not operating in a vacuum, however. The bulk of activists simply did not look to SDS for leadership; indigenous leadership developed, local and autonomous projects grew and sustained themselves. Neil Buckley, writing in 1968, suggested that SDS had abdicated its leadership responsibility, pointing to its refusal to support national marches against the Vietnam War organized by other coalitions. Instead of adding to the momentum of the anti-war and student movement, or even leading it, SDS stalled or turned its back. Revealingly, however, Buckley added that these events did not suffer greatly in numerical terms by the organization's failures, since SDSers "as individuals . . . joined the marches in droves."[20] In other words, SDS members or "members of the heart" participated in political activity *whether or not* national SDS endorsed it. The organizational mandate of SDS was not overriding either way. A dilemma was posed: we are failing because we are not providing leadership, but leadership is often ignored anyway. Summing up the situation as he saw it, Buckley said that SDS's efforts to create a resistance and membership in the university, "says more about a mood already there which we articulated and crudely led than anything positive about our leadership abilities."[21]

The majority sentiments must be placed against the concern and commitment to the organizational responsibilities of SDS. Rossman wrote that "Young activists are reluctant to create formal groups . . ." concluding that the organization of opposition is informal. One of the central elements militating against SDS's ability to provide a more coherent program, set of goals and adequate structure, was this powerful current which stood for decentralization and local initiative. Repeatedly SDSers and movement activists said such things as "The distance between "the people" and the leaders who are doing things to and for people is a major problem in America, and must be avoided to the fullest degree in a radical, democratic movement.[22] Or a letter to *New Left Notes* in 1966 said, "SDS is and should be a movement. . . . Movements have spirit, life, energy, motion. They have no defined form. They grow spontaneously and creatively. They die when people in them try to channel them instead of participate in them." It continued:

> Decisions don't occur because people vote. And action does not follow logically from mandates. People do things because they want to. It is best for people to do things when they have thought about a problem and decide freely what to do about it. In fact, if people don't decide freely . . . they probably won't act. . . . People talk about freedom to a large degree because that is what they want for themselves and they join the movement because maybe it exists there. . . .[23]

In a similar view, explicating the decisions at Clear Lake, Ed Richer of St. Cloud State College wrote in *New Left Notes* that the point was not so much to deal with antagonism to national program and the National Office as to redistribute power within SDS, so that everyone could learn what the problems of power entailed through experience at the local level. He questioned whether a national program that "preempts energies, schedules, time, perspective and even constituency from the local places was worth much" and whether one of the failures of the old left was that it could "never shake itself free of national preconceptions of where people were at." Much of SDS committed itself to the building of community through day-to-day local organizing. As one participant put it: "Liberals on the Right and older revolutionary socialists on the Left of the Peace Movement share a devotion to tactics rejected by the SDS convention because, whatever their ideological differences, they are both committed to a traditionally national solution to the problems of American power."[24] This was the predominant sentiment, the heart of rejection of strategic politics.

One source of the sense of urgency facing SDS organizationally, besides the expansion and the escalation of the war, was expressed in late 1965 by Paul Booth: "The most elementary problem of SDS is that it straddles two social functions; it serves as the most powerful and important organized expression of the left in America, and it serves as a radical educational organization for students."[25] Later the next year, Greg Calvert, the new national secretary, articulated the same distinction. He wondered whether SDS's dual role, on the one hand a large student organization and on the other a group of people trying to build a left in America, was responsible for severe difficulties. SDS, the student organization, was forced into a position of financing, structuring and providing leadership for a national left movement, more than just a student movement, because there was no institutionalized left in America. SDS as a student organization had been forced to expand far beyond what it could realistically support in staff, money and resources, filling a need not filled by other organizations.[26] Calvert suggested that many of the structural problems might be solved by SDS becoming a mature political organization with affiliates among student, labor and community groups, i.e., becoming an adult left organization. In other words, he was suggesting that no *internal* structural solution could solve the problems facing SDS; it badly needed allies in other sectors of the population. Its problems were political: it was a student movement forced into a position of assuming the burden of a national left.

The tension between organization and movement would not have been solved if there had been a viable adult left in the United States during the 1960s; I think it is true however, that the tasks facing SDS were exacerbated by that absence. Kirkpatrick Sale locates SDS's failure as an organization at the heart of the new left's failure to survive.[27] He has this in common with much of the literature on the new left (and on social movements) which is uniformly critical on the grounds of organizational failure. Many lessons have been drawn from the history and sociology of the new left, the most prevalent being, not unexpectedly, that organizational failure meant new left and student movement failure. I suspect that the conclusion is inadequate; organization could not have "saved" the student movement or new left. It, in fact, appears to have undermined other social movements. Organization can neither create nor substitute for a movement, and often when it has in the past, there is evidence it becomes either undemocratic, with Bolshevism being the classic example, or electorally inclined and integrated into the system, with the late nineteenth and twentieth century agrarian revolts of the Farmer's Alliance which developed into the Populist Party, or some of the poor people's movements considered by Piven and Cloward, being examples of the latter.[28]

The rest of this chapter examines the considerations and concerns of those who attempted to create program and coherence in SDS. Their struggle against prefigurative politics in the debates and arguments in and around SDS was constitutive of a strategic definition of politics. Within it were varying degrees of trepidation about national and centralized program and structure, but on balance these were people who believed that if the new left were to succeed there was no alternative to building organization.

ORGANIZATIONAL POLITICS, 1964-1965

In a mimeographed pamphlet entitled "The Anti-War Movement: From Protest to Radical Politics," Paul Booth and Lee Webb stated:

> SDS as an institution of the movement is able to strengthen individuals and groups in the movement in many ways that derive from its permanence; the passing on of accumulated experience, the emotional reinforcement of solidarity, the advantage of collectively allocated resources. It is an institution to which people can affiliate in the expectation that it will play a role in changing America. [29]

This potential of what SDS represented was a minority preoccupation throughout the sixties.

Usually it was the leaders (almost always men) or those who worked in the national office, who experienced and expressed most acutely the organizational problems facing SDS. It was they, reflecting their leadership positions, who articulated the necessity of organization. Those most likely to disagree or to have little interest in such problems were members and activists in the field, on the campuses, who relied only marginally on SDS for guidance and support. The most political and articulate pleas for organizational coherence and responsibility were from SDS leaders or staff who by virtue of their positions felt responsible to new or potential chapters. One after another (generally excluding ERAPers who almost all supported a decentralist, prefigurative politics)—Al Haber, Don McKelvey, Todd Gitlin, Paul Potter, Clark Kissinger, Paul Booth and Greg Calvert, among others—voiced concern for the state of the organization. The old guard who argued and pleaded for organizational responsibility attempted to alter the trend towards a celebration of activism, little or no structure, total participation, and direct, in contrast to representative, democracy.

Organizational debates were at their most intense beginning with the ERAP discussions which proceeded through the spring and summer of 1964 and the school year 1964–65, with most of the disagreement provoked and symbolized by ERAP because of their opposition to national organization and their SNCC-inspired anti-leadership and consensual decision-making projects, highlighted by the December 1965 Conference in Champaign-Urbana, and finally in diminished manner again around the Clear Lake, Iowa, Convention in August 1966, a turning point for the organization. The discussion of organizational responsibility and form slowed down after that, in large part because events in the shape of the black revolt and the anti-war movement created an emergency, changing the priorities and concerns of the movement. Leadership, chapters and ordinary activists had all they could do to keep up with events. In the early years it was the partisans of community organizing who argued, before SDS's rapid expansion in 1965, for decentralization and consensual decision-making. In 1963 to 1965 the discussion was more nearly between friends, the first generation, but it laid down the main lines of the debate which continued into the late sixties.

In March 1964 Al Haber suggested, within the context of the ERAP debates, that:

> *We cannot do all things.* Our resources are limited (not fixed); we must plan their use. This means deciding what is important and it means saying that some things are less important and should be discouraged. What are the *problems* that we, SDS, face in understanding the society and working in it to create radical change? How can we *direct* and *allocate* our limited organizational resources to solve these problems?[30]

This was a clear strategic statement pointing to the need for coherent organizational structure. It suggests, as well, the dilemma of shouldering the burden of being both a radical student organization and a national multi-generational left, with Haber arguing for concentrating on realistic goals for a student organization. Like Haber, with the tide against them, leader after leader argued in 1964, prior to the 1965 expansion, for developing the organization through ordering priorities.[31]

Todd Gitlin, president of SDS in 1963–64, wrote in the May *SDS Bulletin* that the upcoming June 1964 convention was to be devoted to the organizational problems which plagued SDS. And by July, Paul Potter, the new president, was focusing much of his energy and concern on the organizational functioning of SDS. Potter wrote that the student generation that built SDS would soon graduate from direct leadership and that it would take with it much organizational expertise and intellectual skill. He wondered what it would mean for SDS and worried whether the large number of "new and uncommitted people" would see themselves as formulators of program. Potter suggested that a "new and expanded network of people who see themselves as the owners of the organization" must emerge or SDS could not survive. He concluded with the suggestion that what was lacking was a "shared organizational vision of the possibility of SDS's becoming an intellectual and political force involving thousands of students effectively and strategically in radical action."[32] Potter's organizational and strategic emphasis is of interest here because he was wrong: SDS *did* become a powerful intellectual and political force without being a strategic and organizational one. For many in the leadership this seemed inconceivable and undesirable; their assumption was that SDS could only be powerful politically as a strong organization.

By April 1965, even before the March on Washington against the war in Vietnam, Potter was talking about the enormous growth of SDS and was concerned with changing numbers into constituencies who would take initiative in SDS and the society. He came up with a plan to increase the number of chapter people who worked for the SDS national staff, insuring in this way more contact between the local level and national SDS. He noted that more people were willing to work for SDS in community projects and on campuses but that it was almost *impossible* to recruit organizational staff from there or to get them to do what SDS wanted them to do. A real gap existed between the national structure and the base, according to Potter, and one of the only ways he could see that gap being bridged was for chapters to take greater responsibility for the national organization. His plan called for each chapter to provide the staff with at least two full-time people each year, each serving for six months. This also guaranteed that SDS would be run by its constituents and not by a professional staff. While his goal was to strengthen the organization, these were not top-down solutions. They indicated, rather, a belief in the efficacy of organization. Defending the plan, Potter said:

> . . . If we take ourselves seriously, *if we believe that our organization is one of the mechanisms for creating a radical movement,* then we must get away from the privatistic notion that organizational decisions are to be carried out by faithful bureaucrats and a small elite of leaders. If we decide that we want a larger full-time staff as one way of creating a movement, then we have to take responsibility for that decision and find ways to distribute the responsibility—for making every member of the organization responsible for providing those staff.[33]

One way to create a movement was to strengthen the organization. Throughout the years other leaders and staff endorsed the idea that building the organization was a powerful tool in creating a radical movement for social transformation.[34] In 1964 Clark Kissinger, the new national secretary, in a parody of bureaucratic energy very unlike most new left energy, proudly reported that for the first time in its history the National Office had a file and bookkeeping system, a fairly efficient staff and a periodical report sent bi-weekly to officers, ERAP projects and chapters. This made it possible for the staff to begin to coordinate all SDS operations.[35] Such achievements were not high on the list of priorities of movement activists, or perhaps more accurately, were not even contemplated by most. There was a lack of interest in all facets of organization by most of those not connected to the National Office or in leadership positions. Often the inefficiency, insulation and disarray of the National Office was an indication of the confusion about or indifference to its functions. Kissinger's attempt to "organize" the office derived from a sense that this would provide a basis for "organizing" and strengthening the organization itself.

DECENTRALIZATION

In 1964 Dick Flacks had written that one of the excellent qualities of SDS was permitting decentralized decision-making. He said that this was allowed not only because new leftists believed in decentralization but also because ". . . only those on the spot really knew what the situation was."[36] Yet as we have seen, one of the themes of organizational discussion was the lack of communication between the leadership in the national office and chapters, the distance problem. A proposed solution to this was strengthening and emphasizing regions and chapters rather than the national office and central program. Potter, too, as we have seen, was one of those who advocated decentralization as a way of strengthening SDS. In early 1965 Flacks again advocated decentralized decision-making, stressing the fact that bitter internal struggles among the staff did not reflect the interests and concerns of ordinary student activists. He said the in-fighting was being conducted at a level of intensity that was "weirdly irrelevant" and that regardless of their outcome ". . . people will generally undertake such actions as seem pragmatically appropriate for their situation (irrespective of alleged "principles" which may be involved)."[37] This was in itself a pragmatic appraisal of how most activists related to SDS. Still more significantly it suggested that *even if* the national staff decided on certain policies and politics, people would do primarily what seemed most relevant and appropriate for their situation and, if appropriate, ignore national SDS.

In a letter probably written in late spring 1965 to the National Office, Roy Dahlberg and Carolyn Craven of the San Francisco chapter wrote that there was a lot of frustration among people on the West Coast because they felt there was no way to make their thinking known to the national organization. People joined SDS, they complained, because they felt they had little control over their lives, and then found out, rhetoric to the contrary, they had little input into the organizational nationally. Communication problems existed between chapters and national staff and from chapter to chapter. Dahlberg and Craven's solution was regional organization at the expense of national organization. Unlike viewpoints which supported the movement at all costs and eschewed organization, the authors did not argue that organization was unnecessary. Rather they believed that decentralized organization "allows the most efficient means of communication, a formally recognized and dependable forum for the dissemination of ideas, it creates the discipline that comes of knowing people are dependent on you to do certain things (like write a paper or organize some activity), and it gives the reinforcement that comes of being with people who share your values."[38]

Such decentralized viewpoints, as we have seen, were often the basis of pro-movement, anti-organizational politics. But Flacks, Dahlberg and Craven, Potter's 1965 plan, and others' concern for decentralized organization was not anti-organizational; it derived instead from a pragmatic, democratic political sense that made sense. It stressed the practicality of decentralized and localized initiative, the impracticality of centralism. It recognized, too, that people were not members of SDS in a traditional sense and consequently could not be disciplined or coerced to behave in particular ways.

There was concern on the part of organizationists about the real gap between the national structure and the base. From the center Potter urged chapters to take on more responsibility for the national organization. But from the chapter perspective it often appeared there was little possibility of having input and feedback. The National Convention was the one place where major directions and formulations were supposedly decided and at which delegates were elected who met as the National Council four times a year. But this was not a reliable means of insuring participation and communication. Part of the problem stemmed from the fuzzy boundaries between the organization and the movement. When people "joined" the movement they generally did not want to be part of structured organization. As we saw in "The Politics of Community" in chapter Four, they often became involved as a reaction to bureaucracy, to unresponsiveness and unreasonableness on the part of the university and the government; and if there were active groups on their campuses, local involvement was sufficient. In part, too, those who felt ignored or frustrated by the way the national officers and staff proceeded were themselves new left leaders, people who believed in organization, and who were searching for organizational forms that could include local and regional participation. The inadequacy of traditional representative structure pointed to by Fruchter, the difficulty in devising adequate new forms, whether an organization can *ever* adequately "represent" a movement: all these were at issue.

ECONOMIC RESEARCH AND ACTION PROJECT (ERAP)

The Economic Research and Action Project, or ERAP (the subject of chapter 7), was a series of community organizing projects in northern urban ghettos organized and staffed by SDS members in 1964 and 1965. These were attempts, modeled on SNCC, to organize poor people in the north against racism (although it turned out that most of the projects were in black neighborhoods) and economic exploitation, with the goals of attaining significant power in the cities and ultimately of linking with the southern civil rights movement. Many of the important early SDS leaders

and activists were involved in ERAP, dropping out of school and, effectively, the student movement, in order to live in the ghetto and organize
full-time. They still were considered, and considered themselves, part
of SDS, although the resources and jurisdiction of the national organization vis-à-vis the projects were bones of contention, as were the politics.
Most importantly for our concerns, the ERAP projects were strongholds
of prefigurative politics. By and large, they attracted activists whose main
priority was not the health and viability of national SDS, or any national
organization.

During these same years the community organizing projects, too, were
experiencing similar organizational tensions. Simultaneously with the
SDS leadership's plea for acceptance of organizational responsibility, a
few lone voices in ERAP spoke up for a centralized and organizationally
sound administration. Throughout the fall of 1965, Richard Rothstein
criticized the disbanding of the national ERAP office and structure as
well as the lack of structure in JOIN (Jobs or Income Now), the Chicago
community project with which he was affiliated.[39] Rothstein worried about
JOIN's lack of structure, which had initially been instituted so that people
would be *encouraged* to participate. This association of lack of structure
with more participation was characteristic of new left politics. However
Rothstein noticed that the student organizers, in contrast to community
people, had an inordinate amount of power over what sort of program
JOIN developed, given that they "spend much greater amounts of time
working out political strategy, spend much greater amounts of time working in JOIN and are held in high esteem by the active community people."

Rothstein suggested counteracting this by lodging *formal* powers in
the hands of community people, in other words, reinstituting formal
structure. "With an informal structure, influence, not formal power,
rules."[40] In line with this Rothstein said he and Rennie Davis had decided
to reopen the national ERAP office again early in 1966. He was willing
to take responsibility for this and enumerated the functions he deemed
critical but that had not been performed since the ERAP national office
and director had been abolished in March 1965. As we have seen, Rothstein later wrote that the dismantling of the national administrative staff
and functions of ERAP, resulting from the ideal of participatory democracy and an attack on hierarchism, was *destructive* of democracy; he saw
this impulse spread from ERAP to the rest of SDS. These "ultra-democratic" reforms, according to Rothstein, were responsible for elitism and
undermining of all but the strongest projects, since the "financial assis-
tance, staff recruitment and morale building the national ERAP office
had provided was essential to the weaker projects."[41]

But Rothstein was one of the few in ERAP who wanted to centralize
functions in a national office: political education, recruiting students for

ERAP, training staff, maintaining and building contacts with other community groups, and stimulating research. Most ERAPers felt these could all be accomplished by individual projects, or were not necessary functions at all. In 1964 and 1965 the organizational debates concerned not only the relationship of ERAP to the national organization of SDS, but the necessity of a national structure and office within and servicing ERAP itself. The general sentiment was demonstrated by the fact that all national ERAP functions *had* been abolished, just as the Kewadin National Convention in June 1965 had abolished the office of SDS National Secretary and downgraded the role of the President. A shared and growing opposition to national structure and an emphasis on local initiative was brought in with the new breed of recruits and reflected in the politics of the SDS National Convention in 1965, the first convention after the anti-war demonstration earlier that spring. The strong assertion of participatory democracy and anti-centralism accompanying the expansion of the movement is explained by the experience and outlook of the newer membership. They had much less a traditional political outlook than the older and original members of SDS as most of the old guard, with similar politics, had turned their efforts to community organizing.

Carol McEldowny, reporting on the June 1965 ERAP Institute, in which the structure of ERAP was discussed at length, said there had been informal agreement among the people there that ERAP should not have a highly centralized national office. The feeling was that everyone should be working in communities and not in an office. It was agreed that certain functions which the National Office had performed should continue to be carried out, though not by an office.[42] ERAP members decided that the individual projects should experiment with assuming the functions that the central office (Ann Arbor) had provided before it was abolished. The point was to decentralize office and national functions so that no one was required to work full time in an office, in order to prevent power from accumulating in any one place or person. No project felt comfortable having a national officer speak for it; this, of course, made centralized organization difficult. McEldowney reported that people felt that "when there were decisions to be made, people would find ways to get together and make them and that we shouldn't create structures"; and that in general people felt more comfortable having no formal mechanisms for decision making. Rothstein and Davis were alone in their sense that the national ERAP office be opened again and that structure was essential for the successful operation of ERAP. By the end of the summer of 1965 most of the ERAP projects had failed and the structure-organization debate within ERAP died with them. The differences within and about ERAP were a microcosm of the differences within the movement at large.

DECEMBER CONFERENCE AND AFTER

In December 1965 a "Rethinking Conference" for SDS was held in Champaign-Urbana, Illinois. This was an important conference because of its attention to organization. It was primarily fascinating, however, for its characterization of itself. A leaflet calling for the meeting said in part: "SDS was formed by radical intellectuals, influenced by C. Wright Mills, Paul Goodman and Camus. They saw the intellectual as central to social change; they saw themselves as a 'new left' pointing to the oligarchic distribution of power as the central humanist concern." It enumerated the various politics and policies SDS had debated, from third party and reform Democratic politics to "counter-community organizing" and "local insurgency," pointing out that without fail the winning strategy became paramount so that everyone had to revise their personal histories and activities to conform. In a poignant passage the leaflet noted that:

> We have slogans which take the place of thought: "There's a change gonna come" is our substitute for social theory; "Let the people decide" has often been an escape from our own indecision; we scream "no leaders," "no structures," and seem to come up with implicit structures which are far less democratic than the most explicit elitism. How did we get here?

Another leaflet calling for the December Conference said that the phenomenal growth of SDS had taken no one by surprise more than SDSers themselves. "Two years ago we viewed ourselves as 'the intellect of the new left' "; it would have been impossible, it went on, for most of us who had "self-consciously dedicated ourselves to our roles as 'intellectuals in social change,' " to have foreseen a year in which SDS would be identified with the Berkeley revolt, a march on Washington against the Vietnam War, community organizing projects and a major threat to the Selective Service System.[43]

This conference was significant in the history of SDS and the movement. It was called by the "old guard." Sale notes that what they had in mind, although perhaps unspoken, was the "need to recreate Port Huron, to give SDS a second birth."[44] The content of the leaflets indicates that those who had called the conference had also been involved in SDS from the beginning and were shaping the questions and articulating the problems facing SDS. The generational shifts and displacements were nowhere more apparent. The mass movement was developing rapidly, the old guard's place and status ambiguous. Sale suggests they believed that if they could create more cohesion through internal education, agreed-upon social theories, improved internal communication and working democracy, SDS could develop into a "significant multi-generational, multidisciplined, multi-issued, genuinely radical organization on the American left." Sale characterized the December Conference meetings as "a touching symbol. Called by the old guard to reestablish the kind of SDS they had known and loved, it actually served to indicate that, inevitably, the organization was headed in new directions, the clock could not be turned back."[45]

However, the conference did not accomplish what was intended. Among other things, it was historically significant because the issue of women in the new left surfaced in a public way for the first time. This was not planned by the primarily male organizers. The origins of the young and radical women's liberation movement may be traced from SNCC through the community organizing projects to its tentative beginnings at the December Conference and with increasing power from that time on.[46] Sara Evans cites the workshop on women as ". . . the real embryo of the new feminist revolt," whose impact would be delayed for two years.[47] The December Conference was also the occasion of the last intensive attention to organization until sometime in 1968. Paul Booth (National Secretary), Steve Max, Al Haber, Dickie Magidoff, Robert Pardun, Clark Kissinger, Michael Zweig and Jeff Shero (the list of names itself indicating why the new left was creating a "woman question"), all wrote papers on the structure, democracy and organizational problems. Most identified SDS's problems as organizational.

Booth criticized the organization for not accepting the leadership of the anti-war movement, for squandering itself by not taking political responsibility for guidance of the movement. Defending the value of organization and SDS's failure on that front, Booth said:

> People start from scratch when they join the national staff, when they form a chapter, when they come into chapter leadership. A test of strength of an institution is the *ability to pass on accumulated experience.* Only an institution with the paraphernalia of structure, tradition, administrative procedures that translate into responsibilities that people expect to assume, etc., will be successful.[48]

Clark Kissinger's paper, "There's a Change Gotta Come! Notes on Structure," asked significantly, "How do you exert democratic control over day-to-day national programming in a country so large that representative bodies cannot meet frequently? How shall delegated responsibility be limited—who may speak for SDS? He pointed to the growth and size of the movement, as they all did, as sources of crises in SDS, for the December Conference itself. Kissinger posed several difficult questions.

> What does democracy mean and how can it operate in a movement of 10,000—or 100,000 people? How can the person whose conceptions of

democracy derive from small group experience expect to survive in this atmosphere? How can one live his values in the movement and yet change an industrial society of 180,000,000 people?[49]

The critical democratic issues were articulated here: the functioning of participatory democracy in a mass movement and the apparent contradiction between prefigurative politics and changing the society. How could these be reconciled? How could consensual decision-making work in a mass movement?

The opposition to administrative structure in SDS, and sometimes to any structure at all, derived, according to Steve Max, from the "confusion between lack of structure and democracy." The leaders in the strategic camp saw the problem posed falsely between democracy and structure, believing it to be an inaccurate dichotomy. According to Max:

> To destroy formal structures in society is unfortunately no small task, but to do so in one's own organization is not only possible, but easy. The use of parliamentary procedure began to wither last winter, and national meetings came to consist of small discussion circles. Next, the role of chairman vanished; at this year's convention, full plenary sessions of 250 people were chaired by members picked at random, with no regard to ability, while workshops debated having no chairman at all. Convention credentials went unchecked, and some key votes went uncounted . . .

Max concluded that most left-wing organizations recruited people to a position as well as to an organization. However, in SDS that situation was reversed. No theory of permanence guides the organization—". . . it rapidly becomes what its members are and its members change with events."[50] Elaborating on this point, Max suggested that often the mass media determined what issues were important, and brought in recruits on that basis. When Berkeley was glorified, SDS was seen as the "liberator of the campus"; after the Washington March foreign policy was on students' minds, just as earlier SDS had been the recipient of supporters of the civil rights movement. This mean that SDS was the common denominator of the feelings and reactions of thousands of politically inexperienced students. SDS was successful but at the price of its political coherence. Max warned that the confusion between structure and democracy spelled disaster: "If the growth and the trend toward elimination of formal structures continue at their present rates, SDS is in danger of decentralizing itself to a point at which it becomes increasingly the *result* of motion among students (as it is in part now) rather than the *cause* of such motion.[51]

Max's criticism was that SDS *was* the movement as much as it was an organization that represented the movement, a position which we have seen many, in fact, advocate. It became what its members were, and its members were always changing. Max believed that SDS should be an organization that recruited and created programs on the basis of a clear political position. He wanted SDS to provide leadership and an organizational base to the student movement, rather than be an expression of the multi-faceted grass roots movement unable or unwilling to give the movement organizational coherence and power. And underlying it all was the troubling question asked by Kissinger: what does democracy mean and how can it operate in a mass movement?

There were (of course) other voices at the December Conference, voices which echoed earlier interest in decentralization and a wariness about a kind of centralization that seemed to isolate the National Office and officers from the thousands of activists around the country. This point of view, more characteristic, indicated the movements's future thrust. Dickie Magidoff, an SDS activist, laid out the choices facing SDS. He said that they could choose to see SDS as the growing manifestation of the movement or as something much larger that was molded in different ways at the many local levels on which it operated. If the first alternative were the case, then organizational questions were paramount and SDS should make every effort to formalize, integrate and deal with these questions. Magidoff found the second alternative more attractive because it emphasized the most exciting part of the movement, its local dynamism, creativity and diversity. It allowed time to see "whether a movement can really develop organically into an organization." He acknowledged, too, that the first alternative was more challenging because it required discipline if they were to "build a conscious left in this country."[52]

Bob Pardun and Jeff Shero both wrote papers that criticized the lack of democracy in the National Office. Pardun charged that participatory democracy was not practiced in the office, where hierarchy and centralization of power predominated. This meant that membership had little control over leadership. He was worried about bureaucracy forming in the organization and reiterated a common theme in SDS: "We have to make it easy for the membership to participate in the decisions that affect their lives."[53] The fear of bureaucracy always surfaced in organizational discussions. We have seen how those who criticized participatory democracy charged that an informal elite was able to exist, an elite that was even more inaccessible than an elected leadership might be, since it did not have formal power. Pardun may have worried about this. At one time or another all SDS leaders energetically sought democratic organizational forms. Even those who stood for prefigurative politics, like Calvert, worried about the gap in the new left's creativity—the relative weakness of adequate organization.

Shero, in his paper, "The SDS National Office: Bureaucracy, Democracy and Decentralization" suggested that old leadership dominated the organization by being familiar with the issues and more sophisticated politically, which made it difficult for younger people to learn and grow into leadership positions.[54] In these examples it seems apparent that "bureaucracy" was used when the speakers were referring to elitism. Shero and Pardun were articulating the problem Rothstein first pointed to in ERAP in 1965 (and developed in his 1972 article), and the perennial problem of organizers: certain people had a monopoly on skills and time and as a result democracy was weakened. Unlike Rothstein's call for more formal democratic structure, Shero and Pardun, echoing Flacks and Craven and Dahlberg, stressed abolishing national and centralized offices and resources and encouraging regional offices and leaders as solutions to the distance problem. Both expressed the point of view, too, of newcomers on the fringes who could see the problem created by a tight network of friends who had a great deal of influence in SDS, Later, analysts would describe this as a problem of movement generations and as the shift from a primary group to a mass movement. SDSer Helen Garvey had asked earlier that year:

> How do we permeate an informal leadership that grew from the days when SDS was a small group of friends? How do we create new leadership, people who know and trust each other and are committed to working to build an organization and a movement? Or, perhaps, how do we minimize leadership rather than merely replacing the old with the new?[55]

Hers were representative remarks, typical of the concerns and perceptions of many active in SDS who were aware of the political problems the changes were bringing. The material basis of the difficulties, the shift from a small informal group to a mass movement, was as real a problem as the ideological opposition to leadership and hierarchical structure. Garvey's queries combined them. She recognized that the original group and organizational structure were no longer possible or adequate, at the same time indicating a characteristic uneasiness with leadership itself.

A double bind presented itself to many who participated in the debate. They understood the limitations of the organization: poorly functioning representative democracy and lack of communication and internal education for many in the grass roots; and yet they were simultaneously committed and wary, some even afraid, of creating strong leadership and organization. Various concrete proposals were made, centering around regional offices and networks. They were never effectively implemented because adequate determination, interest and reception were lacking, not on the part of advocates of strategic politics, but in others. Determination could not be enough in a social movement characterized by antiauthoritarianism and spontaneous direct action. There was in fact little grass roots support for stronger organization. Protest and confrontation continued apace, attracting new participants, many of whom joined or identified with SDS, and most of whom did not support the proposals made at the December Conference. The 1965 December Conference in Champaign-Urbana resolved very little, certainly nothing organization-ally, other than the future direction of the movement and SDS in favor of activism and grass roots initiative. The SDS convention in Clear Lake, Iowa, in the summer of 1966, a half year after Champaign-Urbana, was an affirmation of prefigurative politics and of the new breed, of the mass movement and activism, and of anti-authoritarian politics. It signified disinterest in the concerns of early SDSers who had identified themselves as intellectuals in social change and who wanted to strengthen SDS as a national and centralized organization.

From the summer of 1966 onwards almost all the discussion and debate about organization was anti-organizational. The predominant sentiments had been expressed at the Clear Lake Convention that summer. This was not an encouraging period for those who were convinced that a strong organization was vital to the success of the movement and SDS. *New Left Notes* did print several articles objecting to the politics ratified at the Clear Lake Convention and the manner in which this had been accom-plished. Both Paul Booth and Paul Buhle wrote to *New Left Notes* ex-pressing discontent with the convention. But, on the whole, they lacked support. Buhle charged that decentralization was a "cop-out," that SDS needed to develop an ideology and that participatory democracy simply could not substitute for concrete analysis or be used as that ideology. Furthermore, he argued, it was incumbent on SDS to ascertain what sort of structure would permit the organization to make decisions coherently and systematically.[56] Booth felt that *no* organizational decisions and pol-itics had emerged at Clear Lake; nothing was clarified, and consequently there was no way for people to participate in decisions or to chart the course of the organization i.e., no programs, no structure, no clear pol-itics.[57] These were lone voices.

Through 1967 and 1968 there was almost no written discussion of organization as central to the failure or success of the movement. After Clear Lake, those voices, which advocated strategic politics, were heard less and less. They lost out to the more dominant ideology embracing direct democracy and direct action politics. In early 1967, after SDS approved a full-scale draft-resistance program at the Berkeley National Council Meeting, enthusiastically endorsed by Calvert in his "From Pro-test to Resistance" essay and cited in the last chapter as an example of prefigurative politics, there were several responses. An article appeared in *New Left Notes* entitled "In Defense of Politics," which criticized

Calvert for his defeatism and sense of alienation which led, according to the author, to his sounding like a martyr; Calvert had allegedly created a picture of a new left pitted against an indomitable monster, a new left which might create a space for love and freedom, but which could do no more.[58] The author pointed out that from Calvert's point of view, organizational and ideological considerations seemed boring and banal; alienation and simply acting to make ourselves feel better had taken the place of politics. Calvert's assumption seemed to be that the movement could not reach out to organize people; he did not appear to believe it could bring about social change; the author charged that subjectivism replaced concrete politics.

The author of the critique of Calvert insisted that there was a great need for education, communication and coordination within the organization and that the only way SDS could survive was to create a structure that made these possible. The solution to SDS's problems, according to the author, was clear organizational structure; regional educational directors, organizers, representative bodies, regional councils. Only in this way could SDS organize other people and develop an analysis, strategy and program. A solid organization would prevent SDS from reveling in its own despair, defeatism, alienation and isolation. Finally he urged that radicals accept it as their responsiblility to be as *effective* as possible, to make the transition from alienation to radical activism. This was a statement of strategic politics, a pro-organization rebuttal that echoed the strategic political arguments against the ERAP impulse and of the old guard against the newer recruits. This ideological attack on prefigurative politics zeroed in on its emphasis on alienation, subjectivism and search for community and characterized it as self-indulgent and defeatist. Only by organizing others into a strong organization, according to these critics, would social transformation be possible.

In March 1967 Todd Gitlin also replied, unhappy with Calvert's definition of a politics of resistance, and asked why activists should struggle only when the spirit moved them. "If we do, we end up with a huddled resistance, smug with our raging honesty, doomed to be small voices in a thunderstorm . . ." Gitlin suggested that in the final analysis such an approach would not appeal to many people, since "their lives will not be changed, nor will America." He concluded saying that SDS believed in a movement that ". . . imports to students a sense of what it means to be an organizer, and leaves a lasting imprint on American power."[59] Here, too, the cry was to be effective in institutional terms, not simply to change lives. In a later piece Gitlin appraised the movement's attempts at forming counter-institutions as a failure, saying that none of the reforms the movement had embodied in itself had lasted because the pressure from society was so fierce that they were either

destroyed or tolerated because they posed no threat.[60] Counter-institutions drained the movement's energies and directed them from changing
the institutional fabric of the society. Gitlin emphasized the failure of the
new left to organize itself and others strategically in order to attack institutional power.

Those leaders whose ideas and perceptions we have been examining
believed that SDS should fashion itself into "an institution with the par-
aphernalia of structure, tradition, administrative procedures that translate
needs into responsibilities" (Booth), "an institution to which people can
affiliate in the expectation that it will play a role in changing America"
(Booth and Webb). Potter had urged the membership to take responsibility for SDS "if we take ourselves seriously, if we believe that our
organization is one of the mechanisms for creating a radical movement . . ."

Many from the old guard who had high hopes for the December Conference withdrew after this point, and particularly after the summer 1966
Clear Lake convention. As a group of young men, the early SDS leadership, due to background, training and experience in their families and
schools, were interested in politics and perhaps political careers.[61] Their
concerns were more strategic and traditionally political than those of
younger activists; in spite of this, younger activists were greatly influenced
by the movement and counter-culture's questioning of conventional values and institutions, including careers and traditional political organization. Newer generations were socialized by the movement; many were
"prairie dogs," less traditional in all ways. They were brought in by the
urgency of the war and through their attraction to direct action. "Putting
your body on the line," taking a stand, saying "no," took precedence over
organization and program.

Part of the reason there was so little written organizational debate and
concern during 1967 and into 1968 was because the terms of the debate
shifted. The issue of agency surfaced again in the ERAP debate and in
the new working class discussion. Organization and structure were sub-
merged, literally, by the shifts in the movement, from the first to newer
generations, from a small to a mass movement, from a small to a large
war. Resistance politics, or what Norman Fruchter called "identity politics,"[62] framed the issues away from strategic concerns.

INTERNAL EDUCATION

One final issue, internal education, graphically demonstrates the conflicts
over organizational responsibility. The need for internal education was
a recurrent theme throughout the early new left's history, exposing di-
vergent organizational impulses. The Radical Education Project (REP)

had been authorized at the December Conference for the express purpose of providing political education for the thousands of new members entering SDS. Supporters believed the organization had a political responsibility to new membership and that the viability of the organization depended on it. As early as 1964 Sara Murphy had pointed to the astonishing lack of political sophistication and knowledge among younger and newer recruits. She observed a growing trend toward action with little interest in learning and understanding and said, "We would be incapable of stemming the tide of activism even if we tried, but it is all too easy to drift with it without attempting to match political education with activism."[63]

With the same concern, Jeremy Brecher wrote a proposal for a Leadership Training School. According to Brecher new members and chapters lacked the basic skills and understanding to articulate and implement SDS's position; he suggested that each chapter send three students to a two-week training school in which organizing skills were taught, a sense of commitment, a feeling of the "style" of SDS transmitted, and political understanding and background developed, which would enable people to respond to the political environment. The difficult problem of organizational continuity would be eased in this way.[64]

Paul Booth had stressed in his December Conference report that SDS needed a publication, otherwise "we lose 95% of the accumulated wisdom."[65] Written materials and structure were required so that people did not have to start from scratch when they joined the organization. And McKelvey in a letter to *New Left Notes* on REP said, ". . . I think this internal education is the most important single thing which SDS can do" and again in August in an article entitled "Intellectual Elitism and the Failure of Teaching," chastized the leadership for its unwillingness or inability to commit itself to teaching. McKelvey accused the organization of a total lack of internal education, charging that the conventions and national councils were inadequate vehicles for learning and that the intellectual elite of SDS did not accept as their responsibility a commitment to a thorough internal education program. He suggested that the leadership talked among themselves with little public debate or thinking in evidence; and further that they did not fulfill their roles as teachers.[66] Later that year Carl Davidson, vice-president of SDS, wrote an article proposing an internal education program for SDS which would operate at all levels of the organization.[67]

There was a push again in 1967 to initiate an internal education program, based on the assumption that it was necessary for SDS to create radicals and a powerful organization. A project for training organizers began to surface. An article printed in *New Left Notes*, prepared by Paul Potter after discussion with Greg Calvert, Nick Egleson, Florence Howe and Paul Lauter, suggested that if the student movement were to grow and deepen organizers were necessary. Experienced SDS organizers created the possibility of increased numbers of recruits and improved levels of campus organizing[68]

SDS planned to set up three teacher-organizer summer institutes in which potential teacher-organizers (T-Os) would live together, take seminars, hold regular discussion sessions and undertake field projects.[69] According to Sale, by the end of the summer they hoped to have thirty regional travelers who would initiate and facilitate political education, or radicalization, among students. In evaluating the T-O experiments Sale says there were thirty to forty people committed and educated movement activists by the time it was concluded,[70] which in a mass movement did not signify a serious internal education program for SDS membership, although it did train some organizers. The T-O institutes of the summer of 1967, thus, did not address the problem that McKelvey in particular had raised, the responsibility of the leadership to educate the new membership, to radicalize and include them so they became committed radicals. This was never accomplished through internal education.

As usual, though, there were articulate spokespeople, who usually predominated, for an opposition point of view. In a position paper for a 1967 National Council meeting, "Internal Education and Institutes," Tom Condit had criticized Brecher's and others' conceptions of political education institutes. He said they were very similar to what used to be known in the old left as "cadre schools." Members of local branches who were deemed to have "leadership potential" were singled out and sent to school to be educated in the organization's (in this case, the Communist Party's) world view and in organizational skills. A solid group of knowledgeable and skilled members was assumed necessary for a stable political movement. This cadre could be built, according to old left assumptions, by a well-organized system of selection and training of "professional revolutionaries."

Condit thought the first assumption correct: a movement depended on people who agreed and knew what they were talking about and had certain organizing skills. But he disagreed that the way these people were produced was in a "school." He pointed out that cadre schools, even for democratic-centralist organizations, "were somewhat dysfunctional, mainly because they reinforced all the most negative aspects of democratic centralist organization." That is, they created great distinctions between the party and the masses, the cadre and the membership. This meant that the party became increasingly alienated and distant from the real needs and experience of ordinary people. Condit asked why the proposed courses were relevant and why radical faculty people knew more about radicalism than students. "Do we want the authoritarian classroom situation repeated in our movement?"

He underlined the fact that he thought chapter work and movement activities were the "main school of 'internal education' . . . and that decentralized conferences and projects tied to local and regional programs and aimed at involving a maximum number of local and regional people" were more desirable. According to Condit, all such conferences should be limited and devoted to a specific topic so that no one was discouraged from participating and all could come prepared. In addition, he suggested that all conferences should include "technical" workshops on mimeographing and poster production so that more people would learn these skills.[71]

Condit's criticism of the internal education institutes was a characteristic, if more knowledgeable, movement reaction based on anti-hierarchical and participatory political notions. For those who supported strategic politics, internal education was seen as a responsibility of the organization, vital to its future and the future of the movement. The concern with continuity and the inheritance of accumulated wisdom, with a certain solidity and permanence which the movement might derive from a strong organization, the hope that the student movement might play a role in changing America over a long period of time, all led a minority of leftists to plead and work for a strong SDS. They were unsuccessful. It seems appropriate to conclude the organization thread with this statement by Paul Booth in June 1966. It captures the viewpoint and sentiments of the organizationally inclined: "What is amazing is that the organization refuses to admit the fact that it plays an important role in American politics, and as a consequence refuses to create responsible mechanisms for making its decisions from week to week."[72]

POLITICS IS ABOUT POWER

Writing after the sixties about a central problem in SNCC, James Forman said:

> Many people in SNCC failed to distinguish between SNCC as an organization fighting for the creation of a better society, and SNCC as that better society itself. They could not distinguish between a revolutionary organization seeking power, and power as it had been corruptly wielded by the managers of capitalist America.[73]

Beyond and below the organizational differences informing the strategic position and its criticisms of prefigurative politics was the new left's relationship to power. It was the subterranean concern of all sides of the debate, at the heart of both strategic and prefigurative politics. Forman indicates its crux: most movement activists could not distinguish between an organization seeking power and power as it was used in the society. How could they be sure that power, even *seeking* power, would not transform or corrupt them? The fundamental suspicion was that there *was* no way to distinguish between the two, that power and politics corrupted. Historically, in fact, there is little evidence to the contrary. The distance between leaders and citizens in ordinary electoral politics, specialization and hierarchy embodied in bureaucracy, an emphasis on ends and not means—all characteristics of traditional power politics— served as warning and example.

During the summer of 1966 Jeff Shero had written that SDSers had to decide whether SDS was seriously committed to political change. If they decided they were, then, Shero wrote, ". . . we must develop political programs that go beyond marches, fasts, personal witnesses, and other symbolic forms of protest. *We must deal with questions of power rather than act out our generation's alienation.*" (Emphasis mine.) Shero underscored his conviction that SDS's reluctance to deal with more serious questions of power led people into personally acting out their alienation instead of politically channeling it. SDS had to develop programs that dealt with achieving power rather than offering "the dead end of continued acting out [of] our disaffection."[74] Around the same time, a letter from Frank Joyce appeared in *New Left Notes* criticizing the Detroit Committee to End the War in Vietnam and the new left in general, accusing it of following "in the SDS tradition of being, in the final analysis, apolitical, anarchistic, not concerned with fundamental questions concerning power." All the talk that went on in SDS about creating alternative and dual political structures and counter communities, he added, ". . . avoids the critical question of how the newly created structure is to achieve power. *Power, after all, is what politics is all about.*"[75] (Emphasis mine.)

This was the central criticism of prefigurative politics from within the movement, an appropriate perspective with which to close this consideration of strategic politics. It was expressed from the early days of the new left in criticisms of ERAP and continued to characterize the differences between activists throughout the decade. Joyce's criticism of SDS and the new left as "apolitical" was shared traditionally by leftists, conventional politicians, and academic sociological analyses of social movements, and derives from the assumption that "power is what politics is all about." The distinction James Forman proposed SNCC was unable to make, between SNCC as an organization fighting for social change and SNCC as the "better society itself," the "beloved community," gets at the heart of prefigurative politics: there *was* no distinction. Counter-institutions, dual structures, demonstrations, community organizations in which new democratic forms and new relationships unfolded during the sixties were, in essence, attempts to structure power differently. They were efforts to share equally and to structure "in" participation, to prefigure a more egalitarian future, a way of living and struggling for social change. Organizational advocates rejected these efforts as utopian, romantic or unrealistic, and often irresponsible, because they seemed to avoid dealing with power both in the movement among activists and more importantly, in relation to the most powerful people and institutions in America. These perceptions, if not their evaluations, were correct. New leftists and student activists did not want to achieve power in socially and politically prescribed forms; they did not want to become powerful by accumulating power. Their dilemma lies exposed.

Students as Agency

AGENCY AS AN ISSUE

The search for a legitimate and plausible agency of social change was central to new left politics and theorizing. Until now we have considered new left debates about organization and the actions which held the new left together and gave it meaning. No mention has been made of a preoccupation with the *legitimacy* of the student revolt. Yet through the decade many new leftists disparaged students' grievances and belittled them as actors and agents of social change. Chapter Seven examines the community organizing projects of early SDS, ERAP, particularly the debate about whether students should act politically *as* students or rather—the position of the more powerful contingent—shed their student status and thereby become "ordinary" people. Those who supported the latter position believed this was the only way students could be legitimate and effective political actors.

A political affirmation of students would seem to be a corollary of prefigurative politics. Throughout the decade, however, there were persistent accusations and doubts about the validity of students' acting politically on their own issues. Students were considered unimportant in contrast to more oppressed sectors of the population, and consequently, their revolt was considered illegitimate. They were, in fact, often considered unimportant *because* of their privilege. I do not refer to the realistic concern with developing allies in other sectors of the population if social change, even ending the war in Vietnam, were to be achieved. Rather, there was a strong sense that due to their privilege students were unimportant in the political scheme of things in this country, that it was the working class, the poor and/or minorities who were strategically placed and had cause for revolt. The source of this negative view of students (by students) was often guilt. New leftists felt guilty about being better off financially and socially, about being in college, about having promising (or secure) futures, about feeling discontent, about seeming ungrateful, about their rage. The logical political outcome was that students should divest themselves of their studenthood in order to be more like "everyone else."

Throughout the sixties the focus of this debate and concern was the issue of agency: who was able and who was interested to make social change in America? In sharp contrast to the rest of the decade, from spring 1966 until late 1967 there was in new left theorizing an intellectual and political affirmation of students as legitimate actors in history with real grievances and a reservoir of power. It was during these years that the student movement came of age; the now all-but-forgotten debate on the new working-class theory was its theoretical expression. Very briefly, the community organizing projects of SDS did not prosper after the summer of 1964, although they got a boost in the summer of 1965 from the burst of student activity on the campuses and in the anti-war movement. Community organizing in poor urban ghettos was not to be the wave of the future of the student movement. The momentum shifted in the fall of 1964 from the civil rights movement and community work to the student movement on the campuses. The pendulum swung back from what Hayden had called the "grass roots," in the community, to the campus; the earlier desertion of the student movement by SDS community organizers in ERAP was upstaged and reversed by the Free Speech Movement, the Vietnam War and the anti-war movement. Sale points out that the tension created by the issue of whether students operating within the university can be "truly agents of social change, or must they leave the campuses and operate in the 'real' world outside?" lasted throughout the decade. However, beginning with the Free Speech Movement, it seemed possible that the university might be as important as the ghetto. A sentence in an SDS publication expressed it well, if laconically: "The revolution may come from the universities after all if Berkeley is any indication."[1]

The new working class discussion, which held currency for no more than a year, was an attempt on the part of student intellectuals of the new left to explain their own formation into a radical movement. What makes this episode unique is its theoretical affirmation of the student, and cultural nature of the student revolt. This theoretical affirmation of students paralleled and reflected the self-generated political activity of the student movement. Dramatically, the search for community and agency come together in this short period; acting on one's own behalf, creating meaningful political activity in both a public and private sense, enabled students to create alternative relations and political forms and to serve as a political catalyst for others as well. Their sense of efficacy enabled them, for a short time, to construe themselves as an agency to be reckoned with. We have seen how grass roots political activity reinforced a rejection of centralized and hierarchical organization; for a time it also encouraged theorizing that students might be central to political change.

Paradoxically, new working class theory, *as theory,* was not "prefigurative." Its project was not to ratify the political experiments characterized by spontaneity, direct democracy and utopianism, although it did not preclude them. A distinction must be made between the theory, which was a step into Marxist analysis, and the significance and purpose of the theory in the context in which it was developed. Although there is a tradition of prefigurative politics within Marxism, Marxism is primarily a strategic theory of politics. With its goal of political and economic transformation from capitalism to socialism, it focuses on the proletariat as the agency of change, and on strategic political possibilities. The predominant Marxist political tradition has few qualms about hierarchical organizational forms. [2] Strategic and Marxist critics of prefigurative politics pointed to its weaknesses vis-à-vis established power and strategy. New working class theory, however, combined strategic concern with agency (reflected in notions of student syndicalism and student power), with prefigurative characteristics.

The sense in which new working-class theory was linked to prefigurative politics was articulated by Greg Calvert in his 1967 "In White America" speech, a hallmark of this period and its politics:

> There is only one impulse, one dynamic which can create and sustain an authentic revolutionary movement. The revolutionary struggle is always and always must be a struggle for freedom. No individual, no group, no class is genuinely engaged in a revolutionary movement unless their struggle is a struggle for their own liberation. [3]

Struggle in one's own name, and not only in that of another group more oppressed, personal investment in the fight for freedom and democracy, were part of the impetus behind new working class theory. Calvert's statement must be understood in the context of alternative justifications of opposition and revolt on behalf of others more disadvantaged than students, other versions delegitimizing student revolt and students' grievances. A sense of political significance grew as the movement grew and created the context for this theorizing. It was expressed by a delegate to the Clear Lake Convention who "pleaded with his peers . . . to believe themselves to be those agents of historical change we are forever debating about." [4]

Before considering new working class theory itself, I want to direct attention to the fact that this theorizing was an attempt by the new left to locate and account for itself. It was theory developed by a social movement, not by theorists separated from it. Just as the development of a theory of community unions and community organizing was dialectically enmeshed in the experience of the civil rights movement, SDS's community organizing projects and the urban riots with their spotlight on the poor, usually black urban dwellers, student power and new working class theories were intimately linked to the explosion of the student movement and the sense of power and importance it brought with it and, in fact, had.

THE UNIVERSITY: NEW REALITIES, OLD NOTIONS

One of the major contributions of the new left was to stimulate and contribute to an analysis of the changing nature and role of the university in the United States. This evolved out of the effort to comprehend why a student movement had arisen, as well as out of growing evidence of the centrality of the university to the war effort and the military-industrial complex. Basing themselves on the writing of Clark Kerr, Seymour Martin Lipset, Daniel Bell and others,[5] as well as their own experiences in the university, new working class theorists argued that universities were no longer communities of scholars, but in Kerr's phrase, "multiversities" closely tied to the federal government and large corporations. In 1963 Kerr pointed to new knowledge as the most important factor in national economic growth; knowledge, the multiversity's product, had become the most powerful element in our culture and economy. And he suggested that power had moved from inside to outside the institution, with the administration's function growing as it had increasingly to mediate between contending interests.

Federal support of research for scientific, military and technological development skyrocketed after the Second World War, with the result that ". . . the federal govenment and the leading universities entered into a common-law marriage . . ."[6] This meant the loss of significant autonomy for the universities. Federal influence, particularly in the form of research funds, meant the growing power of scientific faculty and researchers and the depreciation of undergraduate teaching. According to Kerr, the two worlds of the university and industry were "merging physically and psychologically," with the professor taking on the characteristics of an entrepreneur.[7] Kerr's statement about the "knowledge industry" was quoted repeatedly in the 1960s:

> What the railroad did for the second half of the last century and the automobile did for the first half of this century may be done for the

second half of this century by the knowledge industry: that is, to serve
as the focal point for the national growth. And the university is at the
center of the knowledge process.[8]

The university had become one of the motors of economic growth in the
United States. With the federal government at its heart, it funded the
production of knowledge and manpower in the fields of defense, space,
atomic energy and technological development. Research had taken priority over teaching, graduate over undergraduate education, and service
functions over scholarship and education. Furthermore the university
had been subjected to industrial methods of operation and instruction.

Both Bell and Lipset elaborated versions of this changing university.
Bell proposed that the new men of the post-industrial society were the
scientists, mathematicians, economists and engineers of the new com-
puter technology housed in the dominant institution of the new society,
the university. Lipset pointed to the reduced informal influence of students in the university as a result of the increased "professionalization"
of the faculty; ". . . teaching as such has declined as the main identification
of the role of being a professor."[9]

Carl Davidson, one of the important new working class theorists,
turned the social scientists' analysis of the university on its head. Kerr
had reported accurately but without understanding the picture's other
side, its negativity. Kerr assumed the multiversity to be inevitable and
beneficent, while Davidson suggested that these developments were in
fact responsible for the increasing division of labor, bureaucracy and
depersonalization in the university, causing feelings of irrelevancy,
boredom and meaninglessness in mass higher education. Education had
become a "mechanistic process of homogeneous, uncritical absorption of
'data' and the development of job skills,"[10] replacing freedom and equality
as the goals of education: ". . . we are a people required to know more
and more about less and less . . ." He stated that ". . . our educational
institutions are becoming appendages to, and transformed by, U.S. corporate capitalism."[11] Furthermore, and fundamentally, the knowledge
factories were deeply involved in producing *the* crucial commodity for
capitalism, labor power. A central function of the university was the
training and indoctrination of future personnel for the system. All the
restrictive regulations, grades and disciplinary procedures were appara-
tuses used to enforce this training in order to turn out appropriately
docile "manpower."

In light of persistent accusations against the new left for being anti-
intellectual, we have seen in the Free Speech Movement how the early
new left critique of the university stemmed from precisely its esteem for
and ideals of learning, thinking independently and sharing ideas in a
community of scholars, very old notions indeed. Davidson himself defined

the purpose of education as development of the "free, autonomous, creative and responsible *individual*—the 'citizen' in the best sense of the word."[12] Numerous leaders, beginning with Tom Hayden in 1962 (who nevertheless consistently disparaged staying in the university soon after), upheld the ideal of the university as a place for the pursuit of truth and the moral development of an independent individual. Hayden argued that the university's concern "must be the unfolding and refinement of the moral, aesthetic and logical capacities of men in a manner that creates genuine independence . . ."[13] and that such a vision had to underlie any university reforms or no qualitative change could occur. The dependence on authority, elites and specialization had to be replaced by participation, democracy and autonomy for the individual.[14]

Throughout the early years the new left's respect for intellectual activity and the university was much in evidence. But the new left notion of the intellectual was strikingly different from that outlined by post-industrial theorists. The cool scholar as technician of the future, dealing in abstract, symbolic knowledge, was rejected by new leftists. Hayden said, "Do not study as a student, but as a man who is alive and cares. . . . Allow your ideas to become part of your living and your living to become part of your ideas."[15] Another SDS leader, Paul Potter, stated in a pamphlet entitled "The Intellectual as an Agent of Social Change" that "the home of the intellectual is in social movements: in political actions and agitation."[16] The early new left notion was not one of intellectual activity as a life of the mind which took one out of the world or kept one controlled by professional or scholarly codes. *Studies on the Left,* a new left radical journal which began publication in 1959 at the University of Wisconsin, devoted itself to intellectual work: developing a left theory that could comprehend American reality. It argued for the intellectual as critic.[17] For early new leftists, being in the university and being an intellectual required that one act in the world according to humane beliefs and values.

While they realized that a community of scholars no longer existed in the multiversity, it remained an ideal. Another leader, Paul Booth, suggested that because it now functioned in the service of the status quo, the new university could not provide a social vision. He pointed out, however, that it was one of the only places in the entire society in which one might construct a vision critical of existing institutions, aiming beyond them to the transformation of reality. He, too, retained an ideal notion of learning and intellectual life perverted by corporate and military links with the university and by technocratic departmentalization of learning. Addressing himself in 1962 to learning and the university, Hayden referred to cherishing "the sunlight of the mind."[18] The shock of recognition that reality was usually shabbier and more immoral than anyone had dreamed was a powerful source of new leftism.

STUDENTS AS AGENCY

In 1961, C. Wright Mills had wondered why new left writers clung so "mightily to 'the working class' . . . as *the* historic agency . . ." of change in the face of the evidence that now stands against this expectation. "Such a labor metaphysic, I think is a legacy from Victorian Marxism that is now quite unrealistic." With the eruption of a mass student movement in the middle of the decade, it did not escape new left theorists that they were moving in a direction Mills had pointed toward in 1961. The movements for social change were located solidly on the campuses, with students the constituency, not simply the organizers of others more unfortunate or, presumably, structurally more basic, than themselves. After 1965 the continued escalation of the war in Vietnam assured the growth of the movement on the campuses. Mills had continued his query: "Who is it that is getting fed up? Who is it that is getting disgusted with what Marx called 'all the old crap'? Who is it that is thinking and acting in radical ways? All over the world the answer's the same: the young intelligentsia."[19]

Broadly speaking, there were three sorts of theoretical efforts to deal with the phenomenon of the student revolt. The first and narrowest simply incorporated students into the proletariat; the term the "knowledge factory," of course, encouraged this. A more interesting and varied effort, the second, broadened this in an attempt to account for the uniqueness of the student revolt by including issues of democracy, culture and consciousness among its sources. This effort included French theorizing which focused more on the educated technical worker in the workplace, while American versions were more preoccupied with students in the university. Finally, a strong suspicion surfaced among a few that traditional explanations and models, including Marxism, were inadequate in the face of the spontaneous, utopian and participatory nature of the new left. Forcing students into the constraints of "producers" and production, according to these theorists, stripped the revolt of its uniqueness.[20]

Most of the more sophisticated contributions to new working class theory were based on the work of French theorists Serge Mallet (*La Nouvelle Classe Ouvrière*) and André Gorz (*Strategy for Labor*).[21] In 1967 Gorz's *Socialism and Revolution* was published in France and probably had an impact on a small group of American new left intellectuals, although by the time interested Americans read it, the peak of new working class theorizing in this country was past. Carl Davidson, drawing on Andre Gorz, contributed irregular "Praxis" supplements in 1967 to the SDS newspaper *New Left Notes* (initiated by the authors of the "Port Authority Statement," which first articulated a new working class analysis on the American new left); and numerous speeches and articles by Greg

Calvert comprised the main contributions during the period under review, a period of hardly more than a year in 1966 and 1967, after which new working class theory was by and large rejected by new left leadership. However, the extent of new left theorizing about a new working class was far more important than its lack of bulk indicates.

In its most coherent form, the first version of new working class theory held that the university had become central to the forces of production in the advanced capitalist countries.[22] If knowledge and technical process were part of the productive base of capitalism, the university occupied a position analogous to the industrial factory in an earlier period. It had become part of the material base of society. Because of its increasingly important role in the production of knowledge and science, the multiversity had taken center stage in the political economy and social structure.[23] With frills removed, the university produced, formed and socialized the new working class.[24] This line of argument pointed to the university as one of the strategic institutions of an advanced capitalist society. Students were at the heart of this institution, and crucial in their student status for the transformation to socialism. Students and intelligentsia were objectively part of an expanded proletariat, their alienation rooted in the material conditions of existence, the product of their labor expropriated, a commodity itself. The university was organized along the lines of a factory, reproducing capitalist relations of production. In Carl Davidson's words:

> The teaching and learning workers . . . are alienated from each other, isolated and divided among ourselves by grades, class ranks and the status levels of the bureaucratic hierarchy. Secondly, they are alienated from the product of their work, the content and purpose of which have been determined and used by someone other than themselves. . . . What should be an active creation and re-creation of culture is nothing more than forced and coercive consumption and distribution of data and technique.[25]

In August 1966 at the Clear Lake Convention Davidson had passed out his pamphlet calling for "A Student Syndicalist Movement." Kirkpatrick Sale interprets that document in the following manner:

> . . . a document for a new generation of SDSers who want once again to turn their attention to the campuses, once again to show the need for students to control the decisions that affect their lives, once again to get students to operate on their immediate felt grievances, once again to radicalize them by having them see the connections between these grievances and the national malaise.[26]

Other theorists defined students and youth as an exploited class.[27]

A second version, more closely connected with French theorizing, suggested that the product of the university was not only science and technological knowledge but educated workers; new technology and new occupations required educated workers, most of whom serviced and ideologically reproduced the dominant society. In this view radicalizing students in the university was important because of their future occupational positions as a new working class in the corporate structures of advanced capitalism. Students were being trained to become a new proletariat, but were not that proletariat while in the university. Students were seen as "trainees" for the new working class and/or the factory, depending on their class background and training. The multiversities were critical for preparing them for their slots in the bureaucratic machinery of corporate structures.[28]

In the United States, the coercive notion of training and channeling was given more currency at the time by the widespread distribution of the Selective Service System's "Channeling" memorandum of 1965. The function of ". . . developing more effective human beings in the national interest . . ." was spelled out under the notion of "channeling manpower," which said in part:

> Many young men would not have pursued a higher education if there had not been a program of student deferment. Many young scientists, engineers, tool and die makers, and other possessors of scarce skills would not remain in their jobs in the defense effort if it were not for a program of occupational deferments.[29]

The idea of students as cogs in a machine, channeled and trained to fill society's empty slots was the critical imagery first introduced by the Free Speech Movement. It was now reinforced by the draft manpower channeling memo and picked up by new working class theorists, who stated that students were "becoming the most structurally relevant and necessary components of the productive process of modern American capitalism."[30]

The Frenchmen Serge Mallet and Andre Gorz both suggested that the new working class was a highly educated and skilled stratum of the traditional working class which required a significant degree of autonomy and democracy in order to perform its work.[31] The demands of educated workers for control and participation, demands generated by the fact that it had become necessary for skilled workers (in certain industries and sectors) to exercise their autonomy and adaptability at work, clashed with capitalism's need to control labor to prevent autonomy. The existence of educated labor signified a challenge to the hierarchy and subordination required by capitalism; it raised demands the system generated but could not possibly meet, given its reliance on authoritarian social control. Gorz elaborated on this struggle, suggesting that once a certain level of culture and education had been reached, the need for autonomy and free development "is experienced with the same intensity as an unsatisfied physiological necessity."[32] The basis for liberation, the need to overcome alienation, had become concrete in advanced industrial society; precisely those traits needed, and frustrated, by advanced capitalism formed the basis for the socialist organization of society.

American new leftists appropriated the idea that it was education itself which developed an expectation of meaningfulness. "Students perceiving both the *productive* potential of society, and the *social* uselessness of the jobs for which they are being trained, are alienated from a system that offers them no socially meaningful work."[33] Students were able to see the waste, hierarchy and inequity *because* of their university education, which was precisely time and space away from the workaday world. The various strands of the second theoretical effort all located the oppositional nature of the new working class, whether in the university or the workplace, in consciousness of its lack of freedom, democracy, and control over the quality of life. Frustrated by its lack of autonomy and participation, controlled by bureaucrats, administrators or managers, this new stratum or class was potentially revolutionary in its desire and need for a different society. The new working class was generated by and further exacerbated a crisis in values, a cultural rupture.

In the latter part of the decade both Alain Touraine and Richard Flacks, two university-based theorists, continued to use new working class theory to speculate on the student revolt. They both utilized the theme of cultural rupture. Referring to May 1968 in France, Touraine suggested that students "are the representatives of all those who suffer more from social integration and cultural manipulation directed by economic structures than from economic exploitation and material misery.[34] And Flacks attempted to work out an explanation culturally specific to the United States.[35] In his view the contradiction between society's technological capacities and its capitalist social organization resulted in a lack of meaningful institutions or culture for those who were not defined by material insecurity. The people who were located or who made a living *outside* the goods-producing sector, in the production and distribution of knowledge, culture and human services, were an oppositional force inside capitalism. Family, education and occupational experiences led them to feel critical of the prevailing culture, social order and its career opportunities precisely because they had a greater sense of alternative and more liberated futures. What Flacks called "post-industrial consciousness" was rooted in a definite class. He proposed that the student movement and youth culture could be seen as the first expression of a new consciousness of a potentially revolutionary working class, the decisive component of which could be called the intelligentsia, engaged in "the production, distribution, interpretation, criticism and inculcation of cultural values." In 1968 Greg Calvert and Carol Neiman attributed the rise of the new left to "an acute sense of oppression and meaninglessness in the multiversities and of alienation from the culture of consumption and materialism."[36] The student and youth movements, according to Flacks, resulted from the convergence of certain social structural and cultural trends in late capitalism. This "class" opposed capitalism because the system as presently organized could not absorb its cultural aspirations, because its vocations were turned into "cogs in the machinery of repression rather than into means for self-fulfillment and general enlightenment . . ." and because its numerical size and concentration made concerted oppositional political action possible.[37]

American theorists broadened the moral and cultural basis of opposition from a highly educated sector of the working class to include students and youth as well as service, intellectual and consumption workers. This was clearly related to the existence in this country of a powerful youth culture and student movement throughout the decade. During the 1960s it was in fact only the student and youth part of the potential new working class which was activated in opposition. By the end of the decade sectors of young health and education workers, to name two, began to be active politically. Flacks emphasized the liberating aspects of the university which reinforced dissatisfaction and alienation from the society at large, proposing that "critical feelings about capitalist culture—particularly negative attitudes towards symbols and ideology which support competitive striving, acquisitiveness, narrow nationalism, and repressive moral codes—are enhanced by exposure to higher education."[38] In both positive and negative senses, the university was identified as an important source of the student movement. The students themselves focused on its bureaucratization and cooperation with the federal government and military, while others stressed its function of providing alternative values and critical ways of thinking about the world, both paths leading to rejection of existing society and to the student movement.

More recently the late Alvin Gouldner suggested that the university has not been totally transformed into a post-industrial, technological-knowledge-producing multiversity. This, Gouldner argues, is partially due to the ideology of intellectual autonomy that has not completely disappeared, but also to the fact that the modern university tends to be a contradictory institution. According to Gouldner the state and hegemonic classes produce two sorts of people: those with the desired vocational and professional skills, and those in the more "isolated" faculties in the humanities and social sciences whose product is not as marketable as those from professional and technical schools. He suggests that these isolated and useless parts of the university "tend to support and produce deviant and rebel ideologies." These segments "cling to older, humanistic virtues from whose perspective they could reject the successful techni- cians, as narrow, servile, venal and hypocritical careerists."[39] Ironically Lipset, too, identifies this phenomenon and condemns it as a "backlash" by humanist intellectuals against the inevitable technological values and expertise which have overtaken the university, and which encourages student revolt. This "backlash," of course, may be viewed alternatively as an expression of the humanist tradition in Western culture.[40] In a series of more recent articles published in book form as *The Future of Intel- lectuals and the Rise of the New Class,*[41] Gouldner points to the possibility of students learning rebellion in spite of the intention of the managers of the status quo. He proposes the existence of a new class, a speech community, characterized by a culture of critical discourse. The role of public education and modern universities and colleges, according to Gouldner, is in the production of this new class, an elite, however, rather than a new proletariat. Gouldner suggests that education undermines authority through the encouragement of situation-free language and the development of reflexivity and auto-critique. But the alienation of the new class is based not only on critical discourse but on the blockage of its upward mobility. He accounts for the 1960s student rebellions pri- marily by students' training in the culture of critical discourse, found mostly in the humanities and liberal arts. The new class is progressive, according to Gouldner, but represents a potential new hierarchy and elite. *The Future of the Intellectuals and the Rise of the New Class* pursues some of the implications and concerns of new working class theory gen- erated during the sixties in more depth and range. Gouldner's recogni- tion, in conjunction with the social structural changes in the university and occupational trajectory of students in middle class and elite univers- ities, that language (free speech) is an important factor in visualizing and articulating liberatory alternatives and in creating community, provoca- tively highlights and extends our understanding of the student rebellion of the 1960s. The synthesis of social structural and linguistic analyses improves upon those that utilize either one or the other.

Within the broad second current of new working class theorizing two other insights are worth considering. Both of these concern the political significance of the middle class in the student revolt, the first suggesting the conservative influence on students of the use of the term and category "middle class," and the second questioning whether all students in the sixties were in fact middle class simply by virtue of their being in the university. I have interpreted new working class theory as a moment of theoretical validation of the student movement. An essential part of this effort by a number of SDS leaders consisted of a battle to justify revolt by the middle class, specifically, middle class students. Calvert's articulation of new working class theory attempted to pierce the "myth of the middle class." According to Calvert almost everyone in American society accepted the political notions that white America was mostly middle class and that being middle class meant not being oppressed; as a result, there was no possibility for discovering the basis for a radical movement in white America. New working class theory, on the other hand, suggested that the vast majority of middle-class Americans were members of a new working class. Calvert suggested that the term "middle class" was ideological in that it promoted false consciousness by obscuring the real class relations in America. Many students were, in fact, sons and daughters of the old working class, but were repeatedly told they were "middle class" and being trained for "middle-class jobs." According to Calvert, ". . . they were overwhelmingly a stratum of pre-workers being trained for new sectors of the new working class."[42]

Along the same lines, Carl Oglesby defended new working class theory and the significance of the student revolt by locating shifts in the class struggle from the factory in the 1930s to the university in the 1960s. He agreed with Kerr and Bell that the university had become the characteristic institution of advanced capitalist society, but one in which the struggle of the proletariat was continued over generations into the present. He and Calvert underscored the recent working-class backgrounds of growing numbers of university students and their future in more highly educated but nevertheless working-class jobs:

> What if it is partly in the multiversity that the proletariat has banked and stored up its enormous achievements in technology? What if the multiversity—the highest realization yet of the idea of mass education and the rationalization of productive labor—is in one of its leading aspects the institutional form through which the proletariat continues its struggle for emancipation? . . . The proletariat, says Marx, will have to prepare itself for self-government through protracted struggle. What if this struggle is so protracted that it actually must be seen as taking place . . . across *generations?*[43]

These analyses made it possible and plausible for students to see themselves as oppressed and manipulated, created by ". . . the meaningless training which is passed off as education and . . . the special coercive devices like the Selective Service System with its student deferments designed to channel them into the multiversity."[44]

In conjunction with Flacks and Gouldner's (among others') proposals of the university as a training ground for the student revolt and critical thinking, with Flacks's suggestion that the student movement and youth culture were the first expression of new class consciousness and cultural rupture, and Calvert's effort to pierce "the myth of the middle class," Barbara and John Ehrenreich's 1977 article in *Radical America* entitled

"The New Left and the Professional-Managerial Class,"[45] is relevant. This is, ten years later, a reinterpretation of new working class theory, a reversal in fact. The Ehrenreichs propose the existence of a new class in monopoly capitalism, the professional-managerial class (PMC), "who do not own the means of production and whose major function in the social division of labor may be described broadly as the reproduction of capitalist culture and capitalist class relations."[46] The PMC was a class on the rise in the 1950s and early 1960s; its material position was advancing rapidly and, they argue, it was *not* becoming proletarianized. Rather the expansion and bureaucratization of the university was mistaken for proletarianization. New left radicalism was an attempt to reassert the autonomy which it had ceded early in the twentieth century to the capitalist class. This radicalism, according to the Ehrenreichs, was characterized by scorn for the capitalist class and elitism towards the working class, which describes new left class consciousness. The Ehrenreichs suggest that the function of the PMC is to expropriate the skills and culture of the working class and to extend its own cultural and technological hegemony over that class. In late 1967 and 1968, however, the Ehrenreichs do grant that large numbers of young people began to develop a critique of their own class and found themselves at odds with it; students began to take a position which ran *counter* to their own class interests, for example, supporting community control of black neighborhoods. The Ehrenreichs conclude that the new left's central achievement was to recognize the conflict between the PMC and the working class and to develop a critique of its own class.

This analysis is in direct conflict with the suggestions and intentions of the new leftists we have just examined who encouraged students in the 1960s to see themselves as oppressed and relatively powerless. It has more in common with Gouldner's proposal of a new class, or a new intelligentsia, whose function is similar but more benign than the hegemony over the working class proposed for the PMC by the Ehrenreichs. It also echoes criticisms of new working class theory by new leftists who accused its proponents of being hostile or indifferent to the traditional working class. From the perspective of my analysis, in which new working class theory is interpreted as a positive moment in new left history, the proposition that the new left as a class was simply defending its own technocratic and social control interests must be rejected. The Ehrenreichs follow in a long line of Marxist critics of the new left who fault it for being elitist because of its social origins and future occupations. They give little credit to new leftists' understanding of their own, often compromised, options. While some of the social structural transformations they indicate were undoubtedly correct, such as the massification of higher education and the changing nature of middle class service and professional occupations, in fact, the new left was to a large extent a rejection of the path laid before it, not simply on the grounds that it wanted autonomy from the capitalist class, but because it was disaffected with the values and goals of capitalist culture and occupations. The Ehrenreichs impute to the PMC, if in fact such a range of occupations and functions *can* be considered a class, a particular consciousness based on its class background or future, especially its expected hegemonic and social control functions. They misrepresent the new left by denying the possibility that middle-class anti-capitalist consciousness may lead to socialist consciousness and political activity; elitist consciousness is not the only available path. The radical content of the student movement is reduced by suggesting that its consciousness was merely a reflection of its PMC background.

In their terms, it appears that the only way the new left could have been genuinely socialist or even truly radical would have been to give up its class privileges and "join" the working class (which many did). They themselves indicate that by the end of the decade many students were repelled by their own class and were filled with guilt and self-loathing, the basis for a politics they reject. But they do not indicate how students might have avoided this, given their analysis of the PMC; "becoming working class" seemed a way to be a bona-fide radical. The guilt and self-hatred that new leftists had a tendency to embrace, and which intensified throughout the decade as the war was escalated and fighting in the ghettos became more savage, were precisely what Calvert, Oglesby and others, in their defense of university-based revolt, tried to exorcise in the development of new working class theory.

NEW WORKING CLASS THEORY AND MARXISM

Although the significance of new working class theory in the context of the development of the new left was to legitimate *students* as revolutionaries, to justify the middle-class youth revolt in white America, much of it fell squarely within the Marxist paradigm, clinging in Mills' phrase "mightily to the 'working class' . . . as the historic agency." It in fact did not drop the "labor metaphysic." Instead the working class was simply extended.

The theory justified the felt oppression of students as *workers* and as a *class*. Because Marxism was the most compelling and perhaps only model of anti-capitalist theory and analysis, it was seized upon and altered by broadening the proletariat to include students and educated labor. The narrowest interpretations never changed the fundamental outline of Marx's analysis: the labor and products of students and intellectuals were expropriated by the capitalist class; these strata were structurally capable of overthrowing capitalism due to their location in the material base of society, which now included the university.

Most of the interesting new working class theorizing did recognize the qualitative nature of the student movement and its demands, and understood that consciousness and education were key to its development. However, theoretical and political confusion was created by the use of the word "class," which has a specific meaning in Marxist terms. Many new leftists adopted the term, stating that the new working class, like the proletariat, neither owned nor controlled the means of production. This, combined with its location in the university, signified its structurally strategic position and politically *legitimated* the student movement. Why was this necessary? Why did the legitimation take the form it did?

These are large questions and the following consideration of this particular theoretical articulation during a year or two in the life of the new left can only begin to suggest some answers. An interpretation of that experience can at most, perhaps, begin to propose the constraints and legacies within which a left in this country must operate. First, the lack of a viable left-wing party and an industrial working class-based left, in conjunction with the obvious weaknesses of an isolated student movement, were probably the most powerful contributing factors. It is here that the interplay between theory and practice is most graphic, the theory shaped by the historical and political absence of a viable left in the United States.

We have seen how SDS felt it had to shoulder the responsibility of creating a new national adult left. It had no party or organization to ally itself with, or to learn from. The magnitude and weight of this task was more than it could possibly bear or realistically accomplish. It certainly could not simultaneously have retained its originality. The new left structurally endowed itself with what it had to be in order to achieve left or socialist goals. Second, in the academy the paucity (and in many cases, the patently corrupt nature) of alternative theoretical analyses of American society combined to create a growing sense among new leftists that Marxism had much to offer. We have discussed how many of the liberal social scientists denounced the student movement, often defending the status quo including the war in Vietnam. The intellectual weaknesses of liberalism and the blatant research and financial connections with government policy led towards more political economic and structural explanations of American society and foreign policy. Third, as witnessed by the later flowering of Marxism in the academy, Marxism did have much to offer— especially in comprehending power and class relations within the United States and in the world. Marxism in an elementary form, however, and in the context of massive upheaval, was simplistically used to defend the strategic location of students, and often black people, within American society; they were part of the proletariat. Finally, the lack of a lively American Marxist intellectual tradition, one which included a recognition of cultural and consciousness factors, might have provided variation and alternatives to orthodoxy. Marcuse did but his single influence was not sufficient.[47] If students had been familiar with the history of Marxism, aware of the debates and issues, more sophisticated than their cold war backgrounds and university experiences permitted them to be, the form which their intellectual legitimation took might have been different. For all these reasons, there appeared no alternative for many theorists but to endow the student movement with a structural centrality and thereby designate it a class. By so doing the student movement was accorded the power that enabled it, theoretically at least, in the absence of other organized sectors of the population, to make a revolution. At the end of the decade, 1968 and especially 1969 and later, many in the new left became orthodox and sectarian Marxists, joining Marxist-Leninist groups. I do not refer to this development in discussing the interest in class analysis and its use in legitimating the student movement. In fact, the orthodox Marxist analysis was primarily used to de-legitimate students in favor of the industrial proletariat.

Mills' references to the labor metaphysic and to the importance of what he called the young intelligentsia provide a clue to the core irony or drama of new working class theory. In the trajectory of the student movement it represents a high point of theoretical affirmation of students and their potentially historic role. I have suggested that in the intellectual history of the new left, the theoretical and political effort to identify oneself as either oppressed or a legitimate subject struggled, generally unsuccessfully, against a much more pronounced tendency to champion others more disadvantaged or more strategically placed in society. Greg Calvert, National Secretary of SDS at the time, stated the impetus behind the new working class idea, a fragile impulse indeed in the trajectory of the new left: "No individual, no group, no class is genuinely engaged in a revolutionary movement unless their struggle is a struggle for their own liberation."[48]

Thus, on the one hand new working class theory represented a positive alternative to the belittling of students and to the growing Marxist orthodoxy and anti-intellectualism of the leadership of the second half of the sixties; *yet at the same time,* the very terms of the theory undercut the innovative character of the student movement and its aspirations. More precisely, the assumed necessity of pinpointing a *single class* which would make the revolution blocked the new left's understanding of its own sources and strengths. And yet Marxist theory was the only, and most compelling, radical theory to which students might turn for an understanding of their situation and for an analysis of American society. New working class theory provided them with legitimacy, coherence and ideology by defining the student movement as a historical oppositional agency, an agency capable of and conscious of its objective interest in overthrowing capitalism.

The relationship of new working class theory and the new left illustrates the difficulty in periods of rapid upheaval and social change of discovering theory adequate to new realities. Familiar formulations are often inadequate and yet nothing appears to take their place, or analysts and actors alike are unable or unwilling to break with the past. In the case of the new left, there were risks and novelty in their praxis and yet that praxis could not find a theory audacious enough to encompass it. Carl Oglesby, a former president of SDS, remarked late in the sixties: "Backwards as it is, our practice is more advanced than our theory, and our theory therefore becomes an obstacle to our practice . . ."[49] New left theorists understood that the appearance of the new left indicated shifts in the landscape of American social life, but they could not extricate themselves from old categories and models. The dilemma noted by Oglesby was itself not new. Marx had long ago dissected the problem in a famous passage from the *Eighteenth Brumaire of Louis Bonaparte*:

> The tradition of all the dead generations weighs like a nightmare on the brain of the living. And just when they seem engaged in revolutionizing themselves and things, in creating something that has never yet existed . . . they anxiously conjure up the spirits of the past to their service and borrow from them names, battle cries and costumes in order to present the new scene of world history in this time-honored disguise and this borrowed language.[50]

American theorists of the new working class pressed hard toward grasping the new configurations of their movement and of the advanced capitalism from which it emerged. But they finally fell victim to the "dead weight of the past," which appeared in the form of Marxism itself. American new working class theory was a case of truncated originality in social theory of the sort Marx warned against.

The preoccupation with the Marxist model and the single agent of revolution to explain the student revolt led Tom Nairn to remark in exasperation that it was much more important to see

> . . . why the university is *not* what the factory once was, why students are *not* a later generation of alienated workers (but precisely the antithesis of this, revolutionary because they negate alienation), and why youth is *not* another "class" fitting into a conventional analysis of the social structure. Where such radical novelties have already come into existence, and a new world has uttered its first cries, theory has to be very audacious merely to catch up with practice.[51]

We have come, finally, to the third strand in this theoretical effort: a strong suspicion of new working class theory and of the constrictions imposed by traditional Marxism. Carl Oglesby stated it clearly in his reply to André Glucksmann's orthodox Marxist reading of the 1968 revolt in France: ". . . [t]he revolt of the students is the revolt against the forces of modern production as a whole—a fact which would doubtless be apparent to everyone if it weren't for the intellectual tyranny of Marxism–Leninism."[52]

Both of these comments represented critical responses to the attempt to squeeze the student revolt into a simple Marxist container which saw students as alienated workers and the university as their factory. Nairn and Oglesby saw the contemporary situation as qualitatively new, requiring a break with old formulations, including Marxist orthodoxy. It is interesting that the left critique of new working class theory was confined to those most familiar with the history of Marxism and consequently, perhaps, most wary of that history. Both Nairn and Oglesby were comparatively sophisticated. The bulk of new leftists had little knowledge of the history and theory of Marxism, and consequently perhaps embraced it uncritically. I suggested earlier that the adoption of new working class theory may in part be attributed to a simplistic Marxism. It seemed obvious to such left critics that students were not a class and that the utilization of "production" concepts stripped the revolt of its uniqueness.

The new left critique of new working class theory presented by Oglesby and Nairn, ironically, converged with that of traditional Marxists, who rejected it from the other side. As one of the latter, Gareth Stedman Jones, pointed out:

> The situation of the working class is a permanent one—it is a life situation. On the other hand, one of the most important social characteristics of students is that their situation is always transient. Furthermore, their social destination is either into professional groups or else into the managerial, technocratic class itself.[53]

From this point of view, students did not constitute a class; the peculiarity of the student movement's politics derived from their social basis as students, an argument echoed in the Ehrenreichs' PMC analysis. As with older Marxist criticism of anarchism, Marxist rejections of new working class theory pointed to the alleged instability or transience of the underlying social group—in this instance, students. From this standpoint, the student revolt was a pseudo-revolt or at least a potential spark for the only real revolt, that of the industrial proletariat.

There was plenty of novelty in new left practice. But its rejection of the norms, relationships, goals and rewards of the existing society and its revolt against hierarchy, authoritarianism, centralization and bureaucracy embodied in the radical experiments, the praxis, could not find a theory "audacious" enough to encompass them. Those engaged in developing new working class theory were faced with the dilemma, in Alain Touraine's words, that the "expression of rejection and revolt constantly went far beyond the revolutionary program . . ."[54] New leftists attempted to create theory about events both unexpected and unparalleled in recent history, and yet most of them could not but conjure up the "spirits of the past" and borrow from them "names, battle cries and costumes."

Finally, there is an interesting paradox. Towards the end of the decade, as new leftists turned away from the university and students and increasingly towards the black revolt, the third world and the working class as sources of inspiration and for political organizing, precisely those leaders who had introduced Marxism into SDS via resurgent neo-Marxism in Europe, and specifically new working class theory, were the ones left defending a version of radical transformation peculiarly adapted to America. As orthodox Marxism and sectarianism made headway in the new left, a revolutionary theory based on post-scarcity values, on individual liberation, participation and cooperation, on participatory democracy and small group political autonomy, became the preserve of some of those new leftists who had introduced Marxism in the first place. It was some of these who had looked to Marxism and who had helped to develop new working class theory in the hope that it might explain and legitimate the student revolt. Ironically, the Marxism adopted by many took, instead, an orthodox form; they were able to proceed in this manner only by disregarding the uniqueness of American society in the mid-sixties.

In spite of my critique of new working class theory for being too timid or orthodox in its emphasis on production and producers, on *a class*, on *one event*, it represented in the history, theory and politics of the sixties, a departure from the traditional leftist notion of the industrial proletariat as the only agent of change, a broadening of the notion of oppression and an emphasis on culture and consciousness. The Marxism adopted by many, however, was a more familiar Marxism, a familiar agency and a familiar outline of struggle, with no place for students or intellectuals, or anyone, for that matter, who did not produce surplus value, thus being strictly exploited. Those who had introduced Marxism were left as bearers of a theory, influenced by the neo-Marxist revival in Europe, which attempted to take into account specific contemporary social developments in America, while the surge of the new left swept past them into an orthodox version of Marxism[55] that had called new lefts everywhere into existence in the first place.

REVERSALS

In the September 25, 1967, issue of *New Left Notes*, Carl Davidson, only months earlier one of the chief theoreticians of student power, student syndicalism and the new working class, wrote an article in which he said, "Students are oppressed. Bullshit. We are being trained to be oppressors and the underlings of oppressors. Only the moral among us are being hurt. Even then, the damage is only done to our sensitivities. Most of us don't know the meaning of a hard day's work." And another article appeared in the same issue questioning whether it was possible for students to be revolutionaries. The author, John Veneziale, maintained that the universities were the training grounds for the "lackeys" of the capitalist class that lived off the poor people of the country; that student struggles were not serious. Not until *students became people* and acquired a base in the community would a struggle against the university assume any meaning. Veneziale wrote, "I don't think the working-class people of this country will ever take the student struggle seriously until students become people again, and come off the campus, and be willing to kill and die for their [i.e., the people's] freedom." He suggested finally that the task of the revolutionary is to bring students *off* the campus. "Programs must be designed on campus to make as many as possible leave."[56]

It was only a year earlier, in August 1966, that Davidson had passed out his "A Student Syndicalist Movement" at the Clear Lake Convention, which had stressed the political importance of the university and students. Davidson's manifesto had urged the formation of a union of students "where the students themselves decide what kind of rules they want or don't want . . ." because only this ". . . kind of student organization allows for decentralization, and the direct participation of students in all those decisions daily affecting their lives."[57]

But by the fall of 1967 student power and new working class notions began to lose whatever small currency they had had. A new aggressive note crept into the deprecation of students, one that had not been present before. The national and international political situation was largely responsible; the 1963–1964 on-campus-off-campus debates in ERAP were repeated with a vengeance, and this time, too, the off-campus anti-student advocates, although more assertive in their attacks than earlier, were powerful and persuasive enough to affect the direction of the organization. The orthodox Marxist-Leninist Progressive Labor Party played its part both directly, by trying to recruit and take over SDS, and indirectly, by the coherence and neatness of its orthodox line. The ideas that students were only useful and significant if they worked off campus organizing the working class, and encouraged others to leave the university as well; that students were members of the capitalist class (to say nothing of one's willingness to kill and die as a sign of seriousness, which sometimes went hand in hand with this denigration of students)—all these ushered in a new phase of the new left. It should be emphasized that this was often accompanied by an increasingly sophisticated analysis of the structural and political-economic organization of American society, of which new working class theory was a part. Political implications and strategies were, however, drawn variously.

Throughout the fall of 1967 letters supporting or objecting to the anti-student statements appeared in *New Left Notes*. The vehemence on the part of those who rejected the legitimacy of the student revolt was striking; differences were couched in a new language, which used Leninist and Third World imagery, violence, militancy and old left vocabulary. The polemics revolved around who was legitimately part of the working class, who could accurately be included in the ranks of the revolutionary or potential revolutionary. It is clear in retrospect that the tide was turning against the affirmation of students, although several writers criticized this politics. A letter in reply to Veneziale stated that ". . . the greatest revolutionary potential today lies with the student and intellectual communities . . ." because the working class was no longer in a position to lead a movement for economic or political democracy.[58] Another reply to Davidson, suggested that ". . . when a person must earn his living solely by his work without benefit of property to 'earn' for him, that person is a worker. Most students become workers . . ." He asked, "Why is it so difficult to conceive of a white-collar worker as a worker?" He outlined why the work force was becoming more white collar, how the universities, by making students obey rules and regulations, carry enormous work loads, not question or think analytically (all factors Davidson himself had earlier pointed to) were training students to obey orders and to accept oppression, qualities necessary for a good worker. Contrary to what others implied, social workers and teachers were not objectively oppressors, but the "salaried employees of the oppressing corporatist class." Service workers were not *per se* oppressors of the working class.[59]

Another reply to Davidson criticized him for belittling students' efforts to end the war and the effect of the war on students and for their attacks on the university. The author suggested that being "trained to be an oppressor is itself being oppressed. These 'lackies' [sic] are being victimized, being used . . . by their oppressors and by the system in which they play such a vital and unwitting role."[60]

And finally a more representative letter of that late fall of 1967 defended Davidson and Veneziale. Youngblood, a "southern white from Uptown and an organizer for JOIN community union," argued that poor working people in this country could see as clearly as students and intellectuals and were as angry and oppositional. There was more "revolutionary potential" in poor and working-class people than in a dozen academic communities. The control of the universities was not important; students ought to leave the campuses since they could do more good as organizers off the campus. Youngblood concluded by saying that he did not want to "put down" students, but they thought of themselves as the whole movement. They had gotten most of the publicity but that did not mean they should "think they're going to make the revolution by themselves." They had to start finding out what was going on in the rest of the country.[61]

Thus just as the student movement was becoming massive, the tide began to turn away from it in SDS leadership circles. While Youngblood's point was not incorrect—students could not make a revolution by themselves—and while he had put his finger on an egocentrism characteristic of the student movement, new left politics swung past this position to a rejection of students and their concerns, of the university, and of intellectual life. In December Les Coleman wrote in *New Left Notes* that white students had initially responded to the cries of blacks and Vietnamese who were now stating clearly they were fighting colonialism. In the face of this statement white students could not help blacks or the Vietnamese "if they themselves were still part of the colonialist power." Whites were being asked which side they were on, "the side of the colonialist or the side of the colonized?"[62] and Coleman asserted that in reply the movement's issues had to be anti-imperialism and racism.

The shift in leadership circles away from students and the university meant the end of interest in new working class theory. The politics embraced by most of SDS leadership had little theoretical space for middle-class radicals.[63] Carl Oglesby wrote in 1969:

> The general adoption of some kind of Marxism-Leninism by all vocal factions in SDS means, certainly, that a long moment of intellectual suspense has been resolved—but much less in response to experience than to the pressure of *tradition*. We have not produced even a general geosocial map of the United States as a society—only as an empire.[64]

Throughout the winter and spring of 1968 the universities and white students' roles in them were attacked by SDS leadership. By April 1968 articles were appearing in *New Left Notes* urging all students to drop out of college, to reject being part of a governing institution and to understand that students could not learn what they needed to know for the struggle ahead in the university. From the university as a potential base, a community, a generator of social ideals and ideas, the position came to be, "The university itself is the enemy."[65]

TRANSITION YEARS, 1967–1968

In early 1967 Greg Calvert had stated, "We must stop apologizing for being students or for organizing students."[66] And in December 1967 he reiterated, in the face of strong pulls in the opposite direction, that the student movement had to develop "an image of its own revolution, about its own struggle, instead of believing that you're revolutionary because you're related to Fidel's struggle, Stokely's struggle, *always somebody else's struggle.*"[67] Two currents began to diverge by late 1967, one emphasizing the issue of racism and anti-imperialism and/or the primacy of the working class, the other confirming the legitimacy of the middle-class student revolt, stressing cultural issues and political process. The latter, more squarely prefigurative, held that a utopian and moral resistance to advanced capitalism on one's own behalf was legitimate and critical to a genuinely liberatory transformation. However, it would be incorrect to give the impression that no part of the movement managed to combine these currents; there were people and groups who affirmed students and participatory democracy and embraced a politics that was primarily anti-imperialist and had a focus on racism in the United States. By and large, however, the new left had a difficutt time synthesizing these strands; it was the prefigurative that lost out.

In September 1967 Andrew Kopkind wrote in the *New York Review of Books*:

> To be white and radical in America this summer is to see horror and feel impotence. It is to watch the war grow and know no way to stop it, to understand the black rebellion and find no way to join it, to realize that the politics of a generation has failed and the institutions of reform are bankrupt, and yet to have neither ideology, programs, nor the power to reconstruct them.[68]

In spite of the fact that the movement became a mass movement and continued to grow during and beyond 1968, the new left moved away from a focus on students towards a militant and orthodox Marxist or Maoist politics. Exactly at the height and power of the student movement, SDS split and collapsed. For many students just entering the anti-war movement it did not matter. The organization had become, or perhaps in many cases had remained, less and less relevant to the grass roots anti-war movement. The growing distance of the leadership from an affirmation of the significance, legitimacy and power of a grass roots radical student movement was in no small way responsible for that irrelevance.

There are at least four factors which lead toward an explanation of the shifts and divergences of late 1967 and 1968. Kirkpatrick Sale suggests that SDS began to feel that a revolution might in fact be possible. SDS leadership felt it could and should forge a broad American left and consequently turned away, perhaps was forced away, from student power and a uniquely "student" movement. It has been proposed in this work, and may be considered the first factor, that SDS was catapulted in the direction of these politics by the lack of major institutional allies, such as a labor or working-class party, with which to link itself. Jim O'Brien analyzed it in retrospect:

> SDS was an embodiment of the New Left, a social movement that was basically limited to a single sector of society (the college campus) and to a single generation of young people. It could not be made to carry the burden of revolution for the whole society. When pressures developed . . . for the New Left to assume that burden, these pressures resulted in an accelerated growth for a time, but they also speeded the movement's ultimate collapse.[69]

The student movement simply could not carry that burden; it was an impossible endeavor. A majority of the population would have to participate in a radical transformation, but in their frustration and isolation many in the white radical movement lost that understanding and took on the burden of social change for the whole society.[70]

The second factor contributing to the new left's difficulty in holding onto its two halves, the libertarian, domestic political emphasis and the strategic, anti-imperialist viewpoint (or the prefigurative and strategic) was the war in Vietnam and the black rebellion that increasingly dominated the consciousness and politics of the nation and the movement. For the movement this happened in such complete fashion that there was less and less possibility for a more cultural, personal and experimental politics since these appeared self-indulgent and unpolitical, the prerogative of the privileged. This was pointed out as early as 1966 by Dick Flacks. Referring to the Vietnam War, he said in *New Left Notes*:

> It has helped to build the Left. But people on the Left can't responsibly worry about much else as long as it goes on. And the more they accept the responsibility for trying to end the war, the more militant they become—and the more they sense their own impotence, isolation and alienation from the larger society. . . . The war helps to build the radical movement, but the necessary obsession to work to end it is, in many ways, incompatible with *achieving* such a movement.

The source of the malaise on the left, according to Flacks, was due to the prolongation and intensification of the Vietnam War, which had sensitized the movement to the international scene but "rendered the domestic strategy of the left largely irrelevant."[71]

The violence perpetrated in Vietnam and at home by the American government, the bloody investment of national military might in defeating the Vietnamese seen nightly on television became paramount, propelling hundreds of thousands to join the anti-war movement and question the legitimacy of the American government. The guilt, horror and frustration compelled the leadership of SDS, and of the new left, to become more militant, angry and revolutionary in ideology. Michael Rossman wrote about the Chicago Democratic Convention in 1968: "Our sound's been growing darker, harder. Guns. Up against the Wall, Mafia threatening our friendly neighborhood dope dealers, sabotage, check the state of your stomach, hard rain's started falling."[72]

A third and critical factor in the changes that took place in 1967 and 1968 involved repression and intransigence on the part of the national government. In a 1968 interview Tom Hayden stated:

> On August 28, 1963 the President welcomed civil rights leaders and 250,000 people to Washington for a sort of joyous celebration. On August 28, 1968 we were gassed in front of the Conrad Hilton and both Kennedys were dead. The difference between those two things, although they're only five years apart, is too staggering to sort out and fully understand right now.

Hayden suggested that the movement was impressively large and had petitioned the authorities, but the authorities were dispensing no meaningful concessions. Instead they were utilizing military means and legal repression to stop the movement in the streets.[73]

Between those two August events in 1963 and 1968, positions had polarized. The national government would not accommodate the growing anti-war movement, and state and local governments were even more opposed to the grass roots youth and student revolts. The difference between them was the loss of hope and of the belief in justice. It consisted of a new sophistication as well. Disillusionment and bitterness grew as the reality of the situation was absorbed. From the movement's perspective the government had not listened to the mass movement, the best liberal leaders were murdered, the official response was military and legal repression. The movement's "darker, harder sound" was built on despair at the government's violence towards the white, black and Vietnamese movements. It was also built on an increasingly realistic analysis of the power of the corporate state and the centrality of imperialism, racism and repression to that state.

The fourth factor involved in the transition period of new left politics was the rejection of participatory democracy. Staughton Lynd wrote of this time that "as participatory democracy, like nonviolence, came to seem the product of a naive early state of protest before the magnitude of the Movement's task was fully recognized, white radicals drifted back toward the political style of the Old Left."[74] The shift away from participatory democracy meant many things. Here Lynd connects its rejection to the political style of the old left, meaning, perhaps, a willingness to forego egalitarian participation for a more effective and hierarchical organization. We have also seen a theoretical progression towards Marxism symbolized by new working class theory and a growing interest in the traditional working class. The movement from late 1967 to the end of the decade was in general moving towards a more traditional Marxism and leftist orientation. Realization of some of the new left's weaknesses did lead to the rejection of early new left emphases in favor of more traditional political activity and theory, although it also led to a politics which stressed anti-imperialism more than domestic issues, a particularly new left characteristic. An article which appeared in *The Guardian* in 1969 by an activist, Bob Goodman, chronicling the development of new left politics, said in part, "To racism we replied with racial brotherhood and love; to war, with nonviolence and peace. To a society which had the forms of democracy, without the substance, we replied to the point of redundance: *participatory* democracy." Goodman continued that the movement's experiences led to a perception that the values and organizational forms of the early new left were not adequate to deal with changing America. This led to a transformation of the new left:

> . . . The values and organizational forms of the early new left gave way to new ones. Idealistic black-and-white-together SNCC was succeeded by black power SNCC and then by the disciplined, organized, ideological, sociological Black Panthers. SDS went from antiwar politics to anti-imperialism, to anti-capitalism, and immersed itself in Marxist analysis.[75]

Discussing the Oakland Stop-the-Draft Week in 1967, Frank Bardacke, one of its architects, summed up its meaning: ". . . We consider ourselves political outlaws. The American government has the power to force us to submit but we no longer believe that it has the authority to compel us to obey."[76] This was a predominant reaction among new leftists in these years, to consider themselves "outlaws," to fashion themselves as a gang of enemies of the state whose presence could not be ignored. The destruction of symbolic property was a central goal. "Weatherman," a militant activist group which grew out of SDS and saw itself as an anti-racist and anti-imperialist military vanguard whose function was the disruption of the state and business-as-usual, was the logical outcome of this perspective.[77] The assumption of the burden of forcing social change for the entire society, of the goal of the de-legitimation of the American government, and a belief in new social and sexual mores as part of revolutionary change were forged into a group and ideology represented most forcefully by Weatherman. In significant ways Weatherman, internally, represented the continuity of egalitarian and prefigurative new left notions disguised, however, by elitism and a militarist notion of politics. In both cases, the one strategic and the other vanguardist, prefigurative politics was lost. The libertarian moment which had affirmed students, counter-institutions and participatory democracy was fast fading.

CHAPTER 7

The Economic Research and Action Project

I conclude this examination of the new left with a consideration of ERAP, the community organizing projects in northern cities sponsored by SDS in the first half of the decade, although several projects survived beyond. ERAP chronologically preceded much of what previous chapters have examined, but since it brings together many of the most important early new left themes, particularly the issues of agency and prefigurative organizational forms, I have placed ERAP at the end. It demonstrates both the dedication and hard work of activists in their attempts to build a new left, and their almost painful self-consciousness, which they were often accused of lacking, about political choices and success and failure. It is a story that needs to be told since the experience and the theorizing form part of the history of later and even contemporary attempts to organize in communities for justice and social change; yet, lacking the media appeal of later new left actions, ERAP has slipped into oblivion. Commentators often remark that Americans have a weak sense of the past: that they know little about and seem uninterested in their history. The left has often shared that trait with the larger culture; I have mentioned that new leftists and student activists were often unaware of earlier left-wing, radical and/or Marxist history. ERAP is an episode with little visibility, familiarity with it confined to those who participated or were aware of it at the time. Yet the ERAP experience is an enlightening and even moving chapter in early new left history. It highlights the strains between prefigurative and strategic politics as well as the dilemmas inherent in prefigurative efforts. It spotlights a new left politics other than demonstrations and direct action, making clear the interplay between theory and practice. It raises issues about reformism and the relationship between reform and revolution, about workplace versus community organizing, of an agency of social change, and finally, about mobilization in social protest organizations. A vital part of the early new left, ERAP may serve as a fitting conclusion to this study.

In the March-April 1963 issue of the *SDS Bulletin,* Tom Hayden proclaimed that President Kennedy's New Frontier was not "coping with problems in ways that will guarantee acceptable levels of democracy and peace." Referring to the civil rights movement, unemployment and American international arrogance, Hayden went on to point out that people working in liberal causes at the grass roots were discontented and that ". . . we may need to transform these invisible rebellions into a politics of responsible insurgents rooted in community after community." He noted that organizers would have to speak to the felt needs of local areas, be very concrete and specific in seeking solutions, and ultimately "create genuinely independent political constituencies who will not be satisfied with the New Frontier. Can the methods of SNCC be applied to the North?"[1] Part of the means to answer this question affirmatively were provided in late summer 1963. Following the August 19 civil rights March on Washington for Jobs and Freedom, the newly created Economic Research and Action Project (ERAP) of SDS received a $5000 grant from the United Auto Workers "to emphasize economic issues on campuses and communities."[2] The October *SDS Bulletin* announced that ERAP is a "response to the increasing crisis in the U.S. economy . . . and the growing awareness of the civil rights movement and of peace advocates that economic issues must be brought into clearer focus and attacked more directly if their particular problems are to be dealt with successfully."[3] One of ERAP's first expenditures sent Joe Chabot, a student from Ann Arbor, where the project was to be administered, to Chicago to explore the possibilities of organizing unemployed youth. Chabot was ERAP's first organizer and as such indicative of a new direction emerging from SDS: away from the campus and into the communities.

This development was not without its critics. By March 1964 Al Haber, among others, was arguing that the "cult of the ghetto has diverted SDS from its primary and most difficult task of educating radicals."[4] In embryo this was the "campus versus the community" debate which unfolded within SDS between 1963 and 1965, and which this chapter will examine. The issues explored here are (1), the initial phase of what would prove to be the new left's protracted internal conflict over the agency of social transformation, a conflict whose subsequent phases, one of which we have examined in new working class theory, not only were never resolved, but contributed significantly to acrimony and the disintegration of the new left at the close of the decade; and (2), the early exploration in practice of organizational forms that encouraged participatory democracy. The tension between prefigurative and strategic politics was clearly delineated. The campus-versus-community debate is reconstructed here as closely as possible in the terms of the disputants themselves. The discussion seeks to recall the lived experience of the debate, the powerful sense of "possibility and urgency" which the founders of ERAP had inherited from the civil rights movement.[5]

In this connection, what the historian Christopher Hill indicates regarding his approach to the radical religious movements in seventeenth-century England is pertinent: "I have given this account mostly in the words of the Agitators or Levellers, not because they are necessarily always accurate but because for our purposes what matters is what men believed to have happened."[6] The following pages focus on the conflict of beliefs about what was happening and should happen, and the experience of participants, which often forced them to reevaluate their beliefs. I, of course, do interpret and evaluate the ERAP effort, but rely largely on the activists in order to comprehend the choices and obstacles they faced and to avoid judgment in hindsight that disregards their values and politics.

THE DEBATE: POOR PEOPLE OR STUDENTS; OFF-CAMPUS VS. ON-CAMPUS ORGANIZING

There were several central impulses behind the community organizing projects known as ERAP. An ERAP brochure said:

> We are young people in search of effective forms of action and new possibilities for change. We have chosen to work with people who most desperately need alternatives to poverty and economic voicelessness, and to devote ourselves to the development of a community organization capable of achieving a better deal for the poor in a democratic fashion.[7]

And Rennie Davis wrote in a 1964 *SDS Bulletin,* "Certainly there is conviction among us that without this effort to bring poor whites into loose alliance with the Negro freedom movement on economic issues, the country faces the alternative of increasing racial violence."[8] The first of these pronouncements centers around "effective forms of action," the activist impulse basic to new left politics. Drawing inspiration from what they believed to be the heroism, dynamism, and dedication of southern blacks, young northern whites in SDS sought a new style and program of social activism of their own. The activist impulse led students into ghettoes of the north with the SNCC model uppermost in their minds. Opposition to racism and the belief that white people would have to be educated and organized to understand that blacks were not their enemy were powerful impetuses to the program. Specifically, ERAPers believed that unemployed and poor white people were often carriers of racism and that to avert a backlash against the civil rights movement and black people generally, it was politically important to work in such neighborhoods.

The second factor informing ERAP was a vision of economic justice which directed the initiators to "work with people who most desperately needed alternatives to poverty and economic voicelessness." The vision was reinforced by predictions of chronic unemployment in the near future and the recent exposure of widespread poverty in the United States. Two examples were the publication of Michael Harrington's *The Other America* (1962) and the "Triple Revolution Statement," a manifesto published in 1963 by liberal and radical intellectuals, to the effect that automation was the wave of the future in production and would drastically increase unemployment. It was signed by many prominent figures including W. H. Ferry, Michael Harrington, Gunnar Myrdal, Robert Theobald, Linus Pauling, Robert Heilbroner and Ben B. Seligman. The "economic" in the ERAP title originated with the idea that community organization "can be developed among persons whose economic role in the society is marginal or insecure. . . . Our immediate identification is with the Negro movement and the problems of the unorganized poor."[9]

These two ideas culminated in a vision of an "interracial movement of the poor," the title of a paper written by Tom Hayden and Carl Wittman and published by SDS as a pamphlet in 1963. It was influential in the thinking behind ERAP. The goals were to develop community control and economic reforms among whites in northern cities, linking these efforts to the black southern civil rights movement. In this way an integrated grass roots movement of the poor would be forged.

The years 1963 and 1964 in America were the height of enormous activity and controversy generated by the civil rights movement. The "America and the New Era" document adopted by the SDS Convention in June 1963 reflected this by pointing the way to a different kind of political activity, a "new insurgency." The document focused on a "new discontent, a new anger" in the country leading toward insurgent protest, particularly the civil rights movement. People were discovering that mass protest was more effective than suffering quietly. The document linked the efforts of the civil rights movement with larger problems in the society, a "prevalent pattern of national, political, economic, and social oppression," and suggested that the civil rights demand for freedom is a "demand for a new society." "The outcome of these efforts at creating insurgent politics could be the organization of constituencies expressing, for the first time in this generation, the needs of ordinary men for a decent life."[10] This was the rationale behind ERAP, the development of local, independent political organizations around everyday needs.

With abundant evidence that times were changing, from Bob Dylan's music to the "New Frontier" to the civil rights movement and its support on northern campuses, new leftists began the school year in the fall of 1963. ERAP was foremost in most SDSers' minds, not least because a good many of the leaders were interested and involved. In December Todd Gitlin's "President's Report" discussed the potential of "social change through community work" and stated that this was quite new for SDS. "The clear trend in the leftward student movement over the past two or three years has been, paradoxically, its departure from the campus." Gitlin continued:

> The hope is that a new variety of "radical vocation," of off-campus work, will be created: one that requires full-time dedication similar to that of SNCC field secretaries, yet one in which students can participate, if less actively, while still regarding the campus as their (temporary) home. Another problem becomes clear: how to do real work outside the campus while maintaining educational and programmatic liaison with the campus.[11]

Gitlin pointed to an important tension in SDS which revolved around the appropriate constituency and political work for a national student organization. Furthermore, his proposal was, in hindsight, impossible. SDS could not possibly have accomplished such a task: full-time off-campus work in SNCC fashion could not be undertaken by people who were students and whose home was the campus. Gitlin held out the hope that students might participate in the new community work and still maintain a campus orientation, indicating at the same time, the inherent difficulties of such a possibility. Gitlin and others viewed community organizing with an enthusiasm and hope not shared by everyone in SDS. The emergence of ERAP created critics who, while a minority and soon swept aside, raised vital questions. Looking back, Kirkpatrick Sale summarizes these tensions—tensions that lasted throughout the decade—paraphrasing questions raised by the new left as to whether the university and its constituency were a base of social change or part of the capitalist system, inextricably rooted in the cold war. Sale asks, "Is the university the nest for those who can create real social change, or the hothouse for those who would resist it? Are students operating within the university truly agents of social change, or must they leave the campuses and operate in the 'real' world outside?" Does the university produce the system's negation or its minions?[12]

These were the options as new leftists saw them—extreme, dramatic, the source of vehement polemics throughout the decade, as we have seen in the later new working class debate. By 1968 the original ERAP impulse had triumphed, in an extreme and perhaps deformed way, when new leftists could argue that no one who remained in the university could be considered a radical. The choices available to students had become ideologically polarized.

Those critical of ERAP pointed to a complicated factor underlying the popularity of community organizing work. Steve Max presciently observed: "I would suggest that the tension springs not from an objective need for a hard differentiation between campus and community organizing but from the *sometimes-whispered, sometimes-silently believed notion that the campus is really unimportant compared to the ghetto.*"[13] (Emphasis mine.) Max correctly disclosed an underlying theme of the student movement. But this cannot be interpreted in an exclusively negative light; students wanted to break out of their privileged and insulated lives, to leave the university and participate in political activity that involved risks. This was part of the appeal of the civil rights movement as well. The desire for activism was no less an impetus behind ERAP than was glorification of poor people and denigration of students and their "middleclassness."

At the December 1963 SDS National Council meeting in New York City the opposing positions clashed with a vengeance. Haber argued that students should concern themselves as students, avoidthe "cult of the ghetto," and use their own talents on the campus. Hayden countered that SDS had to *"leave all that academic crap behind it,* has to *break out of intellectuality into contact with the grass roots* of the nation. ERAP, by getting off the campuses and into the ghettoes, would get to the grass roots, *get to where the people are.*" He argued that here, finally, was "something for SDS to do."[14] (Emphasis mine.) In a way neither whispered nor silent, Hayden, with all his influence, made it very clear that the campus was insignificant compared to the ghetto, that moving off the campus and away from "intellectuality" meant leaving an unreal world for a real one with real people.

Writing in the *SDS Bulletin* after the overwhelming victory of the Hayden proposal, Haber stated his critique of the politics behind ERAP: "The 'into the ghetto' enthusiasm has become linked with an anti-intellectualism, a disparagement of research and study, an urging of students to leave the university, a moral superiority for those who 'give their bodies,' etc."[15] Along with others, Haber was suspicious that SDS, contrary to its formal minority resolutions and statements, did not seriously intend to stress campus political work. Gitlin himself admitted that the off-campus-on-campus tension, about which he had earlier been sanguine, had intensified. Haber was the most outspoken critic of ERAP and its implications, anti-intellectualism and the denigration of students and the university. He queried the membership about the relevance of community work for a growing student organization and formulated issues that became central several years later when the movement developed into a mass student movement consisting in part of many college graduates with no radical organizational base. Striking at the heart of the matter, Haber asked, "Is radicalism subsisting in a slum for a year or two, or is it developing your individual talents so you can function as a radical in the 'professional' fields and throughout your adult life? Can a teacher be a radical in his profession? or an artist? or a lawyer?"[16] These questions, asked prematurely, would become critical only as soon as a number of academic generations began to face their futures.

Bitterness and frustration may be detected in Haber's comments, derived in part from his insulation from the upsurge of political activism and enthusiasm that made ERAP and community organizing seem so right to so many in SDS at the time. He felt isolated and worried about SDS's desertion of the student constituency (which came to fruition in late 1967 and 1968). He believed that the role of a radical student movement was to educate students and to make radicals of them regardless of their future occupations. Students and professionals could be radicals, in Haber's view, and SDS's task was to give them an education and a home of sorts. Although in several years' time, Radicals in the Professions, the New University Conference (NUC), and radical caucuses in many professional organizations developed as expressions of problems graduate students and young adults had in the university and workplace, in 1963 and 1964 it was too early. The student movement and new left, characterized by an immediacy and an orientation to the present, combined with a growing desire to escape middle-class insulation, found the appeal of the civil rights movement and projects like ERAP strong indeed.

Gitlin tried to bridge the gap, suggesting that what was needed were movements in the middle classes with radical goals and strategies for radicals in the professions that *combined* with lower-class movements.[17] No one, of course, could disagree; it was just what the new left hoped for and never achieved. Gitlin added that Haber was wrong to assume that students had defined their futures in professional terms; in many cases the student was "confused about his future." This was a critical point in the developing student movement; the movement's many facets, particularly the civil rights movement and ERAP, but movement activism and values in general, were beginning to undermine the assumed futures of these mostly middle-class activists. Or perhaps movement activism, like ERAP, was an expression of the rejection of professional futures. Hayden made clear that the ERAP projects in part represented a rejection of the paths set out for students, an experiment in a different way of living. In 1963 and 1964 Haber's idea of student radicalism lacked more adherents precisely because students and ex-students were in the process of shedding their professional aspirations (only for the time being for some).[18] This made Haber's student and organizational concerns seem distant and irrelevant.

Writing in the spring of 1964, Don McKelvey remarked that the national leaders of SDS were primarily clustered around ERAP, and while they were nominally students ". . . they are more concerned with social change activism outside student groups." They focused their energies on adults and not students. And he asked whether it made sense that people with this point of view determined the "tone and direction" of a campus-based organization?[19] McKelvey, SDS's Assistant National Secretary working in the National Office, raised two key issues in the on-campus-off-campus debate, issues reiterated by others. The first was that students *qua* students and the developing of a national left student organization did not appear to be prime concerns of SDS. Pointing out that there were only a few strong SDS chapters at the time and many more struggling for existence, waiting for aid and encouragement from SDS, McKelvey considered it SDS's organizational responsibility to help these chapters and to politicize students on the campuses. He echoed Haber in articulating two opposing roles SDS could play: "One involves the developing of *future social change* as its main goal, the other involves the development of *future social changers* as its main goal. . . . We must view SDS, not as the 'Movement' or an organization which seeks to do everything . . ." SDS must be seen as part of a plethora of groups seeking to change America. *"300 or 2000 of us simply cannot change the United States by ourselves, much less the world."*[20] (Emphasis mine.)

That the new left by itself could neither make "the revolution," nor create social change, was a critical insight, no matter how self-evident in hindsight. By organizing the poor and ignoring students, SDS, McKelvey argued, was acting on the principle that it could "do everything." The exhaustion of the old left and the lack of institutional allies on the left burdened SDS, as we have seen, with the sense that it had to do and be everything. Haber, too, had argued in these years, "We cannot do all things." In 1964 Paul Potter, the new president of SDS, illuminated the problems facing SDS:

> The development of SDS to date has much more represented the attempt by a few to pull together the organizational and intellectual conception of an American new left than it has the development of a student organization, radical or otherwise. Some of the early issues that attracted people to the organization were "student" issues, such as university reform, but these kinds of issues have consistently diminished in their importance, almost from before the official birth of SDS at Port Huron.

He continued that the issue was especially important because the drift away from campus issues was characteristic of SDS leadership but not of the organization as a whole.[21] Potter insightfully drew together various strands of the problems. Like McKelvey and Haber, he characterized the efforts of SDS as an attempt *by students* to pull together a new American left rather than an effort to build a *student* left, exemplified by the leadership's focus on community and non-campus issues. This was McKelvey's second key point as well. Almost all the early SDS leadership went into ERAP.[22] This had serious political repercussions for SDS organizationally in that the original leaders, with their political experience, expertise, and skills, abandoned the student organization for community work at a time of steady growth on campuses. Sale suggests that their absence was deeply felt. Exaggerating, he states ". . . They were, after all, some of the best talents, the brightest minds, the most committed souls in the organization, and there they were, off in almost utter isolation, rarely participating in ongoing SDS business." Younger people, new recruits into SDS, according to Sale, had few mentors.[23]

Steve Max criticized the June 1964 SDS convention, which had reaffirmed ERAP politics, saying it was not a convention for students, but rather for young adults interested in community work. The leadership lamented the tension between the campus and the community but did nothing to correct it, according to Max.[24] The leadership's abdication in favor of community work had repercussions for the morale and energy devoted to the campus and organizing students. These problems were inextricably bound together. The interest in immediate political activity and commitment, the unease with being students, the lack of a left in the United States, were reflected in the leadership's involvement off-campus; and they all created or reflected political and organizational dilemmas for SDS.

A year later, in the spring of 1965 this debate was still raging in SDS. Although the height of ERAP enthusiasm had by that time passed, feelings and tensions inspired by differences were just as strong. At the December 1964 National Council meeting in New York City, ERAP people had again dominated the discussion and tempers were sharp. Bob Ross stated that the "gentlemen from New Jersey" (Hayden and others from the Newark Community Union Project, NCUP) dominated the National Council meeting and turned it from its agenda; at the same time he argued that "they have little interest, as ERAP organizers, in the content of what has come to be called 'students' concerns' . . ." Ross accused them of obstructing discussion with their inordinate influence, and of "arrogance and contempt" in their remarks. These remarks implied ". . . a) students as such were wrong for being students, and b) the 'role' of the intellectual or academic was *prima facie* bad." He concluded that given their personal and political influence in SDS, it was no wonder it was demoralizing for so many people and that there was no "satisfactory program for, or rationale for, SDS campus groups." In part this was due to the fact that the most influential people were in ERAP and uninterested in students: Ross suggested that ". . . the 'old' people should stay out of the argument, forcing upon new leadership the problems of *their* organization."[25]

Dick Flacks, too, spoke of being "upset that a lot of polarization has occurred around the figures of Steve Max and Tom Hayden." He said they should be reminded that they had implicitly agreed to withdraw from top leadership in an effort to encourage new and younger leadership. Those who were distressed felt that it was inappropriate for ERAPers to force the organization to deal with ERAP problems when these were neither student concerns nor organizationally within SDS's jurisdiction, and when ERAPers demonstrated little interest in general SDS organizational questions. Bob Ross suggested that ERAP decision-making should be separate from SDS and that SDS should divest itself of formal connection with the community unions.[26]

The dichotomy between campus and community political work had been posed sharply and bitterly for two years. The bitterness stemmed from ERAP's appeal and power, and an attitude of self-righteousness on the part of its spokespeople, as well as from frustration and lack of clarity about what students and a radical student organization should and could be doing politically. However, the sharpness of the positions was modified by the upsurge of the student movement on the campuses beginning with the Free Speech Movement in the fall of 1964. The community focus suffered from then on, not only because of dramatic activity on the campuses but from difficulties in ERAP as wll. Before continuing the examination of ERAP, a qualification is in order. Although these exchanges among the leadership in SDS corresponded to real choices and tensions, they were not as dramatic and exclusive for most ordinary activists. The inner guard of SDS was attempting to formulate policy for the organization, and thus the debates took on an urgency, and the strategies an exclusivity, irrelevant for most movement activists. While many activists did drop out of school to go south or work in a community organizing project, many more managed to do so during the school year or summer at the same time as they were active on campus in Friends of SNCC, anti-war work, and other campus-based political activity, such as FSM. The options so wrenchingly posed in the leadership *debates* were not sc acutely *experienced* by many in the movement, for whom being a studen was not experienced in flatly negative and useless terms. The polarizec positions captured, however, a real tension which deepened throughou the decade. The emotion of the debates reflected the stakes as they wer evaluated by SDSers, which for many meant nothing less than a nev chance for America.

THE THEORY OF COMMUNITY UNIONS

In the spring and summer of 1964 *Studies on the Left* published a series of articles, the main contributor to which was James O'Connor, around the theme that contemporary working-class agitation was increasingly generated by poverty, slums, inadequate educational facilities and insufficient public services—not job issues. This amounted to a shift in the traditional leftist notion of agency from the working class to the poor and the marginal.[27] This exchange continued into 1966, and included essays by O'Connor, Stanley Aronowitz, Norman Fruchter and Robert Kramer, who all argued that due to various developments in advanced capitalism, the residential community, not the workplace, had become the main site of anti-capitalist protest and rebellion. Whether these articles were used as after-the-fact rationalizations for community organizing or were, in fact, theories of poverty and of the potential power of the poor which provided an impetus for ERAP is unclear. They did, however, provide a theoretical framework for the ERAP projects and were both influential on and influenced by ongoing community work, an e ample of the connection and interaction of theory and practice in the new left. As the ERAP projects were experimenting with new organizational forms and a different agency, people not traditionally considered "organizable," a parallel theoretical exploration was undertaken. The civil rights movement provided the initial model of local community-based protest and organization, which in turn forced socialists and Marxists to review traditional theory.[28]

In "Towards a Theory of Community Unions I," O'Connor argued that long-run unemployment was concentrated among semi-skilled and unskilled workers. These categories of workers would not find their interests defended by the entrenched and conservative trade unions, and as a result, the expression of work agitation and political activity, where it emerged, shifted to "the neighborhood, the community, the region."[29] Although working-class agitation derived from the lack of jobs and income, it was not immediately focused on these issues. "Long-run unemployment is revealed as poverty, slum housing, inadequate educational facilities, insufficient public services. . . . In the future the social base for working-class organizations will lie more and more in the community where today there is largely a political vacuum. Community unions clearly will be the appropriate mode of working-class organization and struggle."

He pointed out that the central problem of community unions was one of tactics, since there was not a political weapon analogous to the industrial strike, and suggested that civil disobedience might be the seed from which more effective tactics would grow.[30] In a second article O'Connor argued that the residential area was being politicized and supplanting the workplace as the center of political activity. The lack of jobs was translated into and experienced as housing, health and other domestic problems; political questions were "thrown back into the community."[31]

Aronowitz, too, pointed to the potential power of community organizations neither managed nor organized from the top down. He was concerned about cooptation by the War on Poverty and other federal poverty programs in urban areas and supported the possibility of the development of community unions as the basis of a strategy for major economic and institutional changes.

Martin Nicolaus continued this line of analysis in a pamphlet entitled "The Contradiction of Advanced Capitalist Society and its Resolution." He suggested that a consensus seemed to be emerging among Marxists that the industrial proletariat in the advanced capitalist societies was no longer a potentially revolutionary force. The working class was no longer able to pose a threat to a carefully managed capitalist system, and no proletarian demands for higher wages or for any other strictly economic goals were "likely to raise the spectre of revolution." At the basis of Marx's thought, according to Nicolaus, was the vision of the liberation of humanity as the liberation *from* labor, "the vision of a world without work."[32] He suggested that two contemporary movements could be interpreted as protests against and demands for the resolution between capital as a productive force and capital as a social relationship: the hippies and the urban ghetto uprisings. The meaning of the ghetto riots and looting and of the counter-culture of the sixties was "the surplus population appropriating the surplus wealth." He went on to note that "For Marxist theory, this poses the problem of rethinking the entire labor union tradition, even the entire class struggle notion, in order to discover exactly what role the concept of community in addition to the concept of class can play in social change models."[33] Community unions were an appropriate form of organization in the struggle between unemployed capital and unemployed people.

In this departure from traditional Marxist notions of workplace and working-class strategies, the community became critical in the transformation of capitalism. In part these theories were based on the incorporation of unions into the prevailing system and the absence of grass roots labor radicalism. There seemed no alternative but to organize in neighborhoods, where the impact of unemployment and low-paying jobs was felt and where radicalization might thus take place. The theories were also informed by a sense that marginal people, particularly blacks and students, were on the move. Norman Fruchter and Robert Kramer's "An Approach to Community Organizing" argued that the urban poor, for whom "the increasingly repressive systems of socialization and control seem to reach down less thoroughly" had an objective, real need for change, and that students were searching for such constituencies that might yield activity. The hope was that the impetus which had led to community-wide movements in Montgomery, Alabama, the Harlem rent strikes, the integration fights in Chester, Pennsylvania, Cleveland, Cambridge, Maryland and Philadelphia, could be expanded from civil rights protest to a "general non-racial protest against continued ghetto existence and whether from that protest durable movement for change could be built."[34]

The value and interest of these theoretical analyses is their wide speculation on the basis of real developments, their break with traditional leftist notions by pointing out the apparent weakness of "production" and work as the sole lever of radical action in poor people's lives. The theories sought, as did the activists, agents of social change other than the traditional working class, because other social forces, including students, were in motion. They tried to account for revolts of the "marginals" of America, theorizing the contemporary political situation in which capitalist structures were attacked at points other than that of production.[35]

The ERAP effort to organize communities for community control, although not an impressive success, struck a chord that has lasted until the present, particularly in black and ethnic communities. The simple idea that people in their community and citizen capacity should be able to control the resources and decisions affecting them was a powerful one. Ironically it "kicked the labor metaphysic"—which C. Wright Mills had implored the new left to do—in favor not of students and the intelligentsia, as Mills had intended, but of poor people. Although community organizing in poor neighborhoods may not have been the most fruitful effort for a burgeoning student movement, it represented the deepening of political experiences and of theoretical insight for the new left, part of the process of building a movement.

COMMUNITY ORGANIZING: ORGANIZATION AS COMMUNITY

In 1964 ERAP Director Rennie Davis stated that ERAPers know no "satisfactory blueprint" for equality, abundance and democracy, and that they had only limited ideas about the strategy for changing this society. "We have found little information on organizing in the 1930s that has proved relevant to our operations. . . ."[36] With this candid statement of the vague notions characterizing the community organizing projects, ERAP began its first and most significant summer in ten urban ghettoes of the north (almost all black). In this June 1964 Director's Report, Rennie Davis enumerated all the obvious questions that inexperienced radicals living in unfamiliar surroundings and trying to "organize" people very different from themselves, might ask: Whom should we organize, men, women, youth? Around which issues? On what basis, block-by-block or neighborhood-wide around issues? How should we deal with racism in white communities? What kind of organizations should we try to build? Over the next several years people who worked in ERAP projects groped to answer these questions. ERAP did not last long as a formally administered centralized organization,[37] although several of the individual projects continued into the late sixties (Chicago, Newark, Cleveland), often generating other community organizations and political activity.

Initially there was a debate among the organizers in the various projects about which issues around which to organize. Richard Rothstein explained that some, like Baltimore and Chicago, arqued that social change could only come about if fundamental economic issues were attacked, particularly unemployment. These were the JOIN projects (Jobs or Income Now). Other projects such as those in Newark and Cleveland believed that movements had to be built around issues which community residents felt were most relevant and these were called "GROIN" projects (Garbage Removal or Income Now).[38] The Join-Groin debate was intense, continuing on and off throughout ERAP, since different projects had varying success with particular issues. By the winter of 1965 most projects had, however, stopped trying to organize the unemployed because the effort had been unsuccessful, largely because unemployment was decreasing due to the war in Vietnam. They had adopted instead the "community union" approach (GROIN): organizing poor people around felt grievances. Organizers continued to search for ways to link these grievances with national political and economic issues, a political task which always faces community organizers, particularly when they are addressing local issues with no clearcut national repercussions. Organizing around felt grievances, such as a traffic light or a welfare check, continually placed ERAPers in the difficult situation of having to draw the connections between reform goals and larger, structural configurations of power.

In the following pages, we will look at what they thought they were doing in ERAP, how they organized, and what their experiences, on balance, were. "Today an ERAP community union is probably the only institution in the world where a destitute alcoholic can stand up and give a lecture, occasionally brilliant but usually incoherent, on political strategy and be listened to with complete respect."[39] In this statement and the next Richard Rothstein gives a picture of their values and goals. Referring to an ERAP community union office he described how the neighborhood people "call it their own" and that keys were distributed by the organizers throughout the neighborhood. There was activity there of all sorts at every hour of the day or night, from leaflet preparation to sleeping. ". . . An ERAP community union is one of those rare organizations where the founders define their task largely in terms of *how successfully they give away their own power.*"[40] (Emphasis mine.)

The organizers attempted to build a sense of trust and support between themselves and the community, part of which entailed creating an office where people felt comfortable and where they might go to discuss neighborhood problems. From the other side, running an office in this manner was a means of becoming a presence in the neighborhood and perhaps gaining acceptance. But even the creation of a "place" was not simple. Often neighborhood youths would behave disruptively and discourage others from entering. The Newark project reported that, when at first young boys came into the office to talk and play, the organizers were delighted. But when they refused to quiet down or leave and became nasty besides, the ERAPers made a decision to concentrate on the "more mature" members of the community.[41] The Trenton project had the same problem and worried that if they were very strict and kept the boys out, they would lose an important contact with the community and ". . . they may be even more of a nuisance when they start breaking windows."[42] Very soon it became quite clear that the process of building trust and establishing a constituency, which an open and available office symbolized, would be a long and slow one.

In addition, it did not take long to comprehend that building supportive and pleasant personal relations was not the ultimate purpose of the community projects. The point was to mobilize people. And there is little question that ERAP was unsuccessful in mobilizing people, a matter taken up below. At this point it is enough to say that the organizers were chastened by the large quantities of time and energy that organizing entailed, often with unclear or negative outcomes. Everything went extremely slowly with no spectacular results. After the important summer of 1964, Rennie Davis suggested that all the ERAP workers had "developed a deeper sense of the extreme slowness of building permanent community organization on a program of fundamental change . . ." He said an organizer could spend two or more hours with one individual, and through "hundreds of conversations, slowly, clusters of unemployed contacts are made and identified on city maps." The organizers then approached one person in a large area of unemployed about having a meeting. If that person agreed, he usually did not have the time to contact neighbors, so the JOIN worker called every unemployed person on the phone or went to his home. "Thirty people are contacted; eight turn out. One is a racist, but his arguments get put down by the group. One (maybe) is willing to work. . . . The others go round and round on their personal troubles. The process is slow."[43]

The goal was to be non-directive, "let the people decide." And yet, as Sara Evans points out in *Personal Politics*, organizing in the north was not like organizing in the south, where there had been self-organization and a collective racial consciousness. The urban lower classes, even blacks in a period of growing racial consciousness, were not easily moved to collective action, and the organizing was often unrewarding and frustrating. Going into a neighborhood, canvassing every apartment, hoping that either issues or people would present themselves, required a belief in the ability of people to be conscious of and to articulate their grievances, and to see the importance of collective political action. It was difficult to maintain that confidence when the results were not encouraging. A Cleveland organizer's letter in July 1965, one whole year after the first summer, stated that their organizing had been "on the level of building personal relationships." This was true for two reasons. The first was purposely as a way to change people's lives and the second was because of the "difficulty of creating enough organization to have an organizational focus instead. People who have been here a year seem frustrated with building personal relationships with no action resulting."[44]

Most of the organizing was indeed based on building personal trust, and yet even when trust was achieved, it did not insure a political outcome. Often ERAP organizers were unsure of the trajectory of their organizing because the whole process was so open-ended; it was difficult to measure progress. This form of organizing required that they live among the people they were organizing, listen carefully and attempt to let *them* determine the direction of whatever actions or organizations arose. Yet the organizers began to see that much of this work would not lead to political change and sapped their energy as well. In discussing his experiences organizing young men in Chicago, Rennie Davis pointed out that ". . . to work with them really requires that you live their way . . . that you run, and fight and drink and do the things they do, and still have the capacity to direct it towards something."[45]

How was it possible to create an "organizational focus" as well as a personal one? And how was it possible to have the capacity to direct one's work towards political and strategic goals when everyday life for the organizer meant hours talking to one person, slowly learning, by observation and living in the community, what was of concern to the residents, all of which required tremendous energy, and most of all, an unfailing political sense of the possibilities and goals.

Another letter from an organizer echoed the same problem. "I, and others, too, I think, tend to become immersed in the day-to-day affairs of ghetto organizing . . .," things like organizing for a meeting, working with a particular person, figuring out a new issue. "You rarely, if ever, stop and think of the relationship of what you're doing to what you want, much less what you want."[46] Summing up his history of ERAP, Rothstein noted that the life of an organizer was physically and emotionally draining and the victories and defeats tended to be exaggerated to create "drama in the midst of the painfully slow process of building a movement." He continued, suggesting that morale was threatened by the "irresistible comparisons with the student movement; it is sometimes hard to keep the faith in the difficult, gradual, yet solid building of a community union when the example is presented of a spectacular, though possibly more ephemeral, student demonstration."[47]

The compelling excitement of student actions and their often immediate results made the slow and not particularly successful work of community organizing seem even less rewarding by 1965. The speed-up of the pace of events had begun.

DEMOCRACY

> ERAP organizers have been among the few in SDS who have tested theories of "participatory democracy" in reality.[48]

Much of the difficulty stemmed from the organizers' ideology about what kind of community organizations they were creating and the process it required. We have seen how Rothstein proclaimed that ERAP organizers evaluated themselves on the basis of how successfully they *gave away* their power. Sara Evans points out that the vision of participatory democracy was a key one in the community projects. The idea of organizing held by most of the organizers was to talk to people without imposing any preconceived concepts and to follow their lead in developing issues and organizations. "We just talked with the women. They decided they wanted to do something. We said we'd help them in whatever they wanted . . ." according to a staff member in Cleveland.[49] And Tom Hayden said, "The most significant thing is the development of a group of people with no previous political connections who are able to speak and act without being embarrassed or dependent on the higher-ups."[50] The overriding concept motivating most new left community organizers was one of "powerlessness." Stokely Carmichael, the architect of black power in SNCC, stated a goal strikingly similar to Tom Hayden's: "I place my own hope for the United States in the growth of belief among the unqualified that they are in fact qualified: they can articulate and be responsible and hold power." And Casey Hayden, an ERAP organizer, said, "You can't talk about a kind of democracy unless those who are affected by decisions make those decisions whether the institutions in question be the welfare department, the university, the factory, the farm, the neighborhood, the country."[51]

Their goal was to create organization in which community people truly participated, began to feel more powerful and were able to act on this sense. The process of joining with others, feeling comfortable enough to speak, and developing self-confidence for political purposes, was central to the organizing and their notion of politicizing people. Success in part consisted of community people who felt strong and confident enough to talk about their grievances with city officials and not be cowed by the trappings of expertise and professionalism that the power structure promoted. It began the process of de-mystifying the power of government and experts, of de-legitimation. The Port Huron Statement had said, "As a *social system* we seek the establishment of a democracy of individual participation, governed by two central aims: that the individual share in those social decisions determining the quality and direction of his life; that society be organized to encourage independence in men."[52]

The effort to put participatory democracy into practice entailed, as we have seen, an emphasis on process and viewing that process as part of the goal. The powerful thread of prefigurative politics ran through these new left experiments, creating similar dilemmas in every situation. The only way people would begin to feel powerful and create democratic organizations was by learning to participate democratically and responsibly in local community organizations. Writing in 1966, based on their experience in the Newark project (NCUP), Norman Fruchter and Robert Kramer expressed this idea. They characterized the ERAP effort as a "dual attempt to build a movement and to achieve specific concrete changes" which generated continual tension in the projects. Organizers came quickly to understand the extreme difficulty of achieving even the most minimal changes (e.g., forcing a landlord to make repairs, forestalling an eviction or getting a traffic light installed), and also to understand that the process of committing residents to the project and building the project into a movement of opposition were dependent precisely upon the efforts to force those limited and minimal changes. In other words, without some results the project was unable to recruit or keep members. Fruchter and Kramer unequivocally state a central notion of ERAP: the two attempts, to achieve change, and to politicize and build a movement, go together, and therefore normal definitions of success and failure are inadequate. Success means the achievement of "specific change and the commitment of a resident to participate in the project's work (which occurs, at least in NCUP, more often through failure of a specific activity, directed toward change, than through the success of such activity)."[53]

The work of community organizing required this dual process; it was the central, and by now familiar, tension that ran through prefigurative politics: ERAPers were attempting to build the new society and the movement at the same time that they fought for concrete changes.

Participatory democracy had two serious political ramifications for

ERAP. The first was the problem of leadership within the community organizations and the second was the "contradiction," articulated above, between the goal of social change and achieving concrete reforms and the desire for new relationships within the movement, or put in question form, whether it is possible to construct an instrument of social change which is itself a microcosm of new relationships or a new social system. These two are related in that instrumental organizational relations and leadership (or the lack of them) create certain kinds of organization, more (or less) suited to functioning within the ongoing political system.

Rothstein wondered at the time why there was such an "inability to resolve the definition of an organizer." He observed that the word "manipulation" arose whenever projects were on the verge of decision making. He suggested that the cultural differences between middle and lower-class people were great and not easily overcome, and that students had condescending attitudes towards ghetto residents. As a result, any political persuasion took on the psychological implication of manipulation. Until cultural differences were overcome and a mutual respect existed between organizers and residents, Rothstein thought "persuasion *would* be manipulative." There needed to be recognition of the legitimacy of both groups' experience and knowledge before manipulation would disappear.[54] Locating the possibility of manipulation in the differences between middle and lower-class people, Rothstein highlighted a difficult problem for middle-class organizers, not peculiar to ERAP; but there was more than this involved for ERAPers. The current of middle-class guilt that ran through the new left was especially pronounced in ERAP. Middle-class students *were* more privileged, were often more articulate, had more options in life, and were almost always white; these characteristics were a source of guilt and encouraged the organizers to play an even less directive role than they might have. More importantly, participatory democracy translated into the community organizing context meant that organizers should not be leaders; they should neither dominate nor use their skills, instead giving away their power and teaching their skills to the community. Rothstein pointed out that poor people always had the big decisions made for them, a process organizers did not want to duplicate. Revealing guilt perhaps and certainly their anxiety about recreating domination, Rothstein described how "many organizers asked the questions, 'Why would an organizer be there if he didn't assume that he was better than ghetto residents, had some superior knowledge about a movement which he was imposing on the innocent, unknowing ghetto residents?' "[55]

In addition, at a painful meeting of most of the ERAP staff in January 1965, the image of SNCC loomed large. SNCC organizers were there and they impressed ERAP "with the image of an organizer who never organized, who by his simple presence was the mystical medium for the spontaneous expression of the people.' "[56] All these factors combined to make the role of the ERAP organizer a complex one. It is ironic that their idea was to "give away" their power, since it is not at all clear what power they had to give away. Given their notions of leadership and organization, they exercised very little power. Organizers wanted residents to generate their own energy and decisions, to "let the people decide"; at the same time they wanted to build a movement for radical change, to force social change. Referring to an ERAP staff meeting in 1964, the Cleveland Community Project wrote that the meeting raised many questions about leadership. These revolved around the issue of how much the organizers should exert themselves to shape a meeting, how much direction they should provide, and if they did intervene, what the consequences were for the meeting and the community organization. They worried that *they* would become the leaders, the energy, the source of ideas—and they often did. For example, as an experiment, the program committee of NCUP was formed. This committee was composed of representatives from all the blocks, the staff, and anyone who wished to attend meetings. Each person at the meeting had one vote. It made *all* the policy decisions at weekly meetings, and was chaired by an elected president rotated once a month.[57] Newark effectively answered the Cleveland project and others by advocating and providing "no direction" on the part of the organizers. The program committee, with its membership and decision-making provisions, was an extreme example of participatory democracy in action. Anyone could vote who attended meetings, at which policy for the organization was decided and which were chaired by a different person each month. (This was essentially how many SDS chapters were run.) The problem was that the organizers were there for a purpose and *did* have ideas about how to create changes in the neighborhoods, ideas that were in fact communicated to residents. The organizers wanted to develop individuals and the group politically, but were barred by their own ideology from doing so. Rothstein, in a later, more analytic piece highly critical of ERAP organizers and SDS, charged that by denying their own roles the organizers undermined their ability to organize honestly and were prevented from developing a sophisticated notion of the organizer role. Rothstein claims that the slogan "let the people decide" led "the organizers to pretend (at the time even to themselves) that 'the people' were deciding issues that only organizers knew about, let alone understood."[58]

Community organizers who believed in participatory democracy were faced with a perhaps insoluble dilemma: how does one organize people different from oneself on the basis of real equality? If they were there because they had a certain political analysis and goals in mind to which they wished to convert residents, how could these be communicated without playing a dominant and leadership role? While it was probably true that the organizers pretended that "the people" were deciding issues they knew little about, it was also true that the instinct of wanting to encourage indigenous leaders, of wanting to be a catalyst but not a directive or manipulative leader, sprang from a rejection of authoritarianism and of the use of middle-class skills for manipulation and exploitation. Participatory democracy created numerous pitfalls and complexities around leadership and middle-class skills.

Sara Evans sheds some light on the theoretical and practical problem of leadership in ERAP. She suggests that due to the sexism in SDS, the successes of women organizers in ERAP were unnoticed and unacknowledged. She points out that when ERAP changed from a JOIN to a GROIN approach it shifted from men's issues to "issues which sprang from the women's sphere of home and community life."[59] The most successful projects were dominated by women and eventually focused almost exclusively on organizing women. What is interesting for us is that the female organizers were not SDS leaders and consequently were less theoretically preoccupied with questions of leadership. More importantly, however, they were *less* concerned with the manipulation and power of the organizer because they were more successful organizers in *practice* than the men. The whole issue was more abstract for the men. Either because they were women and had been trained in skills that enabled them to talk and relate more easily on a personal basis and/or because they shared a common oppression with community women, the female organizers were more successful than the men in generating political consciousness and activity that acknowledged their own politics but was neither manipulative nor directed from above.

The second problem created by participatory democracy in ERAP is one with which we are by now acquainted: the dualism and contradiction inherent in prefigurative politics. It is my belief that this is what was unusual about ERAP. The unhierarchical and participatory model toward which organizers aimed provides ERAP's fundamental significance. There is little question that organizers became discouraged and often did not sense any progression since so much of their time was spent listening and being nondirective. But the ability to work with people as equals, build trust, create an office people felt was their own, to create a model of how people might relate in a future society, was part of the political goal. Rothstein said of JOIN in Chicago, ". . . We have begun to see JOIN as the focus for building a new community. Building a movement around a community." While they did not want to see JOIN as a charity organization, they were broadening their notion of what was political and of what JOIN might provide the community; this increasingly meant *build-*

ing a community. The idea was to tie people together, "making JOIN a place where people come for various parts of their lives, various normal life activities, which are movement activities as well. To build an alternative community, to build an alternative community around a political movement."[60] Fruchter and Kramer described the process. Once the project attracted enough local people so that it appeared like a cooperative to the neighborhood, with equal numbers of community people and students, ". . . the quality of relationships and values within the cooperative begin to suggest the existence of a new form (a locus of opposition)."[61] Not only the tangible successes, but the quality of relationships and values, were critical.

Carl Wittman, an organizer in Hoboken, articulated this emphasis on community, "it is important to make real what kind of society we want and we think is possible . . . the real power relationships in the society will become apparent as we try to create a new 'counter-society.' "[62] But ERAP was not simply building alternative communities; a central goal was to attain and restructure power, win concessions, change the material and political situation of people's lives. Sale suggests that ERAP never "resolved the contradictions between wanting fundamentally to change the nature of the state and building its projects around all the shoddy instruments of that state."[63] Put very bluntly, did the concern for participatory democracy undermine the prospect of strong organization and leadership? The answer must be yes. Neither ERAP nor any of the other prefigurative experiments could synthesize the two. The effort to build a grass roots movement, a community that foreshadowed the future society, in which manipulation and hierarchy would be absent and participation universal, meant that strong and instrumental organization was weakened. At the same time, the two goals are not irreconcilable: an instrument of social change can be a microcosm of new relationships and a new culture. What has been presented in this book is evidence, however, of the profound difficulty of juggling the two, and thus preventing, to paraphrase Max Weber, the collapse of politics into violence. Our society is peculiarly intolerant of politics that hint at the utopian, politics that are unpragmatic in their notions of power, how to get it, and how to wield it. The response on the tip of an American's tongue, when they hear an ideal, a vision, a humanist goal, is how could *that* happen? Who will pay? How could it possibly work when people are so selfish and competitive? Don't be ridiculous, etc. The only way in which the new left could have effected a reconciliation of the dual goals was through time and experience, neither of which they possessed. It is an historical political process, learned over years. These were fledgling political experiments, the participants for the most part ignorant of earlier experiments, feeling their way towards democratic and effective forms. If ERAP and SDS and the new left in general had not had a vision of another kind of community, they might well have created stronger organization; they certainly would have been less ambivalent about leadership, hierarchy and bureaucracy. There is no question, however, that what was new about the new left would have been lost in that case, and it is by no means a foregone conclusion that it would have meant success in the traditional political arena.

ERAP was, on balance, a failure; the organizers did not succeed in building an "interracial movement of the poor," and rarely established strong community organizations.[64] There are many factors that may explain this, as there are in explaining the weaknesses of any social movement or organizing effort. The democratic nature of ERAP community organizations was probably the least important. Vitally important, however, is the ideology of individualism that pervades American culture. People privatize and personalize their deprivation and failure; they neither band together nor develop adequate political analyses of their troubles easily. Internalizing them, collective analyses and collective political forms are not created. The prevailing pragmatism compounds passivity. The goal of mobilization, which ERAP and SDS share with every other social protest organization, is not easily achieved. And we shall see how some of the organizers began to understand that they did not have much to offer. From the residents' point of view it appeared they were being given the chance to risk the little they had for no clear gains.

But more important than ERAP's strategies and philosophy are national political explanations, social structural causes that do or do not permit populations to act. ERAPers could not, on the basis of will or hard work alone, move ghetto residents in northern cities who were not ready or willing to move in the ways ERAP hoped they might. Frances F. Piven and Richard Cloward point out in *Poor People's Movements*, "Protest wells up in response to momentous changes in the institutional order. It is not created by organizers and leaders."[65] They stress, too, that insurgency and defiance happen only during periods of structural dislocation and change and that institutional patterns shape that insurgency. During the later sixties ERAP's "constituency" participated in ghetto riots and Welfare Rights agitation, among other things, some of which grew out of ERAP efforts, but were never "caused" by leaders. In fact, in retrospect, the theorists and activists of ERAP were correct in their focus on the poor in their communities; insurgency did develop in the ghettos and cities.

By suggesting that institutional life structures defiance and protest, that ". . . people cannot defy institutions to which they have no access and to which they make no contribution,"[66] Piven and Cloward direct our attention to the question of which institutions poor people have access to. They argue, almost none. Another factor, then, in ERAP's inability to mobilize people was an inherent political dilemma in community organizing of poor people: people only marginal to the electoral and power system in this country, in their residential communities, have almost no political leverage, a fact which *they* often understood better than did the organizers. They had little power to wield and consequently expected nothing in return; few concessions could be wrought.[67] There was not much point in mobilization for negative results, not much point in endless meetings. Piven and Cloward help us to understand the attractions of mass insurgency. Unlike boring meetings and petitions to city hall, riots and spontaneous activism at least produced results. In addition they provided a release. We turn finally to an internal critique of community unions, particularly the concern about the relationship between local concessions and successes and large-scale, radical social change in America.

THE CRITIQUE OF COMMUNITY ORGANIZING

Kim Moody, an ERAP activist, criticized the GROIN approach pointing out that demonstrating that the Department of Sanitation is inefficient will not "break through the localism of the poor . . .," will not teach a class analysis, will not lead to revolutionary social change. Issues of the sort ERAP was concentrating on, according to Moody, "do not carry . . . the seeds of a radical movement."[68] He argued that a municipal or even state government could not implement a radical program and that ". . . it is the duty of the organizer to educate on the national nature of the constituency's economic problems—that is assuming that he has been able to get past neighborhood issues."[69] The authors of a project report from Cleveland asked how neighborhood groups move from local issues to making challenges to the system; they remark, "Services, such as help in getting through channels of bureaucracy, are certainly not in any way short range challenges or radical activities."[70]

One of the main criticisms of ERAP was that the organizers had no national strategy, no way of linking everyday grievances and struggles to an analysis of national power, and were doomed, therefore, to political provincialism. This argument, of course, is a version of the strategic critique of prefigurative politics. Steve Max, one of the most articulate spokespeople against the ERAP projects, characterized them as unpolitical because they did not get at the sources of power in the society. He argued that many concessions could be won from the city, state or federal government in areas such as education, housing, sanitation and discrimination, but once some demands were met and the pressure died down, the situation reverted to its former state; ". . . the conditions which produced their grievances in the first place were not changed."[71]

The gap between forcing a landlord to make repairs, tutoring a ghetto child, getting a traffic light installed, or helping someone receive welfare payments, and fundamental social change was enormous; the path between the two uncharted. Criticisms of ERAP focused on the fact that there seemed no way they could achieve social and structural change by providing a service role to the community and by sticking to local issues. "Localism" was not assaulted, revolutionary change not put on the agenda. Without issues and ways of raising questions about national power and control and about the structure of wealth in America, a radical movement could not be built. It was always easier to fall back on the lowest common denominator because it seemed so important to get things moving in a neighborhood, to show some results. Because of that, larger political questions might never arise. The tendency to get "immersed in the day-to-day affairs of ghetto organizing" often obscured the political goals of the community organization.[72]

Fruchter and Kramer contend that the value of community organizations was in disruption and challenges to democratic rhetoric and authority. Members continually questioned who should control programs, make decisions, receive benefits, represent them; and this challenged the bases of power and legitimation in the society.[73] This evaluation is based on their analysis that ". . . the possibilities for fundamental change are obscure . . ." in contemporary America and that any expression of desire for change is defused by making it appear irrational, pathological or utopian. The dual goals, remedying specific grievances and basic structural change, characterized by egalitarian and participatory institutions, meant that the project pursues "an impossibility, posits a utopian aim, since that change is clearly not achievable on the municipal level."[74]

Any opposition movement must, according to Fruchter and Kramer, "create, then enlarge, a space in which the possible alternatives can be developed, and the possible challenge to the status quo be kept alive."[75] Their picture of what ERAP might accomplish was, in other words, based on a pessimistic evaluation of the possibility for radical social change in America. "Lacking a national radical movement, or clear indications of an agency of change, the projects see their task to be the foundation and continuous enlargement of a *permanent* local movement of opposition."[76] The movement's oppositional values, its attempts to implement them, the existence of the movement at all, kept alive the possibility of a different life. Their analysis did not address itself to the issue of strategy because the paths and levers to fundamental change were in doubt, or obscure, and in that way represented a new understanding of power and domination, probably informed by Herbert Marcuse's *One Dimensional Man.*

Another critique of community organizing in ERAP came from the organizers themselves. "I go out every so often, and be friendly (which is often pleasant) and listen to people complain and say that they don't have time to do anything and that you can't do anything and they are moving, and that the neighbors and the kids are bastards. Shit."[77] The discouragement is graphic. Residents did not have time, did not believe they could accomplish anything anyway, and used their neighbors as scapegoats. Writing from Hazard, Kentucky, where he had served as ERAP director for four weeks, Steve Max said that a chronically economically depressed area was often characterized by chronically depressed people "whose struggle for existence leaves little room for organizational activity from which there is no very immediate personal benefit, particularly when they stand to lose what little they have."[78] The hopelessness and difficulty of most people's lives created fatigue and cynicism. Furthermore, it was not clear, as Max pointed out, just what they would gain by joining a community organization. I have suggested that part of ERAP's difficulty lay with the phenomenon of self-blame in our culture, which organizers began to understand; the resistance to thinking politically was monumental. And the differences between various strata within their areas began slowly to be learned. An organizer wrote in the *ERAP Newsletter* that he was beginning to see how working-class people responded differently than lower-class people to events around them. The first group tended to work towards moving out of the neighborhood and/or electing someone to represent them for their area (often a crooked politician). The second group seemed characterized by alienation or apathy. They were unable to move out and yet they always planned to leave, their subjective intentions keeping them from making any commitment to ERAP and so ". . . it's often really hard to get started with them."[79] Organizers began to comprehend the ways in which the society kept people from acting on their own behalf by scapegoating others or themselves, or through chronic depression and apathy.

Nick Egleson, working in Hoboken, New Jersey, with immigrant factory workers, said that he was coming to see that people, in fact, understand their situations quite well (something ERAPers were unable to comprehend earlier). If they did not join a community organization it was because they did not think it would get them anywhere "because they perceive the smallness of the organization compared to the enormity of the problem much better than we . . . do." He said he was ready to recognize that they were not willing to become involved on the basis of sound perceptions of where it would get them: ". . . if they fail, they get fired, if they win, they still have to work at the same stuff and live in almost the same way: they won't be much better off." Egleson continued that the kind of adjustments and coping and compromises people made to "go along with the game" ("Don't mess with the cops," "Keep your mouth shut," etc.) meant that they were probably better off.[80]

They began in other words to understand the limitations of their own organizing projects, to learn how people coped with poverty and powerlessness, what the options and concerns of their constituency were. Often they were not the concerns that ERAPers had initially thought they were, but the organizers were willing to listen and learn and to be open enough to acknowledge their own misconceptions. One could almost say, reversal though it is, that ERAPers were the community's constituency. They learned a great deal about life in America. They also learned a lot about themselves, a not insignificant result. An understanding of what it is like to be poor and neglected and of how few the options are, of the parameters within which community organizations must operate, the complexity of being an organizer of prefigurative politics in a world of hierarchical and electoral power politics, could not help changing them and their understanding of politics in America.

The organizers' commitment to "Let the People Decide," the slogan of the Newark Community Union Project, signifying their commitment to egalitarian participation, stands as the main ERAP contribution. Their desertion of the campus in favor of organizing poor people in their communities, while notable, a "to-the-people" movement reminiscent of the Russian youth movement of a hundred years before, is less significant than the *kind* of community organizations ERAP attempted to build. SNCC and ERAP stamped the first half of the sixties with their participatory and egalitarian organizing projects, experiments inspired by optimism and a democratic social vision. ERAP is an important chapter in the new left's dedication to social change in America. The concept and term "community organizing" contained fateful and contradictory impulses for ERAPers, impulses that capture the two sides of the tension between prefigurative and strategic politics. "Community" connoted direct participation by all, the lack of hierarchy, and a full connection between people, while organization implied the opposite; hierarchy, control and instrumentality. ERAPers devoted themselves to combining aspects of the two, attempting to create instrumental organizations for social change characterized by the lived ideals of a community. It was a remarkable early chapter in new left history, one that contained the seeds of subsequent achievements and dilemmas.

Conclusion

When they learned, in the midst of a perfectly reasonable conversation, that I was writing a book on the new left, a group of older generation leftists became rancorous, asking me what the new left had *wanted* anyway? They were irritated, as they had been during the sixties, saying they knew what new leftists were against, but never what they were *for*. Why was the new left so inchoate and so negative? What was its strategy? I was struck with their lack of comprehension, similar to that of Lipset and his colleagues, and by their genuine perplexity and anger. Why was it so difficult to understand what the new left was about, to feel sympathy, even if occasionally they felt admiration, for new left principles and the risks taken?

On the other end generationally, as I suggested in the Introduction, students of the late 1970s and early 1980s express a kind of cynicism or fatalism about the new left, perhaps about politics in general, both no doubt born of the current economic contraction and anxiety about their futures. That they are not impressed by the new left's accomplishments is used to buttress their sense that "you can't change anything anyway, so why try?" (Or is the predilection against political activism and risk-taking responsible for their negative assessments of the new left? Both are probably true.) The mood in the early 1980s could not be further removed from that of twenty years ago, a time of hope, expectancy and change. The political atmosphere as I write this is one of retrenchment and reaction. Central to it is the embrace of traditional values of family, religion, gender, militarism and the flag. A belief in the entitlement of individuals to equality, justice, and social welfare in a progressive society in which the state serves its citizens, is unpopular, at least with the government, and daily becoming more so. People nervously cling to what they have. Thoughts of a qualitatively different future are far from their minds.

In such an atmosphere it is easy to look back and say that the new left failed and to portray new leftists as even more foolish in hindsight than they were at the time, with little to show for their political activity. In some cases satisfaction seems to be derived from interpreting the movement as a failure, specifically pinpointing youthful radicalism as a phase that never accomplishes much. The media has done its share of focusing on the relatively few new leftists who became religious zealots, insurance salespeople, or traditional politicians, allegedly proving that even *they* recognized they had been crazy or merely going through a phase.

On one generational side, exasperation and intolerance; on the other, rejection and disdain. The new left in retrospect seems surrounded by those who have little sympathy or understanding for its project. Young and old, leftists and liberals, to say nothing of conservatives, converge in a chorus of condemnation, impatience or disinterest.

I have undertaken to demonstrate that there were many in the new left who took seriously the imperatives of its critics to be realistic and practical, to organize for social change and to build organization. It was, however, a different kind of organization than most critics had in mind. The new left worked to give life to politics as community; it is this that appears to elude commentators. New left politics rejected the criteria of narrow efficiency, efficacy, compromise, discipline and the "rules of the game" as they are played in politics today. This core of the new left project, easily missed or facilely dismissed, is surely its most vital contribution towards a just and democratic society.

My attempt to reconstruct sympathetically the prefigurative and utopian features of the new left may be faulted in various ways, but not for being fashionable. I see the demise of the new left and its virtual expulsion from America's memory as a major sign of the impoverishment of our political culture. The absence of a vigorous and visionary movement increases the contemporary malaise. We become inclined to hope for less and to accept virtually everything. Nor can it be said that the new right has picked up where the new left and women's liberation movement ceased. Far from being two sides of the same allegedly extremist coin, as some would have it, the new right and the new left are fundamentally different phenomena. Where the latter sought economic, political and racial justice, the former opposes these; where the new left sought community and an end to domination, the new right thrives on the latest techniques of manipulation and entrenched, monied elites; where the new left sought peace, the new right presses for bigger and better military build-ups; where the new left joyously affirmed life, the new right fears and constricts it.

The new left provided values by which to measure how we are forced to live, what we accept in the name of freedom, equality, democracy, or the "free world." I have tried to show that the new left of the 1960s grappled, in a more serious and sustained way than a great many commentators have been willing to recognize, with what is probably one of the most pressing issues facing any and every egalitarian social movement: the issue of community and organization. I hope I have contributed to the sociological and historical records, and beyond them to prefigurative movements of the future, which may recognize in the new left of the sixties both a living heritage and a dilemma to resolve.

Notes

Preface

1. See, for example, Christopher Hill, *The World Turned Upside Down* (New York: Viking, 1972); E.J. Hobsbawm, *Primitive Rebels* (New York: Norton, 1965); and his *Laboring Men* (New York: Doubleday, 1967); Eugene D. Genovese, *Roll, Jordan, Roll* (New York: Random House, 1976); Herbert Gutman, *Work, Culture and Society in Industrializing America* (New York: Random House, 1976); and his *The Black Family in Slavery and Freedom* (New York: Pantheon, 1976); and E.P. Thompson, *The Making of the English Working Class* (London: Victor Gollancz, 1963).

2. See Elizabeth Fox-Genovese and Eugene D. Genovese, "The Political Crisis of Social History," *Journal of Social History* X (1976): 205–220.

3. Underground newspapers provided sporadic analysis of the political situation in this country, depictions of the student and youth scenes in the 1960s, and discussions of local situations and events connected to campuses and the war. While the underground papers offer a rich source of reports on demonstrations, riots, vigils, protests and so on, they rarely include in-depth analyses of the mechanisms of protest; of the ways in which participants related, decided, organized and resisted; or of the meaning of the events for the participants. Personal reflections on these important dimensions can be found in such first-person accounts as Michael Rossman, *The Wedding within the War* (Garden City, N.Y.: Doubleday, 1971); Michael Ferber and Staughton Lynd, *The Resistance* (Boston: Beacon, 1970); and Dotson Rader, *I Ain't Marchin' Anymore* (New York: David McKay, 1969). For a very good collection of posters, leaflets, articles and ephemera from the 1960s, see Mitchell Goodman (ed.), *The Movement Toward a New America* (Philadelphia: Pilgrim Press, 1970). See also Massimo Teodori (ed.), *The New Left: A Documentary History* (Indianapolis: Bobbs Merrill, 1969). I have, in addition, relied upon such sociological depictions of the protests as William Friedland and Irving Louis Horowitz, *The Knowledge Factory: Student Power and Academic Politics in America* (Chicago: Aldine, 1970); and such journalistic accounts as Stephen Spender, *The Year of the Young Rebels* (New York: Random House, 1968).

4. Sara Evans, *Personal Politics: The Roots of Women's Liberation in the Civil Rights Movement and the New Left* (New York: Alfred A. Knopf, 1979), p. 112.

5. See Evans, *Personal Politics*, for an historical analysis of this history.

6. See my review of Evans, *Personal Politics*, in *Feminist Studies*, vol. 5, no. 3 (Fall, 1979), pp. 495–506 for a discussion of this.

Chapter 1 • *An Introduction to the New Left*

1. See, for example, Michael Harrington, "The Mystical Militants," in *Beyond the New Left*, ed. by Irving Howe (New York: Horizon, 1965); Irwin Unger, *The Movement: A History of the American New Left 1959–1972* (New York: Dodd, Mead, 1975); James Weinstein, *Ambiguous Legacy* (New York: Franklin Watts, 1975); Michael Miles, *The Radical Probe* (New York: Atheneum, 1973); James O'Brien, "Beyond Reminiscence: The New Left in History," *Radical America*, VI:4 (July–August, 1972); and his "The Development of the New Left in the U.S., 1960–1965," unpublished Ph.D. dissertation, University of Wisconsin, 1971; and Philip Altbach, ed., *Student Politics in America: A Historical Analysis* (New York: McGraw-Hill, 1974), especially the essays by Daniel Bell, Nathan Glazer and Seymour Lipset.

2. Philip Altach and S.M. Lipset, eds., *Students in Revolt* (Boston: Houghton Mifflin, 1969), pp. 498–499, 512.

3. Daniel Bell, "Columbia and the New Left," *Public Interest*, no. 13 (Fall, 1968), p. 100.

4. Edward Shils, "Dreams of Plenitude, Nightmares of Scarcity," in *Students in Revolt*, Altbach and Lipset, eds., pp. 27–28.

5. Eugene D. Genovese, *In Red and Black* (New York: Pantheon, 1968), pp. v and vi.

6. In *The Berkeley Student Revolt*, ed. by Seymour Martin Lipset and Sheldon S. Wolin (New York: Doubleday and Co., 1965), see Nathan Glazer, "Reply to Selznick" and "FSM: Freedom Fighters or Misguided Rebels?" and Seymour M. Lipset and Paul Seabury, "The Lesson of Berkeley;" in *The University Crisis Reader*, Vol. II, ed. by Immanuel Wallerstein and Paul Starr (New York: Vintage Books, 1971), see Irving Howe, "The Agony of the Campus," and Sidney Hook, "The Trojan Horse in American Higher Education"; Daniel Bell, "Columbia and the New Left," *Public Interest;* Edward Shils, "Dreams of Plenitude, Nightmares of Scarcity," in *Students in Revolt*, ed. by Altbach and Lipset; S.M. Lipset, "The Possible Effects of Student Activism on International Politics," in *Students in Revolt*, ed. by Altbach and Lipset; Christopher Lasch, "Where Do We Go From Here?," *New York Review of Books*, vol. XI, no. 6, October 10, 1968, p. 5; Lewis Feuer, *The Conflict of Generations* (New York: Basic Books, 1969).

7. "Freedom Fighters or Misguided Rebels?," p. 338.

8. "The Possible Effects of Student Activism on International Politics," p. 512.

9. "Dreams of Plenitude, Nightmares of Scarcity," p. 12.

10. "The Agony of the Campus," p. 438.

11. "Freedom Fighters or Misguided Rebels?" p. 338.

12. Ibid., p. 338.

13. *Union Democracy* (Glencoe, Ill.: The Free Press, 1956), p. 401.

14. "Dreams of Plenitude. . .," p. 12.

15. Ibid., p. 13.

16. Ibid., p. 13.

17. *The Conflict of Generations*, p. 389.
Throughout this book I have added "her" or "woman" where feasible. The original documents use "him," "his" and "man" exclusively.

18. I want to thank Frances Fox Piven for emphasizing this point in conversation.

19. Nisbet, *The Sociological Tradition*, pp. 47–48. See also Raymond Williams, *Keywords* (New York: Oxford, 19-6), p. 66; and Francis Hearn's discussion of community in his *Domination, Legitimation and Resistance* (Westport, Conn.: Greenwood, 1978).

20. See Francis Hearn, "Remembrance and Critique: The Uses of the Past for Discrediting the Present and Anticipating the Future," *Politics and Society*, V:2 (1975), for a provocative argument along these lines. See also his *Domination, Legitimation and Resistance: The Incorporation of the Nineteenth Century English Working Class*, pp. 270ff.

21. See Michael Young and Peter Wilmott, *Family and Kinship in East London* (Baltimore: Penguin, 1975), for a description of a working-class community.

22. In contrast to this perspective, see E.J. Hobsbawm's equation of political with political organizations, and his dismissal of primitive and preindustrial social movements as "pre-political," in his *Primitive Rebels*, p. 2. Frances Fox Piven and Richard Cloward have pointed to a number of difficulties arising from the equation of "political" and "organization" in their *Poor People's Movements* (New York: Pantheon, 1977). See also Hobsbawm's rejoinder in his review of their book, *New York Review of Books* (March 23, 1978).

23. "The New Left and American Politics After Ten Years," *Journal of Social Issues* XXVII (1976):23–24.

Chapter 2•*Emergence of the New Left*

1. For a detailed history of SDS, see Kirkpatrick Sale, *SDS* (New York: Random House, 1973).

2. It will be obvious to anyone familiar with the new left that the role of the Progressive Labor Movement (PL) in the development of the new left has been omitted. This is primarily because PL was not a new left organization but a Marxist-Leninist one that tried to infiltrate and reorient the politics of SDS. It did not develop out of the new left but was an offshoot of the American Communist Party and held to an orthodox Maoist politics. It represented the presence of an old left variant in the midst of the new left, but the Communist Party was the traditional left with which the new left primarily engaged, theoretically at least. It might be said that had the new left dealt head-on with PL, the latter might not have been able to successfully take over SDS at the end of the decade, but an open democratic organization is vulnerable to well-disciplined and hierarchical intrusions.

3. See James O'Brien, "The Development of a New Left in the United States," pp. 19–25. In this section of his study, entitled "A. J. Muste and Radical Pacifism," O'Brien makes the point that the radical pacifists rejected the conventional limits of political realism, and saw political problems in terms of individual morality and responsibility.

4. Jonah Raskin, *Out of the Whale: Growing Up in the American Left* (New York: Links Books, 1974), p. 215.

5. See, for example, Robert and Michael Meeropol, *We Are Your Sons* (Boston: Houghton Mifflin, 1975); Jonah Raskin, *Out of the Whale;* Kenneth Kenniston, *Young Radicals* (Harcourt, Brace and World, 1968); Jane Lazarre, *On Loving Men* (New York: Dial Press, 1978), particularly the chapter "Father and Daughter; Vivian Gornick, *The Romance of American Communism* (New York: Basic Books, 1977). It is interesting that at an SDS reunion in the summer of 1977 the children of new leftists were discussed as virtual "biological bearers" of socialism who, in the absence of others, could at least be counted on to transmit new left values.

6. These criticisms are closely connected to Marxist theory as a dimension of the old left and have wide theoretical implications which can be seen in the development of neo-Marxist, critical theory and feminist paradigms. The theoretical aspects will be touched on in Chapter Six on new working-class theory.

7. See Richard Gombin, *The Origins of Modern Leftism* (Baltimore: Penguin Books, 1975); Richard Gombin, *The Radical Tradition: A Study in Modern Revolutionary Thought* (New York: St. Martin's Press, 1979); *The Unknown Dimension: European Marxism since Lenin*, ed. by Dick Howard and Karl E. Klare (New York: Basic Books, Inc., 1972).

Chapter 3 • The Great Refusal

1. Todd Gitlin, "The Dynamics of the New Left," *Motive* (November 1970), p. 45 and (October 1970), p. 55.

2. *The World Turned Upside Down* is the title of Christopher Hill's study of radical ideas during the English revolution of the seventeenth century.

3. Miles, *The Radical Probe*, p. 64.

4. Alain Touraine, *The May Movement* (New York: Random House, 1971), p. 178.

5. Eric J. Hobsbawm, *Primitive Rebels* (New York: W.W. Norton and Co., 1965), p. 12.

6. See James O'Brien, "The Development of a New Left in the United States, 1960–1965," unpublished Ph.D. dissertation; Miles, *The Radical Probe;* Irwin Unger, *The Movement;* George Vickers, *The Formation of the New Left* (Lexington, Mass.: Lexington Books, D.C. Heath, 1975).

7. For some who did understand the cultural origins and aspects of the revolt see Richard Flacks, *Youth and Social Change* (Chicago: Markham Publishing Co., 1971); Herbert Marcuse, *An Essay on Liberation* (Boston: Beacon Press, 1969); Gregory Calvert and Carol Neiman, *A Disrupted History: The New Left and the New Capitalism* (New York: Random House, 1971); and Goodman, ed., *The Movement Toward a New America.*

8. M. Teodori, ed., *The New Left*, p. 363.

9. A. Touraine, *The May Movement*, p. 270.

10. Stephen Spender, *The Year of the Young Rebel*, said: "Some critics sneer at the students for their equating what are called in America 'pareital rights' with issues like Vietnam, as though to do so is frivolous. I think these critics are wrong. That the students want to relate intimate personal values of living with public values is one of the most serious aspects of their movement," p. 12.

11. See, for example, James O'Brien, "Beyond Reminiscence: The New Left in History," *Radical America*, vol. 6, No. 4 (July-August, 1972). In this view a distinction is made between support for issues based on moralism and a politics based on the self-interest of an oppressed group, the latter of which is properly radical.

12. See Richard Rothstein, "Representative Democracy in SDS," *Liberation* 9 (February 1972), p. 11; Todd Gitlin, "The Dynamics of the New Left," *Motive* (October–November 1970); Staughton Lynd, "The New Radicals and Participatory Democracy," SDS pamphlet, reprinted from *Dissent* (Summer 1965); conversation with Bob Ross, Worcester, Mass., September 29, 1977.

13. The ". . . remarkable liberation of energy . . . in which men felt free . . ." to which Christopher Hill refers in his history of the English Revolution may be likened to the eruption of repressed dreams and brief periods of spontaneous democracy and solidarity achieved during the 1960s. *The World Turned Upside Down*, p. 123. Looking at it from the other side, it is equally speculative to assume that an anti-capitalist structural vocabulary and critique of capitalism *necessarily* leads to radical instincts or activity. Students of the history of Marxism must be chastened about the social radicalism which "automatically" follows from a Marxist analysis.

14. Todd Gitlin's phrase, "The Dynamics of the New Left."

15. Thompson, *The Making*, p. 88.

16. Carl Oglesby, "Trapped in a System," in *The New Left*, ed. by Teodori, p. 184.

17. Arlene Eisen Bergen, "Don't Follow Leaders, Watch Parking Meters," *The Movement*, August, 1968.

18. Hal Draper, *The New Student Revolt* (New York: Grove Press, 1965), p. 98.

19. For the function of risk-taking and creation of sect mentality by being separate and different, see Barrie Thorne's dissertation, "Resisting the Draft," Brandeis University, 1971.

20. It is also true that although students were massed in large institutions and could therefore easily collectivize their protests, they were generally there only for four years, which presented serious obstacles to institutionalization on a permanent basis. For discussion of this and other sociological aspects of students, see Altbach and Lipset, *Student Politics*; Altbach, *Student Politics in America*; and for a good overall summary, Jerome Skolnick, "Student Protest," in his *The Politics of Protest* (New York: Ballantine, 1969). See Chapter Five for the changing role of universities and students in American life.

21. Philip Altbach, "Student Activism and Academic Research," introductory

essay to P. Altbach and D. Kelly bibliography, *American Students* (Lexington, Mass.: Lexington Books, D.C. Heath, 1973) states there are at least one hundred and fifty books, articles and doctoral dissertations on FSM.

22. Feuer, *The Conflict of Generations*, p. 441.

23. Larry Spence, "Berkeley: What it Demonstrates," in *Revolution at Berkeley*, ed. by Michael Miller and Susan Gilmore (New York: Dell, 1965), p. 218.

24. Paul Jacobs and Saul Landau, *The New Radicals* (New York: Random House, 1966), p. 62.

25. Mario Savio, "Comments on Berkeley," from *The Free Student*, no. 1, 1965 (Bancroft Library, University of California, Berkeley).

26. See Clark Kerr, *The Uses of the University* (New York: Harper and Row, 1966) and Chapter Six for a discussion of new left theory in relation to these developments.

27. Mario Savio, "The Berkeley Student Rebellion of 1964," in *The FSM and the Negro Revolution* (Detroit: News and Letters, 1965).

28. Larry Spence, "Berkeley: What it Demonstrates," p. 220.

29. *Ibid.*, p. 222.

30. *Ibid.*, p. 222.

31. See Carl Oglesby, "Trapped in a System," the speech delivered at the October 27, 1965 antiwar march in Washington, D.C. for an early analysis of corporate liberalism in which he said of the men responsible for waging the war (Truman, Eisenhower, Kennedy, Bundy, McNamara, Rusk, Lodge, etc.): "They are not moral monsters. They are all honorable men. They are all liberals." And then, "We do not say these men are evil. We say rather, that good men can be divided from their compassion by the institutional system that inherits us all. Generation in and out, we are put to use. People become instruments. Generals do not hear the screams of the bombed; sugar executives do not see the misery of the cane cutters—for to do so is to be that much *less* the general, that much *less* the executive," p. 186. This statement led towards a structural analysis of the power of the system and its institutions to shape lives in its own interests.

32. Savio, "Comments on Berkeley."

33. Cited in Feuer, *The Conflict of Generations,* p. 441.

34. Sol Stern, "A Deeper Disenchantment," *Liberation* (February 1965) and *Revolution at Berkeley*, ed. by Miller and Gilmore, p. 233.

35. Rossman, *The Wedding Within the War*, p. 11.

36. Tape recording made during the 1964 sit-in at the University of California, Berkeley. In *The FSM and the Negro Revolution.*

37. Hal Draper, *Berkeley: The New Student Revolt*, p. 189.

38. *Ibid.*, p. 190.

39. Eric Levine, "Overview of the FMS," *SDS Bulletin*, January 1965.

40. James Petras, "On Mounting Political Action," in *Berkeley: The New Student Revolt*, ed. by H. Draper, p. 224.

41. Rossman, *The Wedding Within the War*, p. 133.

42. Irving L. Horowitz, "Social Deviance and Political Marginality," *Ideology and Utopia in the United States* (New York: Oxford University Press, 1977), p. 388.

43. Stephen Spender, *The Year of the Young Rebels*, p. 111.

44. Spence, "Berkeley: What it Demonstrates," p. 222.

45. Rossman, *The Wedding within the War*, p. 76.

46. Martin Jezer in WIN of the Cornell contingent in the Spring Mobilization to End the War in Vietnam, April 1967, quoted in *The Resistance*, ed. by M. Ferber and S. Lynd, p. 76.

47. Dotson Rader, *I Ain't Marchin' Anymore* (New York: David McKay, 1969), pp. 30, 38, 29.

48. *The Movement Toward a New America*, ed. by M. Goodman, p. 312.

49. Rader, *I Ain't Marchin'*, pp. 116, 117, 118.

50. *Ibid.*, p. 122.

51. Norman Mailer, *The Armies of the Night* (New York: Signet, 1968), p. 130.

52. *The Resistance*, ed. by Ferber and Lynd, p. 136.

53. Thorne Deyer, "Anti-War Battle at the Pentagon," *The Fifth Estate* (Detroit), November 1–15, 1967.

54. Thorne Dreyer, *The Rag* (Austin, Texas), October 30, 1967.

55. Margie Stamberg, "October 21, 1967: White Left Gets Its Shit Together," *The Rag*, October 30, 1967.

56. Tyrone Drever, *The Rag*, October 30, 1967.

57. Dreyer, *The Fifth Estate*, November 1–15, 1967. Emphasis added.

58. George Dennison, quoted in *The Resistance*, ed. by Ferber and Lynd, p. 139.

59. "October 20, Oakland Resistance Termed Peaceful, Friendly!" *LA Free Press*, October 27, 1967.

60. Buddy Stein, "A New Kind of Protest," *Steps*, Journal of Free University of Berkeley, no. 2, p. 35.

61. Text by the Communications Co. of San Francisco, SHSW, n.d.

62. *The Resistance*, ed. by Ferber and Lynd, p. 143.

63. Mike Price, "Report on the Berkeley Strike," in *The Paper*, East Lansing, Michigan, January 16, 1967.

64. "Sit-in at Stanford," in *The Knowledge Factory*, pp. 299 and 300.

65. "Reply to Selznick," in *The Berkeley Student Revolt*, ed. by Seymour M. Lipset and Sheldon S. Wolin, p. 315.

66. "The DOW Protest: A Narrative," *Connections*, November 1–14, 1967.

67. Letter in *New York Review of Books*, September 12, 1968, p. 42.

68. See Sara Evans, *Personal Politics*, for an in-depth discussion of this and my review of her book in *Feminist Studies* (Fall, 1979).

69. Evans, *Personal Politics*, p. 172.

70. *They Should Have Served that Cup of Coffee: Seven Radicals Remember the Sixties*, ed. by Dick Cluster (Boston: South End Press, 1979), p. 22.

71. Spender, *The Year of the Young Rebels*, pp. 53, 54.

72. *The Rag*, May Day, 1967.

73. Spender, *The Year of the Young Rebels*, p. 104.

74. *The Resistance*, ed. by Ferber and Lynd, p. 160.

75. Basil Bernstein, *Class, Codes and Control* (London: Routledge and Kegan Paul, 1971); Jürgen Habermas, *Toward a Rational Society* (Boston: Beacon Press, 1970); Habermas, *Legitimations Crisis* (Boston: Beacon Press, 1975); Claus Mueller, *The Politics of Communication* (New York: Oxford University Press, 1973);

Alvin Gouldner, *The Dialectic of Ideology and Technology* (N.Y.: Seaburg Press, 1976); Gouldner, *The Future of Intellectuals and the Rise of the New Class* (N.Y: Seaburg Press, 1979).

76. Gouldner, *The Dialectic of Ideology and Technology*, p. 19.

77. *The Daily Cardinal*, May 18, 1966, University of Wisconsin, Madison, Memorial Library, archives.

78. *Ibid.*, May 24, 1966.

79. *Ibid.*

80. Statement from the New Haven group, *The Resistance*, ed. by Ferber and Lynd, p. 54.

81. Tom Cornell quoted in *The Resistance*, p. 27; and a description of the Des Moines, Iowa meeting, August 1966, *The Resitance*, ed. by Ferber and Lynd, p. 55.

82. *The Resistance*, p. 49.

83. *Ibid.*, p. 91.

84. *Ibid.*, p. 130.

85. For a discussion of this see Ann Popkin, "The Personal is Political: The Women's Liberation Movement," in *They Should Have Served that Cup of Coffee*, ed. by D. Cluster.

86. *The Resistance*, p. 132.

87. A. Touraine, *The May Movement*, p. 165.

88. E.J. Hobsbawm, *Primitive Rebels*, p. 61.

Chapter 4 • Politics as Community

1. Greg Calvert, "National Secretary's Report," *New Left Notes*, December 23, 1966.

2. Hannah Arendt, *On Revolution* (New York: The Viking Press, 1963), pp. 259 and 265.

3. Michael Rossman, "The Birth of FSM," in *The Wedding within the War* (New York: Doubleday, 1971), p. 110.

4. Arendt, *On Revolution*, p. 249.

5. Allen Green, "For a Revolutionary Ideology," *New Left Notes*, October 14, 1966.

6. See Gregory Calvert and Carol Nieman's book *A Disrupted History: The New Left and the New Capitalism* for a full expression of this politics and an interpretation of the new left from this point of view, written later.

7. "A Statement of Values," *New Left Notes*, November 4, 1966.

8. *New Left Notes*, November 25, 1966.

9. *Ibid.* Emphasis in the original.

10. Sheldon Wolin, *Politics and Vision* (Boston: Little, Brown, 1960), p. 376.

11. Greg Calvert, National Secretary, "From Protest to Resistance," *New Left Notes*, January 13, 1967.

12. Henri Lefebvre, *The Explosion: Marxism and the French Revolution* (New York: Monthly Review Press, 1969), p. 113. See this book for a discussion of the French May in these terms.

13. Michels, *Political Parties*, p. 335.

14. *Ibid.*, p. 70.

15. *Ibid.*, p. 338.

16. *Ibid.*, p. 61.

17. Michael Ferber and Staughton Lynd, *The Resistance* (Boston: Beacon Press, 1970), p. 243.

18. Mario Savio speech, December 2, 1964 in Hal Draper, *The New Student Revolt*, p. 98.

19. Carl Boggs, "Marxism, Prefigurative Communism and the Problem of Workers' Control," *Radical America* (Winter 1977–78), p. 100.

20. Gianni Statera, *Death of a Utopia* (New York: Oxford University Press, 1975).

21. *Worklist*, February 18, 1963.

22. Teodori, ed., *The New Left*, Introduction, p. 50.

23. Tom Hayden, "SNCC, the Qualities of Protest," *Studies on the Left* 1 (1965), p. 123.

24. Young, *An Infantile Disorder?* (Boulder, Colo.: Westview Press, 1977), p. 272.

25. *Ibid.*, p. 80.

26. Richard Gombin, *The Origins of Modern Leftism*, (Baltimore: Penguin Books, 1977), p. 272.

27. Max Weber, "Politics as a Vocation," in *From Max Weber*, ed. by H. Gerth and C. Wright Mills (New York: Oxford University Press, 1973), p. 126.

28. Carl Davidson, "Toward a Student Syndicalist Movement, or University Reform Revisited," in *The University Crisis Reader*, ed. by I. Wallerstein and P. Starr, vol. II, p. 107.

29. For books on participatory democracy, see C. George Benello and Dimitrios Roussopoulos, eds., *The Case for Participatory Democracy* (New York: Viking Press, 1972); Terrence E. Cook and Patrick Morgan, eds., *Participatory Democracy* (San Francisco: Canfield Press, n.d.); Daniel C. Kramer, *Participatory Democracy: Developing Ideals of the Political Left* (Cambridge, Mass.: Schenkman Publishing Co., 1972). For important articles, see Staughton Lynd, "The New Radicals and Participatory Democracy," SDS pamphlet, reprinted from *Dissent* (Summer 1965); S. Lynd, "Prospects for the New Left," *Liberation* 10 (Winter 1971); Richard Flacks, "Revolt of the Young Intelligentsia," in *The New American Revolution*, eds. Roderick Aya and Norman Miller (New York: The Free Press, 1971); "Introduction," *The New Left*, ed. M. Teodori; C. George Benello, "Participatory Democracy and the Dilemma of Change," in *The New Left*, ed. Priscilla Long (Boston: Porter Sargent, 1969); Martin Oppenheimer, "The Sociology of P.D.," *New Left Notes*, November 25, 1966; Bruce Payne, "SNCC: An Overview Two Years Later," *The New Student Left*, ed. by M. Cohen and D. Hale; Richard Flacks, "On the Use of Participatory Democracy," *Dissent* 13 (November 1966); John Cammett, "Socialism and Participatory Democracy," in *Revival of American Socialism*, ed. George Fischer; and scores of articles throughout the decade in the newspapers and periodicals of the movement and the new left.

30. Tom Hayden, "Student Social Action," pamphlet, mimeographed, 1962.

31. This is a direct quotation from the Port Huron Statement.

32. Richard Rothstein, "Representative Democracy in SDS," *Liberation* (February 1972), 11. Lynd also refers to participatory democracy as a form of socialism in "The New Radicals and Participatory Democracy," *Dissent* (Summer 1966).

33. "Some Notes on Participatory Democracy," *New Left Notes*, May 6, 1966.

34. Marcuse, *An Essay on Liberation*, p. 69.

35. Lynd, "The New Radicals and Participatory Democracy," SDS pamphlet.

36. Ibid.

37. Kenneth Keniston, "Young Radicals and the Fear of Power," in *The Politics and Anti-Politics of the Young*, ed. by Michael Brown (Beverly Hills, Calif.: Glencoe Press, 1969).

38. Richard Rothstein, "Representative Democracy in SDS," *Liberation* (February 1972); Norman Fruchter, "SDS: In and Out of Context," *Liberation* (February 1972).

39. Rothstein, "Representative Democracy in SDS." All the quotations are taken from pp. 14–17.

40. Norman Fruchter, "SDS: In and Out of Context," *Liberation* (February, 1972), p. 28.

41. *Ibid.*, p. 26.

42. *Ibid.*, pp. 28 and 26.

43. *ERAP Newsletter,* July 23, 1965 from Richie, Neil and Nina.

44. *Ibid.*

45. "Participatory Democracy, Collective Leadership and Political Responsibility," *New Left Notes*, December 18, 1967.

46. "Prospects for the New Left," *Liberation* (Winter 1971), p. 23.

47. See Marge Piercy, *Vida* (New York: Summit Books, 1980) for a novelistic account of political consciousness and activity of a sector of new leftists in those years.

48. Arendt, *On Revolution*, p. 268.

Chapter 5 • Politics as Organization

1. See Todd Gitlin, *The Whole World is Watching: Mass Media in the Making and Unmaking of the New Left* (Berkeley: University of California Press, 1980) and "Spotlights and Shadows: Television and the Culture of Politics," *College English*, vol. 38, no. 8 (April 1977) for an analysis of how the media controlled and constrained the movement by creating leaders, issues and politics *for* the movement. Further, by simplifying and making immediate the issues and consequently speeding up the timetable of the movement, the organic rhythm and progression was lost and the movement developed *in relation to the media* rather than its constituencies. Gitlin focuses especially on 1965 when he sees the media's "spotlight" transforming SDS into a mass movement with which it was unprepared to deal.

2. "National Secretary's Report," *New Left Notes*, June 17, 1966.

3. "Spotlights and Shadows," p. 8000. Also see Robert Ross, "Primary Groups in Social Movements: A Memoir and Interpretation," *Journal of Voluntary Action Research* (February 1977).

4. Milton Mankoff, "The Political Socialization of Radicals and Militants in the Wisconsin Movement during the 1960s," Ph.D. dissertation, University of Wisconsin, 1969.

5. See Sale, *SDS*, pp. 280ff.

6. Rossman, *The Wedding Within the War*, p. 304.

7. Sale, *SDS*, p. 7.

8. See Hannah Fenichel Pitkin, *The Concept of Representation* (Berkeley: University of California Press, 1967) for a discussion of representation. See also Roland Pennock and John Chapman (eds.), *Representation* (New York: Atherton Press, 1968); Hannah Arendt, *On Revolution* (New York: Viking Press, 1963); N. Fainstein and S. Fainstein, *Urban Political Movements* (Englewood Cliffs, N.J.: Prentice-Hall, 1974), for a discussion of urban political movements; Norbert Bobbio, "Are There Alternatives to Representative Democracy?" *Telos* 35 (Spring (1978); and "Why Democracy?" *Telos* (Summer 1978); and M. Bookchin, "Beyond Neo Marxism," *Telos* 36 (Summer 1978). Also see, Ralph Miliband's discussion of "Class and Party," in *Marxism and Politics* (New York: Oxford University Press, 1978).

9. Cited in Howard Zinn, *SNCC: The New Abolitionists* (Boston: Beacon Press, 1965), p. 36.

10. Mimeograph on internal education workshop during a National Council meeting, n.d., Todd Gitlin's file.

11. *SDS Bulletin*, no. 3 (1962–63).

12. *Worklist*, April 7, 1965.

13. *New Left Notes*, February 25, 1966.

14. "Whatever Became of the New Left?" *New Left Notes*, August 12, 1966.

15. *Ibid*.

16. Shero, *New Left Notes*, August 24, 1966.

17. Michael Useem, *Protest Movements in America* (Indiana: Bobbs Merrill, 1975).

18. Joseph Gusfield, "The Study of Social Movements," in *The Encyclopedia of the Social Sciences*, ed. by David L. Sills (New York: Macmillan Co., Free Press, 1968).

19. *Poor People's Movements* (New York: Vintage Press, 1979), p. xv.

20. Neil Buckley, "Burning Questions of Our Movement," 1968, mimeograph.

21. *Ibid*.

22. December Conference, mimeograph.

23. Peter and Stevie Freedman, *New Left Notes*, March 11, 1966.

24. *Worklist*, January 30, 1965.

25. *SDS Bulletin*, January 1965.

26. *New Left Notes*, December 23, 1966.

27. Sale, *SDS*, p. 215. He is referring to the period just after the Kewadin Convention in the summer of 1965.

28. Michael Schwartz, *Radical Protest and Social Structure* (New York: Academic Press, 1976); *Poor People's Movements* (NY: Vintage Press, 1979).

29. Paul Booth and Lee Webb, "The Anti-War Movement: From Protest to Radical Politics," mimeographed.

30. *SDS Bulletin*, March 1964.

31. Don McKelvey, "The SDS: Where Are We Going?" *Discussion Bulletin,* 1964, mimeograph.

32. Potter, *SDS Bulletin*, July 1964.

33. Potter, *Worklist*, April 7, 1965. Emphasis added, last quotation.

34. In defining organizations, Charles Perrow says, "Organizations must be seen as tools. . . . A tool is something you can get something done with. . . . It gives you power that others do not have." *Complex Organizations* (Glenview, Ill.: Scott, Foresman and Co., 1972), p. 14.

35. *SDS Bulletin*, July 1964.

36. Dick Flacks, special supplement on December National Council meeting, 1964, mimeograph.

37. *Worklist*, January 30, 1965.

38. Ray Dahlberg and Carolyn Craven, mimeographed letter.

39. For an extended criticism of this tendency, see Rothstein, "Representative Democracy in SDS," *Liberation* (February, 1972).

40. *ERAP Newsletter,* October 5, 1965. This is the source of his later critique of participatory democracy and the "SNCC mystique," published in the early 1970s. See pp. 60–61.

41. Rothstein, "Representative Democracy," p. 17.

42. *ERAP Newsletter*, July 23, 1965.

43. SDS leaflets for December Conference, December 27–31, 1965, mimeograph.

44. See Sale, *SDS*, pp. 248–52 for a discussion of the December Conference.

45. *Ibid.*, pp. 248–252.

46. See Sale, p. 252, and Sara Evans, *Personal Politics*, pp. 156ff.

47. *Personal Politics*, p. 157.

48. National Secretary's Report, December Conference, mimeograph. Emphasis mine.

49. Kissinger, mimeograph.

50. Max, December Conference, mimeograph.

51. *Ibid.*

52. Written September 1965 and included in the December Conference packet, mimeograph.

53. Pardun, "Organizational Democracy," December Conference, mimeograph.

54. Shero, December Conference, mimeograph.

55. *Worklist*, April 7, 1965.

56. "Clear Lake: New Answers or New Tactics" *New Left Notes*, September 23, 1966.

57. *New Left Notes*, October 1, 1966.

58. *New Left Notes*, February 20, 1966.

59. "Resistance and the Movement," *New Left Notes*, March 20, 1967.

60. Todd Gitlin, "The Politics and Vision of the New Left," (San Francisco: Clergy and Laymen, REP, mimeograph, Bancroft Library, University of California, Berkeley).

61. See Norman Fruchter, "SDS: In and Out of Context," *Liberation* (Feb-

ruary, 1972), for a discussion of the traits and experiences of the elite of the developing social force created in political clubs and other school activities of their high schools and colleges. Their initial trajectory was to be successful politicians and leaders. Also see Sale, *SDS*, p. 356n, for Nick Egleson's background confirming this.

62. Fruchter, "SDS: In and Out of Context," p. 26.

63. "Some Thoughts on SDS in the Coming Year," from the University of Chicago for the 1964 SDS Convention, mimeograph.

64. Fall 1964, mimeograph.

65. December Conference, mimeograph.

66. McKelvey, *New Left Notes*, June 3, 1966; August 12, 1966.

67. *New Left Notes*, October 28, 1966.

68. "Campus Organizers," *New Left Notes*, April 3, 1964.

69. See Sale, *SDS*, p. 336 for a description of these.

70. *Ibid.*, p. 347.

71. Condit, *New Left Notes*, April 3, 1967. In his proposal, Brecher had acknowledged old left cadre schools *positively*, citing them as examples to be emulated.

72. National Secretary's Report, *New Left Notes*, June 17, 1966.

73. James Forman, *The Making of Black Revolutionaries* (New York: Macmillan, 1972), p. 425.

74. "The SDS Phenomenon," *New Left Notes*, July 29, 1966.

75. "A Letter to the New Left," *New Left Notes*, August 5, 1966.

Chapter 6 • Students as Agency

1. *Worklist*, vol. 1, no. 12½, December 1964.

2. See, e.g., Alvin W. Gouldner, *The Two Marxisms: Contradictions and Anomalies in the Development of Theory* (New York: The Seabury Press, 1980), especially pp. 346–52.

3. Teodori, ed., *The New Left*, p. 414.

4. "Ideology at Clear Lake," *New Left Notes*, September 16, 1966.

5. Clark Kerr, *The Uses of the University* (New York: Harper and Row, 1966); Daniel Bell, "Notes on the Post-Industrial Society (1)," *The Public Interest* 6 (Winter 1967); Seymour Martin Lipset, "The Activists: A Profile," *The Public Interest* 13 (Fall 1968).

6. Kerr, *The Uses*, p. 50.

7. *Ibid.*, p. 91.

8. *Ibid.*, p. 88.

9. Lipset, "The Activists," p. 7.

10. "The Multiversity: Crucible of the New Working Class," in I. Wallerstein and P. Starr, eds., vol. 1, p. 90.

11. *Ibid.*, p. 89.

12. *Ibid.*, p. 90.

13. Hayden, "Student Social Action," 1962, mimeographed pamphlet.

14. *Ibid.*

15. *Ibid.*

16. "The Intellectual as an Agent of Social Change," mimeographed pamphlet, 1963.

17. See James Weinstein and David Eakins, eds., *For a New America: Essays in History and Politics from "Studies on the Left" 1959–1967* (N.Y.: Random House, 1970).

18. Hayden, "Student Social Action."

19. C. Wright Mills, "Letter to the New Left," in *The New Left: A Collection of Essays,* ed. by Priscilla Long (Boston: Porter Sargent, 1969), p. 22.

20. It is worth noting that many commentators at the time and since have remarked that the new left was either ignorant of and/or hostile to the working class. From this point of view, interest in the new working class was an avoidance of the traditional working class or a function of students' own self-interest. For a discussion of an aspect of this, see p. 108 ff. herein.

21. Serge Mallet, *Essays on the New Working Class,* ed. and trans. by Dick Howard (St. Louis: Telos Press, 1975); Andre Gorz, *Strategy for Labor* (Boston: Beacon Press, 1967).

22. For a brief summary, see Gareth Stedman Jones, "The Meaning of the Student Revolt," *Student Power,* ed. by R. Blackburn and A. Cockburn (Baltimore: Penguin Books, 1969).

23. See Bettina Aptheker, *The Academic Rebellion in the United States* (New Jersey: Citadel Press, 1972), and David Smith, *Who Rules the Universities?* (New York: Monthly Review Press, 1974) for an elaboration of this argument.

24. Carl Davidson, *The University Crisis Reader,* vol. 1, p. 69.

25. *Ibid.,* pp. 97, 98.

26. Sale, *SDS,* p. 292.

27. See John and Margaret Rowntree, "Youth as a Class," *Our Generation,* nos. 1-2 (May, June, July 1968).

28. See Greg Calvert, "In White America," *The New Left,* ed. by M. Teodori, for one of the earliest American new left articulations of this idea.

29. *University Crisis Reader,* vol. 1, p. 196.

30. R. Gottlieb, G. Tenney and D. Gilbert, "Praxis and the New Left," from the "Port Authority Statement," *New Left Notes,* February 13, 1967.

31. See Serge Mallet, *Essays on the New Working Class,* ed. by Dick Howard (St. Louis: Telos Press, 1975) and Arthur Hirsch, *The French New Left: An Intellectual History from Sartre to Gorz* (Boston: South End Press, 1981) for later discussions of the significance of Mallet and Gorz's work.

32. A. Gorz, *Strategy for Labor,* p. 105.

33. R. Gottlieb, G. Tenney and D. Gilbert, "Toward a Theory of Social Change in America," *New Left Notes,* May 22, 1967.

34. *The May Movement* (New York: Random House, 1971), p. 365.

35. See "Revolt of the Young Intelligentsia," in *The New American Revolution,* ed. by Roderick Aya and Norman Miller; "On the New Working Class and Strategies for Social Change," in *The New Pilgrims,* ed. by Altbach and Laufer (New York: David McKay, 1972); and his book *Youth and Social Change* (Chicago: Markham, 1971).

36. Gergory Calvert and Carol Nieman, "Where are We Heading?" *Guardian,* June 15, 1968.

37. Flacks, "Revolt of the Young . . .," p. 238.

38. R. Flacks, "Social and Cultural Meanings of Student Revolt: Some Informal Comparative Observations," *Social Problems* 17 (Winter 1970), p. 365.

39. Alvin W. Gouldner, *The Dialectic of Ideology and Technology* (New York: Seabury Press, 1976), p. 188.

40. Seymour Martin Lipset, "The Possible Effects of Student Activism on International Politics," in *Students in Revolt*, ed. by S.M. Lipset and P. Altbach.

41. First published as "The New Class Project, Part I," *Theory and Society*, vol. 6, no. 2 (September 1978) and "The New Class Project, Part II," vol. 6, no. 3 (November 1978); in book form, *The Future of Intellectuals and the Rise of the New Class* (New York: The Seabury Press, 1979). See also, Claus Mueller, *The Politics of Communication* (New York: Oxford University Press, 1973).

42. G. Calvert and C. Neiman, *Guardian*, June 15, 1968.

43. C. Oglesby, "Notes on a Decade Ready for the Dustbin," *Liberation* (August-September, 1969), p. 13.

44. G. Calvert, "In White America," in *The New Left*, ed. by M. Teodori, p. 417.

45. *Radical America*, vol. 11, no. 3 (May, June 1977). Reprinted with ten responses and a rejoinder by the Ehrenreichs in *Between Labor and Capital*, ed. by Pat Walker (Boston: South End Press, 1979).

46. *Between Labor and Capital*, p. 12.

47 See Paul Breines, "Marcuse and the New Left," in *The Revival of American Socialism*, ed. by George Fischer (New York: Oxford University Press, 1971) for a discussion of the new left's resentment of Marcuse and of theory around 1968.

48. Greg Calvert, "In White America," in *The New Left: A Documentary History*, ed. by M. Teodori (Indianapolis: Bobbs Merrill 1969), p. 414.

49. Carl Oglesby, "Notes on a Decade Ready for the Dustbin," p. 15.

50. Marx and Engels, *Selected Works* in two volumes (Moscow: Foreign Language Publishing House, 1958), vol. 1, p. 247.

51. Tom Nairn, "Why It Happened," in *The Beginning of the End* (London: Panther Book, 1968), p. 173.

52. Oglesby, "Notes on a Decade. . .," p. 10. Also see Murray Bookchin, *Listen Marxist* (New York: Times Changes Press, 1971) for inadequacies of Marxism in what he calls a post-scarcity phase. This bitter statement was made in the context of the demise of SDS in 1969 and its takeover by the Progressive Labor Party, an orthodox Marxist organization.

53. "The Meaning of the Student Revolt," in *Student Power*, ed. by Alexander Cockburn and Robin Blackburn, p. 28.

54. Alain Touraine, *The May Movement*, p. 270.

55. And many women swept past all the men, all the left political currents, out of the new left into feminism.

56. This notion echoes Hayden's 1963 statement in ERAP that we have to get off the campuses and ". . . get where the people are. . ." Sale, SDS, p. 107. See text below, p. 128, Chapter Seven for this discussion.

57. "Towards a Movement of Student Syndicalism," *Our Generation*, vol. 5, no. 1, p. 107.

58. Letter from Steven Shank, *New Left Notes*, October 9, 1967.

59. *New Left Notes*, October 16, 1967.

60. Al Spangler, "Hollow Suggestions for Serious Issues," *New Left Notes*, October 16, 1967.

61. *New Left Notes*, November 27, 1967.

62. "Finding Our Direction from History," *New Left Notes*, December 11, 1967.

63. For example, "Consumption: Domestic Imperialism," by D. Gilbert, R. Gottlieb and S. Sutheim was not reissued at that time because it was not anti-imperialist enough, stressing instead domestic and cultural characteristics of advanced capitalism. See *The New Left*, ed. by M. Teodori, pp. 425–37.

64. "Notes on a Decade. . .," *Liberation*, p. 15.

65. Mark Klieman, *New Left Notes*, April 29, 1968.

66. *The New Left*, ed. by M. Teodori, p. 417.

67. *The Movement*, December 1967, emphasis added.

68. Andrew Kopkind, "The New Left: Chicago and After," *The New York Review of Books*, September 1967.

69. Jim O'Brien, "Beyond Reminiscence: The New Left in History," *Radical America* 4 (July–August 1972).

70. For personal and fictional accounts of this political consciousness see Marge Piercy, *Vida* (New York: Summit Books, 1980); Jonah Raskin, *Out of the Whale: Growing Up Left in America* (New York: Link Books, 1974); Susan Stern, *With the Weathermen* (Garden City, N.Y.: Doubleday and Co., 1975); Samuel Melville, *Letters from Attica* (New York: William Morrow and Co., 1972) with a useful introduction by John Cohen.

71. Richard Flacks, "Whatever Happened to the New Left?" *New Left Notes*, August 12, 1966.

72. Michael Rossman, "Chicago, First Day, Last Day," *The Wedding Within the War*, p. 277. See the film "The War at Home," produced by Catalyst Films, Madison, Wisconsin.

73. Interview with Tom Hayden, *The Movement*, October 1968.

74. Staughton Lynd, "Towards a History of the New Left," in *The New Left*, ed. by Priscilla Long. See Nigel Young, *An Infantile Disorder?* for an analysis in this vein.

75. Bob Goodman, "The Southern Student Organizing Committee Folds in Favor of SDS Politics," *The Guardian*, June 21, 1969.

76. Frank Bardacke, "Stop-the-Draft Week," in *Towards a New America*, ed. Mitchell Goodman, p. 478.

77. See *Weatherman*, edited by Hal Jacobs (Ramparts Press, 1970), for Weatherman documents. Also see note 70 in this chapter for personal accounts of members or of sympathizers.

Chapter 7 • Economic Research and Action Project

1. *SDS Bulletin*, March–April, 1963.

2. SDS *Bulletin*, October 1963; see Kirkpatrick Sale, *SDS*, pp. 131-50, for details of ERAP history (New York: Vintage, 1973); see also George Vickers, *The Formation of the New Left* (Lexington, Mass.: Lexington Books, D.C. Heath,

1975); and Richard Rothstein, "Short History of ERAP," *SDS Bulletin*, vol. 4, no. 1, Brancroft Library, Social Protest Report, University of California, Berkeley. Rothstein is reprinted in *The New Left*, ed. by Priscilla Long (Boston: Porter Sargent, 1969); Sara Evans, *Personal Politics*, Chapter Six, "Let the People Decide."

3. *SDS Bulletin*, October 1963.

4. *SDS Bulletin*, March 1964.

5. Todd Gitlin, "On Organizing the Poor in America," *New Left Notes*, December 23, 1966.

6. Christopher Hill, *The World Turned Upside Down* (New York: The Viking Press, 1972), p. 50.

7. ERAP brochure, n.d.

8. Rennie Davis, *SDS Bulletin*, June 1964.

9. Quoted in Sara Evans, *Personal Politics*, p. 128.

10. "America and the New Era," 1963, mimeograph.

11. *SDS Bulletin*, 1963.

12. Sale, *SDS*, pp. 85–86.

13. *SDS Bulletin*, July 1964.

14. Sale, *SDS*, p. 107.

15. *SDS Bulletin*, March 1964.

16. *Ibid.*

17. *SDS Bulletin*, April 1964.

18. This is an alternative interpretation of the ideology and consciousness of students' intentions to what later analysts, particularly the Ehrenreichs (see Chapter Six), suggested was really going on. According to the Ehrenreichs, students could not really "escape" their class origins and were in fact acting on those class interests in ERAP. The students' function, in other words, was not as democratic as they themselves *thought* it was; professionals could not be radicals, contrary to what Haber believed. I have made it clear that I disagree with the Ehrenreichs and other "class deductive" interpretations of the new left.

19. Don McKelvey, "The SDS: Where are We Going?" Spring, 1964, *Discussion Bulletin*.

20. *Ibid.*

21. *SDS Bulletin*, July 1964.

22. Included were Tom Hayden, Todd Gitlin, Rennie Davis, Ken and Carol McEldowney, Paul Potter, Richard Rothstein and Carl Wittman.

23. Sale, *SDS*, p. 147.

24. Steve Max, *SDS Bulletin*, July 1964.

25. 1965 Spring *Discussion Bulletin*.

26. *Ibid.*

27. James O'Connor, "Towards a Theory of Community Unions, I," *Studies on the Left* 2 (Spring 1964); and "Towards a Theory of Community Unions, II"; James Williams, "On Community Unions"; Stanley Aronowitz, "Poverty, Politics, and Community Organization," all in *Studies on the Left* 3 (Summer 1964); Norman Fruchter and Robert Kramer, "An Approach to Community Organizing," *Studies on the Left* 2 (March–April 1966).

28. In spite of "traditional theory," there is evidence that the old left organized

in communities as well as in the workplace, contrary to what new leftists thought and to the singleminded labor organizing image of the old left.

29. O'Connor, "Towards a Theory I," p. 146.

30. *Ibid.*, pp. 146, 147.

31. O'Connor, "Towards a Theory II," p. 101

32. Martin Nicolaus, "The Contradiction of Advanced Capitalist Society and Its Resolution," Radical Education Pamphlet (REP), mimeograph, n.d.

33. *Ibid.*

34. Fruchter and Kramer, "An Approach. . .," p. 35.

35. It is interesting to consider how the community projects foreshadowed organizing and theorizing that developed out of the women's liberation movement. Recent work in women's history, economics, anthropology and sociology has taken a closer look at women's role in the political economy in order to understand their role in society and their participation in social transformation. This has necessitated consideration of the community and the family as crucial institutions in which women are located (and it will be shown below that women were more successful community organizers perhaps because they were more familiar and comfortable with these institutions). An interest in those groups not directly related to the productive process, such as women in the home, the unemployed, the very poor and students, required looking at institutions in which those lives were embedded, especially the community. For students it meant the university.

Much of the feminist material has led to speculation that work has diminished in its ability to determine an individual's consciousness of their class and position in society. Due to enormous economic, political and cultural changes in capitalism in the second half of this century, issues that were once defined as personal and private, whose context is the home and the community, have assumed a political content they did not previously have. The thread connecting these perceptions may, in part, be traced backwards to the ERAP projects and the civil rights movement, which focused attention on the neighborhood and residential community and on the ideology of community control, participation and power.

36. Rennie Davis, *SDS Bulletin*, June 1964.

37. In 1965 ERAP disbanded its central office and staff. See Rothstein on this, "Representative Democracy in SDS," *Liberation* 9 (February 1972), p. 10; and section on ERAP in Chapter Five.

38. Rothstein, "Short History," *SDS Bulletin*.

39. *Ibid.*

40. *Ibid.*

41. Newark, ERAP Project Report, June 20–July 1, 1964.

42. Trenton ERAP Project Report, June 21, 1964.

43. *SDS Bulletin*, September 1964.

44. Letter from Evan Metcalf in Cleveland to Larry Gordon and Nick Egleson in Hoboken, *ERAP Newsletter*, July 23, 1964. James O'Brien interviews with Mark Naison and Evan Metcalf discuss problems of community organizing on tape (Naison interview, June 10, 1969; Metcalf interview, April 19, 1969), State Historical Society of Wisconsin (SHSW).

45. "Chicago JOIN Project," *Studies on the Left* 3 (Summer 1964), p. 113.

46. *ERAP Newsletter*, October 5, 1965.

47. Rothstein, "Short History."

48. *Ibid.*

49. Evans, *Personal Politics*, p. 136; Andrew Kopkind, "Introduction: The Young Radicals," in *Thoughts of the Young Radicals* (New Jersey: Harrison-Blaine, A New Republic Book, 1966), p. 4.

50. Kopkind, "Introduction," p. 7.

51. *Thoughts of the Young Radicals*, pp. 34, 45.

52. "Port Huron Statement," (New York: SDS, 1964), p. 7.

53. "An Approach to Community Organizing," *Studies on the Left* 2 (April 1966), p. 36.

54. Rothstein, "Short History."

55. *Ibid.*

56. *Ibid.*

57. *SDS Bulletin*, October 1964.

58. Rothstein, "Representative Democracy," p. 17.

59. Evans, *Personal Politics*, p. 141.

60. *Studies on the Left* (Summer 1965), p. 123.

61. *Studies on the Left* (April 1966), p. 41.

62. *ERAP Newsletter*, November 22, 1965.

63. Sale, *SDS*, pp. 143–44; an interesting exploration of this tension is Norman Fruchter's film about the Newark project, "The Troublemakers."

64. Newark, Chicago and Cleveland were the strongest and most influential projects in the ERAP network. As they shifted to other than employment issues, housing grievances and welfare rights came to the fore. Newark was most successful in housing through organizing rent strikes, while Cleveland's successes lay in organizing welfare mothers for adequate welfare and for a school lunch program. Chester, Pennsylvania attacked racial discrimination, building a significant community organization and following. Chicago was the only major success in white community organizing. Other projects achieved minor successes, and some offshoots of ERAP developed, whose influence can be traced from the early sixties into community groups that developed later, the heirs of which exist, in a few cases, today.

65. *Poor People's Movements* (New York: Pantheon, 1977), p. 36.

66. *Ibid.*, p. 23.

67. I would like to thank Michael Schwartz for arguing with me that what I have identified in the "transition years" as a shift away from prefigurative politics and a loss of the kernel of new leftism, was in fact an accurate recognition by the new left of the weaknesses of community organizing; the lack of political leverage of ghetto residents and students led organizers to a new recognition of the power of the working class in the workplace. In other words, the shift to a more classical Marxist and left analysis and an interest in working-class organizing resulted from the *failures* of the new left up until then, was a rational shift, (and indicates, in support of part of my argument, the degree of dynamic and change in the thinking of SDS activists as earlier theoretical conceptions intermixed with concrete political activities.) The failures and successes were utilized to redefine and reanalyze former theoretical concepts, and according to Schwartz, to develop a new and

more realistic synthesis with more possibility for constructive political action. I hope I have made it clear that I do not think the shift was as rational or as positive as that. Certainly, real understanding of power in America was involved, but the anti-intellectualism, guilt and *easiness* of it cannot be ignored. With it were lost cultural and participatory components in addition to an affirmation of middle-class radicalism. I don't believe these were incidental losses.

68. Kim Moody, "ERAP, Ideology and Social Change," mimeograph, n.d.

69. *Ibid.*

70. ERAP Project Report, August 9, 1964.

71. "Words Butter No Parsnips," *SDS Bulletin,* May 1964.

72. This raises the traditional left debate of reform vs. revolutionary strategy. Vis-a-vis ERAP, the questions might be whether it was ever possible to achieve reforms, and without achieving them whether it was possible to radicalize people? Even with some success, we have seen how many organizers were not sure of the links between their work and radical social change. Nevertheless, reform and revolution were not separate in organizers' minds, nor were they in reality. Form and content, the duality, were linked; the new social relations in the organization were the heart of social change. ERAP and similar projects cannot be dispensed with as simple reform efforts, and certainly their weaknesses were more complicated.

73. Fruchter and Kramer, "An Approach. . .," p. 51.

74. *Ibid.,* p. 37.

75. *Ibid.,* p. 51.

76. *Ibid.,* p. 43.

77. Letter from Evan Metcalf, *ERAP Newsletter,* July 23, 1965.

78. ERAP Project Report, Hazard, August 10, 1964.

79. Letter from Evan Metcalf, *ERAP Newsletter,* July 23, 1965.

80. Letter from Nick Egleson in Hoboken, *ERAP Newsletter,* July 23, 1965.

Bibliography

NOTE

A good portion of my source material consists of essays, letters, articles, reports on meetings, pamphlets and the like, produced by a group that may be loosely designated as the SDS leadership. Abundant material of this sort is among the holdings of the New Left Collection of the State Historical Society in Madison, Wisconsin and the Social Protest Project in the Bancroft Library at the University of California at Berkeley, both of which I was able to examine, along with documents from my personal files and those made available to me by a number of movement participants. The *ERAP Newsletter, New Left Notes, SDS Bulletin, Worklist,* Radical Education Project pamphlets, "Port Huron Statement," "America in the New Era" statement, and assorted brochures, flyers, articles and mimeographed material are in the private possession of the author, unless otherwise specified. They were originally in the possession of the late Carol McEldowney.

The following movement and counter cultural publications have been consulted in the State Historical Society of Wisconsin and articles from them cited throughout the text (they are not listed separately in the bibliography):

Connections (Madison)
The Fifth Estate (Detroit)
The Guardian (New York)
L.A. Free Press (Los Angeles)
The Movement (San Francisco)
The Paper (East Lansing, Michigan)
The Rag (Austin, Texas)
The Seed (Chicago)

The following SDS publications have been cited throughout the text (articles from them are not listed separately in the bibliography):

ERAP News Letter
New Left Notes

Radical Education Project (REP) pamphlets
SDS Bulletin
Worklist

———

Altbach, Philip G. "Student Activism and Academic Research." In *American Students: A Selected Bibliography on Student Activism and Related Topics*, comp. Philip Altbach and David Kelly. Lexington, Mass.: Lexington Books, D.C. Heath, 1973.

———. *Student Politics in America: A Historical Analysis*. New York: McGraw Hill, 1974.

———, and David Kelly. *American Students: A Selected Bibliography on Student Activism and Related Topics*. Lexington, Mass.: Lexington Books, D.C. Heath, 1973.

———, and Robert S. Laufer, eds. *The New Pilgrims: Youth Protest in Transition*. New York: David McKay, 1972.

———, and Seymour Martin Lipset, eds. *Students in Revolt*. Boston: Houghton Mifflin, 1969.

Aptheker, Bettina. *The Academic Rebellion in the United States*. New Jersey: Citadel Press, 1972.

Arendt, Hannah. *On Revolution*. New York: Viking Press, 1963.

Aronowitz, Stanley. "Poverty, Politics and Community Organization." *Studies on the Left* 3 (Summer 1964).

Aronson, Ronald. "The Movement and its Critics." *Studies on the New Left* 1 (Jan.–Feb. 1966).

Ash, Roberta. *Social Movements in America*. Chicago: Rand McNally, 1977.

Banks, J.A. *The Sociology of Social Movements*. London: Macmillan, 1972.

Bardacke, Frank. "Stop-the-Draft Week." In *The Movement Toward a New America*, ed. Mitchell Goodman. Philadelphia: Pilgrim Press, A. Knopf, 1970.

Bell, Daniel. "Notes on the Post-Industrial Society (1)." *Public Interest* 6 (Winter 1967).

Benello, C. George. "Participatory Democracy and the Dilemma of Change." In *The New Left: A Collection of Essays*, ed. Priscilla Long. Boston: Porter Sargent, 1969.

———, and Dimitri Roussopolos, eds. *The Case for Participatory Democracy*. New York: Viking Press, 1972.

Bernstein, Basil. *Class, Codes and Control*. London: Routledge & Kegan Paul, 1971.

———. "Class, Codes and Control: Social Class, Language and Socialization." In *Language and Social Context*, ed. P. Giglioli, Baltimore: Penguin Books, 1972.

———. "Elaborated and Restricted Code: Their Social Origins and Some Consequences." *American Anthropology* 6 (Dec. 1964).

Blackburn, Robin, and Alexander Cockburn, eds. *Student Power*. Baltimore: Penguin Books, 1969.

Blumer, Herbert. "Social Movements." In *Principles of Sociology*, ed. Alfred McClung Lee. New York: Barnes & Noble, 1951.

Bobbio, Norberto. "Are There Alternatives to Representative Democracy?" *Telos* 35 (Spring 1978).

————. "Why Democracy?" *Telos* 36 (Summer 1978).

Boggs, Carl. "Marxism, Prefigurative Communism and the Problem of Workers Control." *Radical America* 6 (Winter 1977–1978).

Bookchin, Murray. "Beyond Neo-Marxism." *Telos* 36 (Summer 1978).

————. *Listen Marxist*. New York: Times Change Press, 1971.

Breines, Paul. "Marcuse and the New Left." In *The Revival of American Socialism*, ed. George Fischer. New York: Oxford Univ. Press, 1971.

Breines, Wini. Review of *Personal Politics: The Roots of Women's Liberation in the Civil Rights Movement and the New Left* by Sara Evans in *Feminist Studies* 5 (1979): 495–506.

Brown, Michael, ed. *The Politics and Anti-Politics of the Young*. Beverly Hills, Cal.: Glencoe Press, 1969.

Calvert, Gregory. "In White America." In *The New Left*, ed. M. Teodori. Indianapolis: Bobbs Merrill, 1969.

————. "A Left-Wing Alternative." In *The Movement Toward A New America*, ed. M. Goodman. Philadelphia: Pilgrim Press, A. Knopf, 1970.

————, and Carol Neiman. *A Disrupted History: The New Left and the New Capitalism*. New York: Random House, 1971.

Cammett, John. "Socialism and Participatory Democracy." In *Revival of American Socialism*, ed. George Fischer. New York: Oxford Univ. Press, 1971.

Clecak, Peter. *Radical Paradoxes*. New York: Harper & Row, 1973.

Cohen, Mitchell, and Dennis Hale, eds. *The New Student Left*. Boston: Beacon, 1967.

Cohn-Bendit, Gabriel, and Daniel Cohn-Bendit. *Obsolete Communism: The Left Wing Alternative*. Great Britain: Penguin Books, 1969.

Cook, Terrence E., and Patrick M. Morgan, eds. *Participatory Democracy*, San Francisco: Canfield Press, n.d.

Davidson, Carl. "The Multiversity: Crucible of the New Working Class." In *The University Crisis Reader*, 2 vol., ed. Immanuel Wallerstein and Paul Starr. New York: Vintage, 1971.

Draper, Hal. *Berkeley: The New Student Revolt*. New York: Grove Press, 1965.

Ehrenreich Barbara, and John Ehrenreich. "The New Left and the Professional-Managerial Class." *Radical America* 2 (May–June 1977).

Engels, Frederick, and Karl Marx. *Selected Works*, vol. 1. Moscow: Foreign Languages Pub. House, 1958.

Erikson, Kai. *Everything in Its Path*. New York: Simon & Schuster, Touchstone, 1976.

Evans, Sara Margaret. *Personal Politics: The Roots of Women's Liberation in the Civil Rights Movement and the New Left*. New York: Knopf, 1979.

Fainstein, Norman, and Susan Fainstein. *Urban Political Movements*. Englewood Cliffs, N.J.: Prentice-Hall, 1974.

Farber, Jerry. "The Student as Nigger." In his *The Student as Nigger*. New York: Pocket Books, 1970.

Faris, Robert, ed. *Handbook of Modern Sociology*. Chicago: Rand McNally, 1964.

Ferber, Michael, and Staughton Lynd. *The Resistance*. Boston: Beacon Press, 1970.

Fischer, George, ed. *Revival of American Socialism*. New York: Oxford Univ. Press, 1971.

Flacks, Richard. "The Importance of the Romantic Myth for the New Left." *Theory and Society* 3 (Fall 1975).

———. "The Liberated Generation: An Exploration of the Roots of Student Protest." *Journal of Social Issues* 23 (July 1967).

———. "Making History vs. Making Life: Dilemmas of an American Left." *Working Papers* 2 (Summer 1974).

———. "The New Left and American Politics after Ten Years." *Journal of Social Issues* 27 (1971).

———. "On the New Working Class and Strategies for Social Change." In *The New Pilgrims: Youth Protest in Transition*, ed. Philip Altbach and Robert Laufer. New York: David McKay, 1972.

———. "On the Use of Participatory Democracy." *Dissent* 13 (November 1966).

———. "Revolt of the Young Intelligentsia: Revolutionary Class Consciousness in Post-Scarcity America." In *The New American Revolution*, ed. Roderick Aya and Norman Miller. New York: Free Press, 1971.

———. "Social and Cultural Meanings of Student Revolt: Some Informal Comparative Observations." Social Problems 17 (Winter 1970).

———. *Youth and Social Change*. Chicago: Markham Pub. Co., 1971.

Forman, James. *The Making of Black Revolutionaries*. New York: MacMillan, 1972.

Fox Genovese, Elizabeth, and Eugene Genovese. "The Political Crisis of Social History." *Journal of Social History* 10 (1976).

Freeman, Jo. *The Politics of Women's Liberation*. New York: David McKay, 1975.

Fruchter, Norman. Review of Howard Zinn, *SNCC: The New Abolitionists*. *Studies on the Left* 1 (Winter 1965).

———. "SDS: In and Out of Context." *Liberation* 16 (Feb. 1972).

———, and Robert Kramer. "An Approach to Community Organizing." *Studies on the Left* 2 (March–April 1966).

Gamson, William. *The Strategy of Social Protest*. Homewood: Dorsey, 1975.

Genovese, Eugene. *In Red and Black*. New York: Pantheon, 1968.

Gilbert, David, Robert Gottlieb, and Susan Sutheim. "Consumption: Domestic Imperialism." In *The New Left*, ed. M. Teodorfi. Indianapolis: Bobbs Merrill, 1969.

Gitlin, Todd. "The Dynamics of the New Left." *Motive* (Oct.–Nov. 1970).

———. "Spotlights and Shadows: Television and the Culture of Politics." *College English* 8 (April 1977).

———. *The Whole World Is Watching: Mass Media in the Making and Unmaking of the New Left*. Berkeley: Univ. of California Press, 1980.

Gombin, Richard. *The Origins of Modern Leftism*. Baltimore: Penguin Books, 1975.

———. *The Radical Tradition: A Study in Modern Revolutionary Thought*. New York: St. Martin's Press. 1979.

Goodman, Mitchell, ed. *The Movement Toward a New America*. Philadelphia: Pilgrim Press, A. Knopf, 1970.

Gornick, Vivian. *The Romance of American Communism*. New York: Basic Books, 1977.

Gorz, Andre. *Socialism and Revolution*. Garden City, N.Y.: Doubleday, 1973.

———. *Strategy for Labor*. Boston: Beacon Press, 1967.

Gouldner, Alvin W. *The Dialectic of Ideology and Technology*. New York: Seabury Press, 1976.

———. *The Future of Intellectuals and the Rise of the New Class*. New York: Seabury Press, 1979.

———. "Marxism and Social Theory." *Theory and Society* 1 (1974).

———. "Prologue to a Theory of Revolutionary Intellectuals." *Telos* 26 (Winter 1975–76).

———. *The Two Marxisms: Contradictions and Anomalies in the Development of Theory*. New York: The Seabury Press, 1980.

Gusfield, Joseph R. "The Study of Social Movements." In *The International Encyclopedia of the Social Sciences*. Edited by David L. Sills, New York: Macmillan Co. and The Free Press, 1968.

Gutman, Herbert. *The Black Family in Slavery and Freedom*. New York: Pantheon, 1976.

Habermas, Jurgen. *Legitimation Crisis*. Boston: Beacon Press, 1975.

———. *Toward a Rational Society*. Boston: Beacon Press, 1970.

———. "Toward a Theory of Communicative Competence." In *Recent Sociology* 2. Edited by Hans P. Dreitzel. New York: Macmillan, 1970.

Harrington, Michael. "The Mystical Militants." In *Beyond the New Left*. Edited by Irving Howe. New York: Horizon Press, 1954.

Hayden, Thomas. "The Politics of the Movement." *Dissent* (January–February 1966).

———. Review of *SNCC: The New Abolitionists*, by Howard Zinn. *Studies on the Left* 1 (Winter 1965).

Hearn, Francis. *Domination, Legitimation and Resistance: The Incorporation of the Nineteenth-Century English Working Class*. Westport, Conn.: Greenwood Press, 1978.

———. "Remembrance and Critique: The Uses of the Past for Discrediting the Present and Anticipating the Future." *Politics and Society* 2 (1975).

Heberle, Rudolf. "Observations on the Sociology of Social Movements." *American Sociological Review* 14 (June 1949).

———. "Types and Functions of Social Movements." In *The International Encylopedia of the Social Sciences*. Edited by David L. Sills. New York: Macmillan Co. and The Free Press, 1968.

Hill, Christopher. *The World Turned Upside Down: Radical Ideas During the English Revolution*. New York: The Viking Press, 1972.

Hirsh, Arthur. *The French New Left: An Intellectual History from Sartre to Gorz.* Boston: South End Press, 1981.

Hobsbawm, Eric. *Labouring Men.* Garden City, N.Y.: Anchor Books, 1967.

———. *Primitive Rebels.* New York: W.W. Norton and Co., 1965.

———. Review of *Poor People's Movements,* by Frances Fox Piven and Richard Cloward. In *The New York Review of Books* 23 (March 23, 1978).

Horowitz, Irving L. *Ideology and Utopia in the United States, 1956–1976.* New York: Oxford University Press, 1977.

———. *Radicalism and the Revolt Against Reason.* Carbondale, Ill.: Southern Illinois University Press, 1968.

———. *The Struggle is the Message: The Organization and Ideology of the Anti-War Movement.* Berkeley: The Glendessary Press, 1970.

———, and W. Friedman. *The Knowledge Factory: Student Power and Academic Politics in America.* Chicago: Aldine Publishing Co., 1970.

Howard, Dick and Karl Klare, eds. *The Unknown Dimension: European Marxism Since Lenin.* New York: Basic Books, 1972.

Howe, Irving, ed. *Beyond the New Left.* New York: Horizon Press, 1965.

———. "New Styles of Leftism." In *Beyond the New Left.* Edited by Irving Howe. New York: Horizon Press, 1965.

———, ed. *The Radical Papers.* New York: Doubleday, 1966.

Jacobs, Paul and Landau, eds. *The New Radicals.* New York: Random House, 1966.

Jacoby, Henry. *The Bureaucratization of the World.* Berkeley: University of California Press, 1973.

Jenkins, J. Craig and Charles Perrow. "Insurgency of the Powerless: Farm Workers Movements (1946–1972)." *American Sociological Review* 2 (April 1977).

Jones, Gareth Stedman. "The Meaning of the Student Revolt." In *Student Power.* Edited by Alexander Cockburn and Robin Blackburn. Baltimore: Penguin Books, 1969.

Keniston, Kenneth. *Young Radicals.* New York: Harcourt, Brace and World, 1968.

———. "Youth Radicals and the Fear of Power." In *The Politics and Anti-Politics of the Young.* Edited by Michael Brown. Beverly Hills: Glencoe Press, 1969.

Kerr, Clark. *The Uses of the University.* New York: Harper and Row, 1966.

Killian, Lewis. "Social Movements." In *Handbook of Modern Sociology.* Edited by Robert Faris. Chicago: Rand McNally, 1964.

Kopkind, Andrew. "Introduction: The Young Radicals." In *Thoughts of the Young Radicals.* New Jersey: Harrison Blaine, New Republic Books, 1966.

Kraditor, Aileen. *Means and Ends in American Abolitionism: Garrison and His Critics on Strategy and Tactics, 1834–1850.* New York: Pantheon Books, 1967.

Kramer, Daniel G. *Participatory Democracy: Ideals of the Political Left.* Cambridge, Mass.: Schenkman Publishing Co., 1972.

Lasch, Christopher, "Where Do We Go From Here?" *New York Review of Books,* Vol. XI, No. 6 (October 10, 1968).

Lazarre, Jane. *On Loving Men.* New York: Dial Press, 1978.

Lefebvre, Henri. *The Explosion: Marxism and the French Revolution*. New York: Monthly Review Press, 1969.

Lipset, Seymour Martin. "The Activists: A Profile." *The Public Interest* 13 (Fall 1968).

————. "The Possible Effects of Student Activism on International Politics." In *Students and Revolt*. Edited by Seymour M. Lipset and Philip G. Altbach. Boston: Beacon Press, 1970.

————. *Student Politics*. New York: Basic Books, 1968.

————, and Philip Altbach, eds. *Students in Revolt*. Boston: Houghton Mifflin, 1969.

————, Martin Trow and James Coleman. *Union Democracy*. Glencoe, Ill.: The Free Press, 1956.

————, and Sheldon Wolin. *The Berkeley Student Revolt*. Garden City, N.Y.: Doubleday, 1965.

Lynd, Staughton. "The Movement: A New Beginning." *Liberation* (May 1969).

————. "The New Radicals and Participatory Democracy. *Dissent* (Summer 1965).

————. "Prospects for the New Left." *Liberation* (Winter 1971).

————. "Socialism, the Forbidden Word." *Studies on the Left* 3 (Summer 1963).

————. "Towards a History of the New Left." In *The New Left*. Edited by Priscilla Long. Boston: Porter Sargent, 1969.

Long, Priscilla, ed. *The New Left: A Collection of Essays*. Boston: Porter Sargent, 1969.

Mailer, Norman. *Armies of the Night*. New York: Signet, 1968.

Mallet, Serge. *Essays on the New Working Class*. Edited and translated by Dick Howard. St. Louis: Telos Press, 1976.

Mannheim, Karl. *Ideology and Utopia*. New York: Harcourt, Brace and World, 1936.

Mankoff, Milton L. "The Political Socialization of Radicals and Militants in the Wisconsin Student Movement During the 1960's." Ph.D. Dissertation, University of Wisconsin, 1969.

Mansbridge, Jane J. *Beyond Adversary Democracy*. New York: Basic Books, 1980.

Marcuse, Herbert. *An Essay on Liberation*. Boston: Beacon Press, 1969.

————. "The Movement in a New Era of Repression: An Assessment." *Berkeley Journal of Sociology* (1971–1972).

————. "On the New Left." Twentieth anniversary of *The Guardian*, speech given Dec ember 4, 1968. Reprinted in *The New Left*. Edited by M. Teodori. Indianapolis: Bobbs Merrill, 1969.

————. *One Dimensional Man*. Boston: Beacon Press, 1964.

Meeropol, Robert and Michael. *We are Your Sons*. Boston: Houghton Mifflin, Co., 1975.

Melville, Samuel. *Letters from Attica*. New York: William Morrow and Co., 1972.

Michels, Robert. *Political Parties*. New York: Collier Books, 1972.

Michener, James. "The Kent State Four Should Have Studied More." Suzanne

Steinmetz and Murray Straus, eds., *Violence in the Family* (N.Y.: Harper and Rowe, 1974).

Miles, Michael. *The Radical Probe: The Logic of Student Rebellion.* New York: Atheneum, 1973.

Miliband, Ralph. *Marxism and Politics.* New York: Oxford University Press, 1977.

Miller, Michael and Susan Gilmore, eds. *Revolution at Berkeley.* New York: Dell, 1965.

Mills, C. Wright. "Letter to the New Left." In *The New Left.* Edited by Priscilla Long. Boston: Porter Sargent, 1969.

Mueller, Claus. *The Politics of Communication.* New York: Oxford University Press, 1973.

Mumford, Lewis. *The City in History.* New York: Harcourt, Brace and World, 1961.

Nairn, Tom and Angelo Quattrocchi. *The Beginning of the End.* London: Panther Book, 1968.

Nisbet, Robert. *The Sociological Tradition.* New York: Basic Books, 1966.

Oberschall, Anthony. *Social Conflicts and Social Movements.* Englewood Cliffs, N.J.: Prentice Hall, 1973.

O'Brien, James. "Beyond Reminiscence: The New Left in History." *Radical America* 4 (July–August 1972).

———. "The Development of a New Left in the U.S., 1960–1965." Ph.D. Dissertation, University of Wisconsin, 1971.

O'Connor, James. *The Fiscal Crisis of the State.* New York: St. Martin's Press, 1973.

———. "Towards a Theory of Community Unions I." *Studies on the Left* 2 (Spring 1964).

———. "Towards a Theory of Comnunity Unions II." *Studies on the Left* 3 (Summer, 1964).

Oglesby, Carl. "Notes on a Decade Ready for the Dustbin." *Liberation* (August–September 1969).

———. "Trapped in a System." In *The New Left.* Edited by M. Teodori. Indianapolis: Bobbs Merrill, 1969.

Oppenheimer, Martin. "The Sociology of Participatory Democracy." *Our Generation.* Vol. 3, no. 4; Vol. 4, no. 1 (n.d.).

Payne, Bruce. "SNCC: An Overview Two Years Later." In *The New Student Left.* Edited by Mitchell Cohen and Dennis Hale. Boston: Beacon Press, 1967.

Pennock, J. Roland and John W. Chapman, eds. *Representation.* New York: Atherton Press, 1968.

Perrow, Charles. *Complex Organizations: A Critical Essay.* Glenview, Ill.: Scott, Foresman and Co., 1972.

Petras, James. "On Mounting Political Action." In *Berkeley: The New Student Revolt,* by Hal Draper. New York: Grove Press, 1965.

Piercy, Marge. *Vida.* New York: Summit Books, 1980.

Pitkin, Hannah Fenichel. *The Concept of Representation.* Berkeley: University of California Press, 1967.

Rader, Dotson. *I Ain't Machin' Anymore.* New York: David McKay, 1969.

Raskin, Jonah. *Out of the Whale: Growing Up in the American Left.* New York: Links Books, 1974.

Rootes, Christopher. "Students Radicalism: Politics of Moral Protest and Legitimation Problems of the Modern Capitalist State." *Theory and Society.* Vol. 9, no. 3 (May 1980).

Ross, Robert. "Primary Groups in Social Movements: A Memoir and Interpretation." (mimeographed). Revised, *Journal of Voluntary Action Research* (February 1977).

Rossman, Michael. *New Age Blues: On the Politics of Consciousness.* New York: Dutton, 1979.

———. *The Wedding Within the War.* Garden City, N.Y.: Doubleday and Co., 1971.

Rothstein, Richard. "Evolution of the ERAP Organizers." In *The New Left.* Edited by Priscilla Long. Boston: Porter Sargent, 1969.

Rothstein, Richard. "Representative Democracy in SDS." *Liberation* (February 1972).

Rowntree, John and Margaret. "The Political Economy of Youth: Youth as a Class." *Our Generation* 1–2 (May, June, July 1968).

Sale, Kirkpatrick. *SDS.* New York: Vintage Books, 1973.

Savio, Mario. "An End to History." In The *Berkeley Student Revolt.* Edited by S.M. Lipset and Sheldon Wolin. Garden City, N.Y.: Doubleday, 1965.

———. "Introduction" to *Berkeley: The New Student Revolt* by Hal Draper. New York: Grove Press, 1965.

———. *The F.S.M. and the Negro Revolution.* Detroit: News and Letters, 1965.

Schwartz, Michael. *Radical Protest and Social Structure.* New York: Academic Press, 1976.

Selznick, Philip. "The Iron Law of Bureaucracy." *Modern Review.* (January 1950) 157–165.

Semprun, Jorge. *The Autobiography of Federico Sanchez and the Communist Underground in Spain.* New York: Karz Publishers, 1979.

Situationist International. *Ten Days that Shook the University.* London: Situationist International, n.d.

Skolnick, Jerome. *The Politics of Protest.* New York: Ballantine Books, 1969.

Smith, David N. *Who Rules the Universities? An Essay in Class Analysis.* New York: Monthly Review Press, 1974.

Spence, Larry. "Berkeley: What it Demonstrates." *Studies on the Left* 1 (1965).

Spender, Stephen. *The Year of the Young Rebels.* New York: Vintage, 1968.

Statera, Gianni. *Death of a Utopia: The Development and Decline of the Student Movements in Europe.* New York: Oxford University Press, 1975.

Stein, Buddy. "A New Kind of Protest." *Steps,* a Journal of the Free University of Berkeley, 2.

Stein, Maurice. *The Eclipse of Community.* New York: Harper and Row, 1964.

Stern, Sol. "A Deeper Disenchantment." *Liberation* (February 1965).

Stern, Susan. *With the Weathermen.* Garden City, New York: Doubleday and Co., 1972.

Teodori, Massimo, ed. *The New Left: A Documentary History.* Indianapolis: Bobbs Merrill, 1969.

Thompson, E.P. *The Making of the English Working Class.* London: Victor Gollancz, Ltd., 1964.

Tilly, Charles. *From Mobilization to Revolution.* Reading, Mass.: Addison Wesley Publishing Co., 1978.

————, Louise and Richard. *The Rebellious Century.* Cambridge, Mass.: Harvard University Press, 1975.

Touraine, Alain. *The May Movement.* New York: Random House, 1971.

Unger, Irwin. *The Movement: A History of the American New Left, 1959–1972.* New York: Didd Mead and Co., 1975.

Useem, Michael. *Protest Movements in America.* Indianapolis: Bobbs Merrill Co., 1975.

Vickers, George. *The Formation of the New Left.* Lexington, Mass.: Lexington Books, D.C. Heath, 1975.

Walker, Pat, ed. *Between Labor and Capital: The Professional-Managerial Class.* Boston: South End Press, 1979.

Wallerstein, Immanuel and Paul Starr, eds. *The University Crisis Reader.* Volumes I and II. New York: Vintage, 1971.

Weber, Max. "Politics as a Vocation." In *From Max Weber.* Edited by Hans Gerth and C. Wright Mills. New York: Oxford University Press, 1973.

Weinstein, James. *Ambiguous Lagacy.* New York: New Viewpoints, Franklin Watts, 1975.

————, and David Eakins, eds., *For A New America: Essays in History and Politics from "Studies on the Left," 1959–1967.* New York: Random House, 1970.

Williams, James H. "On Community Unions." *Studies on the Left* 3 (Summer 1964).

Williams, Raymond. *Keywords.* New York: Oxford University Press, 1976.

Wolfe, Alan. *The Limits of Legitimacy.* New York: Free Press, 1977.

Wolin, Sheldon S. *Politics and Vision.* Boston: Little, Brown and Co., 1960.

Young, Michael and Peter Willmott. *Family and Kinship in East London.* Baltimore: Penguin Books, 1957.

Young, Nigel. *An Infantile Disorder? The Crisis and Decline of the New Left.* Boulder, Colo.: Westview Press, 1977.

Zald, Meyer and Roberta Ash. "Social Movement Organizations: Growth, Decay and Change." *Social Forces* 44 (1966).

Zinn, Howard. "Marxism and the New Left." Priscilla Long, ed. *The New Left: A Collection of Essays.* Boston: Porter Sargent, 1969.

————. *SNCC: The New Abolitionists.* Boston: Beacon Press, 1965.

Index

"America and the New Era" document, 126

Anarchists, influence of, 13–14

Anti-intellectualism, accusations of, 28, 100–101

Anti-war movement, 12, 18, 120; April 15, 1967, marches of, 31–32; October 21, 1967, Pentagon demonstration of, 33–34

Arendt, Hannah, 46–47, 66

Aronowitz, Stanley, 133–34

Beatniks, 10

Bell, Daniel, 1–2, 5, 99–100, 108

Berkeley Barb, 20

Berkeley, University of California at, 36. *See also* Free Speech Movement

Boggs, Carl, 52

Bookchin, Murray, 14

Booth, Paul, 67, 70–71, 74, 76, 84, 88, 90–91, 93, 101

Brecher, Jeremy, 91

Buckley, Neil, 73

Buhle, Paul, 88

Burlage, Robb, 70

Calvert, Greg, 74–75, 88–89, 91, 98, 118–19; on new working-class theory, 102–3, 106–8, 110, 112; on prefigurative politics, 47–49, 50, 54, 65; on problems of SDS, 63, 76

Camus, Albert, 11, 83

Carmichael, Stokely, 139

Catholic Worker movement, 13–14

Central Intelligence Agency, 37

Chabot, Joe, 124

Chicago, University of, 38

Civil rights movement, 10, 22; and Free Speech Movement, 24–25; impact on new left of, 10–12, 125, 133

Cleveland Community Project, 142, 146

Cloward, Richard, 72–73, 75, 145–46

Cohn–Bendit, Daniel, 30, 45

Coleman, Les, 118

Columbia University, 2, 32, 38

Communist Party, 13–16

Community, search for, 45, 47–50, 58–59; at Berkeley, 26–27, 30, 35; defined, 6–7
Condit, Tom, 92
Congress of Racial Equality, 24
Connections, 37
Cornell University, 31
Corporate liberalism, 22, 26
Council communists, 16–17
Counter-institutions, 52, 89–90
Craven, Carolyn, 79–80, 87

Dahlberg, Roy, 79–80, 87
Davidson, Carl, 57, 91, 100–103, 115–17
Davis, Rennie, 81–82, 125, 135–38
Death of a Utopia (Statera), 53
Dellinger, David, 13
Democratic Party, 1964 convention of, 11–12, 21
Dennison, George, 34
Detroit Committee To End the War in Vietnam, 94
Dow Chemical Corporation, 18, 37
Draft resistance, 31, 71, 88. *See also* Resistance, the
Drugs, 20, 71
DuBois Clubs. *See* W. E. B. DuBois Clubs

Economic Research and Action Project (ERAP), 48, 55, 80–82, 124; influence of civil rights movement on, 11, 133; participatory democracy within, 60–63; practical problems of, 135–49; relation of "campus versus community" debate to, 124–32; theory behind, 133–35
Egleson, Nick, 91, 148–49
Ehrenreich, Barbara, 108–10, 114, 169 n. 18
Ehrenreich, John, 108–10, 114, 169 n. 18
Eighteenth Brumaire of Louis Bonaparte (Marx), 113
Essay on Liberation (Marcuse), 58

Evans, Sara, 38, 83, 137–39, 143
Existentialism, 16
"Expressive" politics, 1, 3, 5–6

Ferber, Michael, 40, 44, 52
Feuer, Lewis, 1–2, 4, 24
Fifth Estate, 33
Flacks, Richard: as analyst of new left, 8–9, 105–6, 108; on participatory democracy, 79–80, 87; as SDS member, 71, 120, 132
Forman, James, 93–94
France, student movement of 1968 in, 21, 30, 39–40, 114
Frankfurt School, 16–17
Free Speech Movement, 2, 11, 23–31, 33; impact of, 12, 97, 104, 132; meaning of, 18, 42, 46–47
"Free universities," 27–28, 32, 34, 55
Friedland, William, 37, 40
Fruchter, Norman, 60–63, 90; on community organizing, 133–34, 140, 144, 147
Future of Intellectuals and the Rise of a New Class, The (Gouldner), 107

Garson, Marvin, 34, 36
Garvey, Helen, 87
Genovese, Eugene, 2
Gitlin, Todd, 18, 21, 67–68, 76–77, 89–90, 127–29, 162 n. 1
Glazer, Nathan, 1–3, 5, 19, 37
Glucksmann, André, 114
Gombin, Richard, 16–17, 55
Goodman, Bob, 122
Goodman, Paul, 11, 14, 83
Gorz, Andre, 102, 104–5
Gouldner, Alvin, 40–41, 106–9
Gramsci, Antonio, 16–17
Guardian, 122
Gusfield, Joseph, 72

Haber, Al, 76–77, 124, 128–30
Habermas, Jürgen, 40–41

Hansen, Pat, 48
Harrington, Michael, 126
Harris, David, 36, 52, 56
Hayden, Casey, 139
Hayden, Tom, 54–55, 57, 101, 121; on community organizing, 97, 124, 126, 128–29, 132, 139
Hill, Christopher, 125
Hippies, 20
Hobsbawm, Eric, 20, 45
Hook, Sidney, 2
Horowitz, Irving Louis, 30, 37, 40
Howe, Florence, 91
Howe, Irving, 2–3

In Red and Black (Genovese), 2
Infantile Disorder? An (Young), 54–56

Jacobs, Paul, 24
Jobs or Income Now (JOIN), 81, 143
Joyce, Frank, 94

Keniston, Kenneth, 59
Kerr, Clark, 25, 99–100, 108
Kissinger, Clark, 76, 78, 84–86
Kopkind, Andrew, 119
Korsch, Karl, 16–17
Kramer, Robert, 133–34, 140, 144, 147

Landau, Saul, 24
Lasch, Christopher, 2
Lauter, Paul, 91
League for Industrial Democracy, 11, 13–15
Lefebvre, Henri, 50
"Let the people decide," 83, 142, 149
Lipset, Seymour Martin, 99–100, 107; as critic of new left, 1–6, 19
Los Angeles Free Press, 34
Lukács, Georg, 16–17
Luxemburg, Rosa, 16–17
Lynd, Staughton: on participatory democracy, 58–59, 63–65, 121; on the Resistance, 40, 44, 52

MacDonald, Dwight, 38
McEldowney, Carol, 82
McEldowney, Ken, 48
McKelvey, Don, 53, 58, 76, 91–92, 130–31
Magidoff, Dickie, 84, 86
Mailer, Norman, 33
Mallet, Serge, 102, 104–5
Mankoff, Milton, 68
Mannheim, Karl, 53
Marcuse, Herbert, 58, 112, 148
Marxism, 13, 17, 98, 102, 110–15, 119, 121–22, 134
Marxism–Leninism, 65, 72, 112, 114, 118
Mass meetings, 36–40, 63
Max, Steve, 84–86, 128, 131–32, 146–48
Michels, Robert, 17, 51–52, 66, 72
Miles, Michael, 19–20
Mills, C. Wright, 11, 25, 83; on "labor metaphysic," 102, 110–11, 135
Mississippi Freedom Democratic Party, 11–12, 58
Moody, Kim, 146
Mueller, Claus, 40–41
Murphy, Sara, 91
Muste, A. J., 13

Nairn, Tom, 113
Neiman, Carol, 106
New University Conference, 129
New working-class theory, 97–115
Newark Community Union Project, 63, 131, 137, 140, 142, 149
Nicolaus, Martin, 134
Nouvelle Classe Ouvrière, La (Mallet), 102

O'Brien, Jim, 120
O'Connor, James, 133–34
Oglesby, Carl, 108, 110, 113, 118; on corporate liberalism, 22, 26, 158 n. 31
Old left, relation to new left of, 13–17
One-Dimensional Man (Marcuse), 148

Pacifists, influence of, 13–14
Pannokoek, Anton, 17
Paper, The, 36
Pardun, Robert, 84, 86–87
Participatory democracy, 6, 16, 21–22, 56–66, 121, 139–46
"Personal is political, The," 44, 48
Personal Politics (Evans), 38, 83, 137–39, 143
Piven, Frances Fox, 72–73, 75, 145–46
Political Parties (Michels), 17, 51–52, 66, 72
Poor People's Movements (Piven & Cloward), 72–73, 75, 145–46
Port Huron Statement, 6, 11, 57, 140
Potter, Paul, 76–80, 90–92, 130–31
Prefigurative politics, 6–7, 20, 30, 45, 47–50, 55, 59, 65, 89, 94–95, 140; contrasted to strategic politics, 7, 15, 30
Primitive Rebels (Hobsbawm), 20, 45
Progressive Labor Party, 12, 116, 155 n. 2

Rader, Dotson, 32
Radical America, 108–9
Radical Education Project, 90–91
Radicals in the Professions, 129
Rag, The, 39–40
Raskin, Jonah, 14–15
Reagon, Bernice, 38
"Red diaper babies," 14–15
Representative democracy, 51, 58, 62
Resistance, the, 31, 40, 43–44, 52
Richer, Ed, 74
Ross, Bob, 131–32
Rossman, Michael, 68–69, 73, 120–21; on Free Speech Movement, 27–29, 31, 33, 46–47
Rothstein, Richard: on community organizing projects, 81–82, 87, 136–39, 141–43; on participatory democracy, 57, 60–64

SDS (Sale), 68–71, 75, 83–84, 92, 97, 103, 119, 127, 144

SNCC: The New Abolitionists (Zinn), 54
Sale, Kirkpatrick. *See SDS* (Sale)
Sartre, Jean-Paul, 39
Savio, Mario, 23–26, 28, 52
Seed, The, 36
Selective Service System, 31, 42–43, 104. *See also* Draft resistance
Shero, Jeff, 71–72, 84, 86–87, 94
Shils, Edward, 1–5, 19
Socialist Workers Party, 13
Soviet Union, 15–16
Spence, Larry, 24–26
Spender, Stephen, 30, 39–40
Stanford University, 37
Statera, Gianni, 53
Stedman Jones, Gareth, 114
Stern, Sol, 27
Stop-the-Draft Week, 33–36, 122
Strategy for Labor (Gorz), 102
Student movement, relation of new left to, 9, 12–13, 20, 68–70
Student Non-Violent Coordinating Committee, 54, 93, 149; influence of, 62, 125, 141–42
Students for a Democratic Society (SDS): conceptualization of students by, 96–122; December Conference (1965) of, 67, 76, 83–88; internal education within, 90–93; National Conventions of: 1963, 126; 1964, 131; 1965, 62, 82; 1966, 68, 74, 76, 88; 1967, 47; 1968, 12; 1969, 12; National Council of, 60–61, 128, 131; as national organization, 49, 60–62, 70–71, 73, 78, 130; origins of, 11; relation of local activism to, 7–8, 68–69. *See also* Economic Research and Action Project
Studies on the Left, 101, 133

Teodori, Massimo, 53
Thompson, E. P., 21
Touraine, Alain, 20, 45, 105, 115
"Triple Revolution Statement," 126

Union Democracy (Lipset et al.), 3–4
United Auto Workers, 124
University, role of: as center for critical thinking, 106–7; as community of scholars, 28–29, 42, 101; in the corporate economy, 12, 18, 25, 42–43, 99–100, 103–4; as "the enemy," 118

Veneziale, John, 116–17

W. E. B. DuBois Clubs, 14
"Weatherman," 122
Webb, Lee, 76, 90
Weber, Max, 1, 5, 25, 49–50, 56, 66, 72

Weinberg, Jack, 24–25, 27
Weisstein, Naomi, 38
Wisconsin, University of, 37, 42–43, 68
Wittman, Carl, 126, 144
Wolin, Sheldon, 50
Women, role in new left of, 38–39, 84, 143
Working class, 12–13, 15, 102, 134. *See also* New working class

Year of the Young Rebels, The (Spender), 30, 39–40
Young, Nigel, 54–56
Young Socialist Alliance, 13
Youngblood, 117–18
Zinn, Howard, 54
Zweig, Michael, 84